Cuba: A Different America

CUBA

A Different America

edited by

Wilber A. Chaffee, Jr.

and

Gary Prevost

Rowman & Littlefield Publishers, Inc.

ROWMAN & LITTLEFIELD PUBLISHERS, INC.

Published in the United States of America in 1989.
by Rowman & Littlefield Publishers, Inc.
81 Adams Drive, Totowa, New Jersey 07512

Library of Congress Cataloging-in-Publication Data

Cuba, a different America

  Bibliography: p. 170
  Includes Index.
  1. Cuba—Politics and government—1959-   .
2. Cuba—Economic conditions—1959-   .
3. Cuba—Social conditions—1959-   . I. Chaffee,
Wilber A. II. Prevost, Gary.
F1788.C765   1988   972.91′064   87-28371
ISBN 0-8476-7503-3

5   4   3   2   1

Printed in the United States of America

To
Catherine and Alice

Contents

Illustrations

Tables

Figures

development of trade unions in Cuba from 1959 to the present. She demonstrates the dramatic turnaround in the role of the unions in the 1970s as they moved from total ineffectiveness in the first decade of the revolution to become an important voice for workers' concerns.

David Craven's detailed analysis of Cuban culture since 1959 concludes that while that while there are some limits to artistic freedom in Cuba, she has not adopted the sterile "socialist realism" practiced in some other socialist countries. Rather, government-subsidized Cuban literature and film, in particular, have achieved international recognition. Professional architect Howard Glazer, who has advised the Cuban government on housing matters, chronicles the serious housing problem in Cuba both before and after 1959. His chapter gives specific emphasis to Cuba's recently enacted housing law, which is designed to redress some of the country's past inadequacies.

Surgeon Jerry Rosenberg surveys Cuban medicine, including health care delivery and its emphasis on preventive measures, the education of medical professionals, and the achievement of high technological levels. Dr. Rosenberg also gives a brief description of conditions prior to 1959 and documents Cuba's significant successes, which include a dramatic lowering of the infant mortality rate. Dawn Keremitsis analyzes the role of women in Cuba with particular emphasis on their role in the workplace. She documents the government's efforts to change the status of women, but shows that significant problems remain. While women make up an important part of the industrial and educational workforce, they still remain responsible for the children and the home. In the final chapter, on Cuban foreign policy, Gary Prevost explores Cuba's relations in the Western Hemisphere and in Africa. The chapter analyzes the long-standing relationship between the Cuban leadership and the Sandinista National Liberation Front (FSLN) of Nicaragua, the importance to Cuba of that revolution, and Cuba's role in Ethiopia and Angola. The author concludes that while Cuba has significant economic dependence on the Soviet Union, her foreign policy must be understood on its own terms with an eye to Cuba's special relationship with the Movement of Non-Aligned Nations.

The authors hope that this volume will help to fill the large knowledge gap that exists in the United States on Cuba, one of our closest neighbors. All the contributors believe this gap will remain significant until full diplomatic relations between the two countries are reestablished and the 1982 ban on American travel to Cuba is lifted. Further, the authors believe that the travel ban and the U.S. embargo on trade with Cuba serves the best interests of neither country and should be ended as quickly as possible.

Preface

The impetus for this book came from a 1984 visit to Cuba by many of the contributors under the auspices of the Center for Cuban Studies. Each contributor in Cuba that summer was engaged in research on some aspect of Cuban society. It was the common feeling of those scholars that a serious study of contemporary Cuba was needed, a study to be accessible not only to scholars of Latin America but also to students and non-students alike who want to become more knowledgeable about a country that is relatively unknown in America today. This collection of essays represents the fruits of that effort.

The opening chapter by Wilber Chaffee provides a brief history of Cuba that begins in the middle of the 19th century but concentrates on the years since 1959. Chaffee concludes that recent Cuban history can be understood completely only by recognizing the nature of Cuba's historic dependencies on Spain and the United States and her current relationship with the Soviet Union. In the chapter on the Cuban political system, Chaffee explores the roles of the Cuban Communist party, the Committees for the Defense of the Revolution, the Assemblies of People's Power, and the organization of the party's Political Bureau. He also analyzes Cuba's electoral system, which, unlike other Communist party-led states, has elections that include a secret ballot with competing candidates, often non-Communist party members. Chaffee also looks at Fidel Castro's place in the government and at the links between the party and the organs of government.

The chapter by Nora Hamilton examines the Cuban economy and its current development. Hamilton traces the history of economic programs since 1959 with particular emphasis on Cuba's successes in reducing economic inequality and in ending the nation's dependence on the U.S. economy. She also analyzes Cuba's mixed record in diversifying its economy and Cuba's choice to become integrated into the Comecon (CMEA) countries. Linda Fuller's chapter focuses on the growth and

Acknowledgments

Many different people and organizations have made this book possible. All but one of the contributors were part of a group that came together to study contemporary Cuba during a seminar sponsored by the Center for Cuban Studies in Havana. We are therefore deeply indebted to the center and to its Executive Director, Sandra Levinson, for making the arrangements that originally brought us together. In addition, the editors wish to commend the continuing work of the center as it seeks to break down barriers between our two countries. We are also indebted to the numerous Cuban institutions that welcomed our research and gave us access to their facilities and their personnel. In particular, we wish to thank the Foreign Ministry, Casa de las Americas, the Committees for the Defense of the Revolution, the Film Institute, the Central Trade Union Confederation, the Institute of Consumer Demand, and the Ministry of Education.

As editors we wish to acknowledge the support, both financial and otherwise, of our home institutions. The departments of government at Saint John's University in Collegeville, Minnesota, and at Saint Mary's College, Moraga, California, provided some of the assistance to bring this work together: long distance telephone facilities, travel funds, reproduction facilities, and secretarial support. Professor Prevost specifically acknowledges the financial backing of a MacPherson Foundation Grant that made possible his trip to Cuba.

The numerous others whose help was invaluable include Jeff Daniel, Monica Fusich-Cheeseman, Edivanir Fontanelli, Benjamin Frankel, and Shelly Detomasi. We especially wish to thank Shirley Zipoy at Saint John's University for her office assistance, and to acknowledge the assistance of Paul Lee and Janet Johnston at Rowman & Littlefield.

1

Cuba: A Background

Wilber A. Chaffee, Jr.

Cuba differs from the nations of the Western Hemisphere in significant ways. It has always been a different America, and today is the only state in the Americas run by a Communist party. Cuba is different in that its 1959 revolution resulted in the greatest political, social, and economic restructuring of any society in Latin America since the 16th-century conquests of Cortes and Pizarro. Cuba is historically different in that it remained a colony of imperial Spain until the end of the 19th century, obtaining independence almost eighty years after most of the rest of Spanish America. Cuba is different in terms of its economic base, sugar. Although other Latin American countries grow and export sugar, in Cuba sugar dominates the economy and therefore the society, since the island is the world's major sugar exporter.

Three major forces have played key roles in modern Cuba. First, leadership has come from organized groups of university students, known as the generations of 1868, 1895, 1930, and 1953, each of which dominated the politics of the country for a period of about thirty years. Second, the sugar economy made Cuba valuable to Spain, gave Cuba a strong African heritage, led to the creation of a sugar workers' union whose leadership was largely Communist, and defined Cuba in terms of its dependence on U.S. and later Soviet purchases at subsidized prices. Finally, geographic proximity to the United States has constrained the political, social, and economic life of Cuba, a small country of about 10 million people that lies 90 miles from Florida. For many Cubans, the United States represents an imperial power that simply took over from the Spanish, imposing its own values and control over the island. Today, even with its close ties to the Soviet Union, Cuba remains limited by U.S. intervention and the threat of further intervention. Cuban exports and products made with those exports are boycotted by the United States, and all commerce in those goods is prohibited by law. Soviet missiles were forced out of Cuba by the United

States in a deal, made exclusively with the Soviet Union, that bypassed the island's leadership, and a U.S. naval base still operates at Guantanamo in eastern Cuba.

Today's Cuba is a product of both its traditions and the policies of Fidel Castro. Tradition includes a background of Spanish rule, North American domination, and an interracial culture. But no understanding of modern Cuba is possible without consideration of the personality of its leader. Most Americans cannot name the leader of Brazil or Mexico, yet Fidel Castro is well known, which is an accurate measure of his place in international politics and his domination of Cuban society.[1]

Early History

Columbus sighted Cuba on his first voyage, and Spanish settlement soon followed; the indigenous Arawak Indians were wiped out by European diseases and the mistreatment of their Spanish rulers. In 1519 the Spanish governor of Cuba sent Hernando Cortes to set up a trading post in Mexico. Cuba became the last stop for ships delivering the riches of Peru and New Spain (Mexico) to Europe. Otherwise the Spaniards had little interest in the island and generally ignored it until the beginning of the 19th century, when the land was found to be well suited to the cultivation of sugar. An African slave trade provided the labor for the growing sugar economy.

When Napoleon invaded the Iberian Peninsula in 1807, most of Latin America used the occasion to gain independence, but Cuba remained Spanish. Yet the move toward independence had been sparked in Cuba, and during the second half of the 19th century Cubans fought three wars against imperial rule. The first, known as the Ten Years War, had an abolitionist component. It began in 1868 with the leadership of landowner Carlos Manuel de Cespedes, who freed his own slaves, and ended with minor Spanish concessions in 1878. Slavery was abolished two years later. A second, inconclusive war lasted a year and ended in 1880. The final struggle began in 1895, led by writer-poet Jose Marti and by General Antonio Maceo, a black who had become a hero when he refused to accept the earlier peace agreement with the Spanish.[2]

When the fight for independence seemed almost won, the U.S. battleship *Maine* blew up in Havana harbor.[3] The resulting war with the United States ended Spanish rule in 1898. Cubans expected immediate independence but instead gained only American occupation. Most European governments expected that the United States, which had twice attempted to buy Cuba in the middle of the 19th century, would annex the island along with Puerto Rico, but Washington promised independence.[4]

The occupation government of General Leonard Wood began re-ordering Cuban life along the lines of North American society. The University of Havana was moved to a prominent location overlooking the city, other schools were organized, public health programs were initiated, and a presidential political system was installed, complete with checks and balances following the U.S. model. A capitol building, scaled down in size from the one in Washington, D.C., completed the picture. Congress made the provision that an amendment to an appropriations bill introduced by Senator Orville H. Platt be incorporated in the Cuban Constitution of 1901. The amendment limited Cuban sovereignty in fiscal and treaty-making matters and allowed the United States to intervene at any time to maintain a "government adequate for the protection of life, property, and individual liberty." The Platt Amendment also provided for a North American naval base on the island.[5] Cuban products now went to North American markets, and the island became, in essence, a political protectorate of the United States. Twice, in 1905 and in 1917, the United States intervened militarily under the Platt provision.

A British-American agreement set up an International Sugar Committee to control the sale of Cuban sugar, dividing the export market exclusively between the two countries and giving them the power to establish the price. U.S. investment in Cuba, in addition to sugar refineries and lands, included mining, communications, and the railways. The U.S. Federal Reserve Bank established a branch in Havana.

Two political parties developed, the Liberals and the Conservatives. In 1924 Liberal candidate Gerardo Machado was elected president for a four-year term. In 1927, Machado changed the Constitution, extending the presidential term to six years and having himself reelected, which in essence destroyed the party system in Cuba.

During the Machado presidency, the influence of the Cordoba University Reform Movement reached Havana. Julio A. Mella, a law student and secretary-general of the Student Federation, organized a national student congress.[6] He later founded the Popular University Jose Marti, patterned on the Popular University Gonzalez Prada, established by Haya de la Torre in Peru, to expand education to the working class. Strongly anti-imperialist and highly critical of the role of the United States, Mella became associated with the Cuban Marxists, a small and splintered group. In 1925, working with Mexican Enrique Flores Magon, Mella (and others) organized the Cuban Communist party. Through Mella's efforts students began to attack the increasingly dictatorial government of Machado, who responded by jailing Mella. After his release Mella left for Mexico. Opposition to the Machado dictatorship continued in the University of Havana, where students organized *the Directorio Estudiantil Universitario,* which focused anti-Machado sentiment in Havana. The *Directorio* leadership was ousted from the University.[7]

The Generation of 1930

The economic collapse of 1929 caused a precipitous drop in the world price of sugar, political unrest, and severe repression. The assassination of Mella in Mexico and the increased repression of Machado led to a second *Directorio* in 1930, which began organizing open demonstrations against the government. *Directorio* leadership included future president Carlos Prio Socarras, Raul Roa (later a foreign minister under Fidel Castro), and Eduardo Chibas, future founder of the *Ortodoxo* party. A clash with police killed one of the student leaders and brought the closing of the university by Machado. Now known as the Generation of 1930, the students turned to urban violence. *Directorio* leaders were arrested, as were most of the faculty, including physiology professor Ramon Grau San Martin. Other groups developed in opposition to the increasingly unpopular Machado. U.S. Ambassador Sumner Welles tried to mediate the conflict between Machado and his opposition. Welles's effort failed, and a general strike, uprisings among the unionized sugar workers around the refineries, and an army revolt forced Machado into exile in August 1933. He was replaced by Carlos Miguel de Cespedes, son of the hero of 1868, who restored the 1901 Constitution. The new government immediately received U.S. backing.

Directorio leaders continued to agitate against the government, accusing Cespedes of being too close to Machado and the United States. Students demanded a new constitution, plus social and economic reforms. Governmental plans to freeze army promotions and reduce pay led to a takeover of the army by noncommissioned officers headed by Sergeant Fulgencio Batista. Batista, who had worked as a stenographer at the military trials of the students under the Machado regime, invited *Directorio* leaders to a meeting. Together they agreed to a coup and on the composition of the new government; Cespedes was ousted in September 1933. Although Batista had not accepted a post in the new government, the action placed Batista, a mulatto, in a position where he dominated politics through the control of the army for the next 26 years.[8]

The new government was headed by Professor Ramon Grau San Martin. American Ambassador Sumner Welles disapproved of Grau, and the United States refused to recognize the government. Batista then forced Grau to resign, established one of his own men as president, and inaugurated a program of social reform. He had himself elected president in 1940 with support from the Communist-led sugar workers, the Havana conservatives, and his power base in the army. The new and progressive Constitution of 1940 was written, and a social security system was established along with a ministry of labor. The Communists changed their party name from the *Union Revolucionaria Comunista* to *Partido Socialista Popular* (PSP). At the completion of his four-year term, Batista turned the presidency over to Dr. Grau San Martin, who won the 1944 election as the candidate of the *Autenticos,* a party he had established in 1936. (Batista had declined to be a candidate to succeed himself but kept the control of the army.) Grau completed his term of office; following the 1948 election the presidency went to another *Autentico* and member of the Generation of 1930, Carlos Prio Socarras.[9]

The *Autentico* program stressed progressive policies but quickly became identified with extremes of corruption. A new political party, the *Ortodoxos,* formed around the leadership of Eduardo Chibas, also a member of the Generation of 1930. University students, critical of the *Autentico* corruption, became a source of support and leadership for the *Ortodoxos.* The party's youth wing was led by Fidel Castro, a law student at the University of Havana. The popularity of the new party indicated that it would win the presidency in the 1952 election, and Castro became an *Ortodoxo* candidate for Congress. Chibas, an emotional yet popular figure, committed suicide while speaking on his regular radio program.

In a surprise move, Batista overthrew the government a second time, removing Prio Socarras. He canceled the upcoming election and again made himself president. The new Batista government catered to U.S. policy interests by adopting an anti-Communist position and by breaking formal diplomatic relations with the Soviet Union. Washington responded with military assistance grants of $1.5 million annually from 1954 to 1956 and doubled this figure during the 1957–1958 period. A military mission assisted in training Batista's army. Cuba was opened up to increased American investment, and Havana became a popular gambling and nightclub center just a few miles off the Florida coast. Organized crime and the Batista government cooperated in personal enrichment.

The Generation of 1953

The opposition to the new Batista government was centered in the student movement. Following the example of the Generation of 1930, the students organized urban guerrilla warfare, using the universities as sanctuaries from the federal authorities. In Havana students formed the *Directorio Revolucionario* under the leadership of Jose Antonio Echeverria. On the other end of the island in the city of Santiago de Cuba, Frank Pais, son of a Protestant minister, organized students at the University of Oriente.

Fidel Castro gathered a number of students around him and sought to begin a national uprising by capturing the army barracks at Moncada in the eastern part of the island. They attacked on July 26, 1953. In the ensuing battle most of the attackers were killed, and Castro was captured. At his trial Castro defended himself, saying "History will absolve me." He was sentenced to prison on the Isle of Pines and was released after twenty-two months as part of a general amnesty by Batista. An agreement between Castro and Frank Pais created the *Movimiento 26 Julio* (M-26-7), named for the date of the Moncada barracks attack. After Castro had made a number of appearances in continued opposition to Batista, he was advised to leave the country, and began to enlist and train a guerrilla army in Mexico. There he met and began work with an Argentine doctor, Ernesto "Che" Guevara, who had been in Guatemala with the government of Jacobo Arbenz until the CIA–backed overthrow of the government. Using some of the money provided by former president Prio, Castro bought a yacht, the *Granma*, from a retired American couple. In November 1956 he loaded the *Granma* with 82 men and sailed for Cuba, landing in Oriente Province. In a coordinated effort Frank Pais tried to divert the attention of Batista's forces to the city of Santiago, but the invaders were met by army units. The survivors, including Castro, his brother Raul, and Che Guevara, took refuge in the Sierra Maestra mountains.[10]

In Havana, Echeverria and the *Directorio* tried to assassinate Batista in March 1957 in an armed attack on the Presidential Palace. The attempt failed and resulted in the deaths of Echeverria and most of the *Directorio* leadership. Shortly afterward, in Santiago, authorities captured and executed Frank Pais. Fidel Castro was left the most visible leader in the battle against Batista.[11]

Students were not the only opposition to the government. Castro and Pais's M-26-7 had a branch in Havana, known as the *Resistencia Civica,* that included Raul Chibas, brother of Eduardo; Manuel Ray, president of the civil engineers' association and Felipe Pazos, Cuba's leading economist. Former president Carlos Prio organized the *Organizacion Autentica,* which unsuccessfully attacked army barracks in Matanzas Province in April 1956. Justo Carrillo, a former student activist and president of the Bank for Reconstruction and Development in the Prio administration, created the *Montecristo* movement with left-wing military officers for a planned coup, which was aborted when Batista arrested the leadership. Carrillo had met earlier with Castro in Mexico and contributed funds to the M-26-7. (Castro had been promised the mayoralty of Havana by Carrillo if the coup succeeded.) Another group of young military officers, the *Puros,* who had been associated with Chibas's *Ortodoxos,* were led by Colonel Ramon Barquin and planned a military revolt. Batista imprisoned Barquin; but in September 1957 a mixed group of *Montecristos, Autenticos,* and M-26-7 supporters, along with naval personnel, took over the naval base at Cienfuegos and held it for a day, hoping for a series of revolts across the country. One group that was not involved was the Communist PSP.

Efforts to unite the anti-Batista forces culminated at a July 1958 meeting in Caracas, Venezuela, of representatives of most of the resistance groups. A *Frente Civico Revolucionario Democratico* was organized, and agreement was reached on the structuring of a post-Batista government. Judge Manuel Urrutia Lleo was selected as president of the provisional government, Dr. Miro Cardono as coordinator of the *Frente,* and Castro as commander-in-chief of the armed forces.

The obvious weakening of support for Batista, defection in the military, and increased revulsion for Batista's excesses of repression led to withdrawal of U.S. backing for the government. In March 1958, under pressure from the Senate, the U.S. State Department placed an arms embargo on Cuba. In December the Eisenhower administration privately sent former U.S. Ambassador and Miami executive William D. Pawley to Havana to tell Batista that he should step down and be replaced with a government led by Colonel Barquin. Batista refused, and a few days later U.S. Ambassador Earl E.T. Smith officially informed Batista that he had to leave. On New Year's Day 1959, Batista and some of his close associates left Cuba, and a provisional government under Judge Urrutia took over. The new government consisted of a mixture of old-line, anti-Batista political figures and revolutionaries from the middle class.

A few days later Fidel Castro entered Havana, the hero of the overthrow of Batista and the most popular man in the nation. He noted that the U.S. military had prohibited the *Ejercito Liberator* under General Calixto Garcia from entering Santiago de Cuba in 1898, and commented that history would not be repeated.[12] Castro took no position in the new government but set about consolidating the military forces under his command. He sent Camilo Cienfuegos to relieve Barquin, who had taken command of Batista's remaining troops. Forces of the *Directorio* initially refused to disarm and had to be persuaded to accept Castro's authority.

In mid-February 1959, Castro accepted the position of prime minister and began to push through measures that would distribute wealth and increase his support in the rural areas. In May the Agrarian Reform Act expropriated large private estates, most of which had been worked on a tenancy or share-cropping basis. Passage of the Rent Reduction Act resulted in the transfer of about 15 percent of the national income from property owners to wage workers and peasants. By July 1959 Fidel Castro, through a series of confrontations, had forced out of the government members not loyal to him, and held supreme power.[13]

Castro in Power

As Fidel Castro consolidated his power, he surrounded himself with persons of determined loyalty. Che Guevara took over the Central Bank. Majors Raul Castro and Sergio del Valle and Captain Rogelio Acevedo, all Sierra Maestra veteran officers, organized National Revolutionary Militias in October 1959. A vote for the leadership of the Federation of Workers (CTC) resulted in Castro's candidate, David Salvador Manso, becoming its secretary-general over the opposition of the Communists, who abstained from the election.[14]

At the same time, potential sources of political competition were eliminated. Major Huber Matos, one of the leaders of the guerrilla action against Batista and then governor of the province of Camaguey, protested the shift of the Cuban government to the left and resigned from the military, along with other officers under his command. Matos and 22 officers were arrested, sentenced, and imprisoned for up to twenty years. Similarly, when Havana students began university politics as before, organizing elections for the Federation of University Students (FEU), Castro personally intervened. The losing candidate, who had been asked not to run, was arrested and sentenced to prison.[15] Meanwhile the exodus from Cuba, which had begun as the flight of persons associated with Batista and his government, increased as large numbers of the middle class and professionals joined the migration.

Despite criticism of Castro's increasing concentration of power and his wealth-distribution policies, the Cuban government maintained the Batista policy toward the USSR, a policy of nonrecognition that had pleased the U.S. government. This policy began to change, and in December 1959 a *Tass* correspondent was admitted to Havana. In February, USSR First Deputy Premier Anastasias Mikoyan paid a visit, and a Soviet-Cuban trade agreement was signed. Che Guevara went to Eastern Europe and lined up $100 million in credits for the industrialization of Cuba. Relations with the Soviet Union offered a balance and an alternative to the dominance of American power in Cuban affairs. Formal diplomatic relations were reestablished between the two countries in May 1960.

The Cuban economy depends on sugar. A U.S. quota system had allocated Cuba a 2.8 million-ton market at a predetermined and subsidized price considerably above the world market price. One of the first actions of friendship by the Soviet Union was the February 1960 purchase of Cuban sugar. As U.S.–Cuban relations worsened, the USSR agreed to purchase up to 2.7 million tons of Cuban sugar if the American government reduced its quota. The Soviet Union also began to supply Cuba with oil. Cuba has a small domestic supply of petroleum, but only enough to meet about 15 percent of national needs. With a shortage of foreign exchange, Cuba found it increasingly difficult to keep the refineries supplied with imported oil, mostly from Venezuela. In April 1960 the first shipment of Soviet oil arrived in exchange for Cuban products. Representatives of the American oil companies, advised by the U.S. Secretary of the Treasury, refused to refine the oil. The refineries were then taken over by the Cuban government, and Washington responded by eliminating Cuba's sugar quota, the backbone of the Cuban economy.

The confrontation between Havana and Washington had been building throughout 1959 and 1960. The Cuban government assumed control of the International Telephone and Telegraph–owned Cuban Telephone Company in March 1959. The Agrarian Reform Law of May resulted in the seizure of many large American properties with an offer of 20-year bonds for payment; the United States, rejecting the bonds, demanded "prompt, adequate, and effective compensation." By December 1959 the CIA began to recruit Cuban exiles, and in March 1960 Eisenhower decided to arm and train an exile force for the purpose of invading the island and precipitating the overthrow of the Castro government. Cuban nationalization continued with a series of expropriations: U.S.–owned properties in August, foreign banks in September, and more businesses in October. The United States broke diplomatic relations with Cuba in October and instituted an embargo on most exports to Cuba.

John Kennedy in January 1961 assumed the presidency of the United States and with it the responsibility for the group of Cuban exiles, now training in Central America under CIA direction. In Cuba, Castro had inaugurated the Committees for the Defense of the Revolution (CDR), organized block by block in the cities, to guard against opposition and to enlist support for the government. In the mountains of Escambray a group of anti-Castro guerrillas maintained a harassment of government troops, but at U.S. request stopped action until the exile forces were ready. In April the exiles invaded Cuba at the Bay of Pigs but were stalled by local militias, while in the cities the CDRs quickly pointed out persons in opposition, who were immediately arrested before any of them could support the invasion. The major result of the American intervention was the consolidation of Castro's position by creating a solid identification between the anti-imperialism of Cuban tradition and the victory of the forces under Fidel Castro. Socialist countries supported Cuba, with the USSR honoring its promise to buy 2.7 million tons of sugar. The People's Republic of China bought a million tons, and other socialist nations 300,000 tons. Fidel Castro openly tied Cuba to the Eastern European nations when he declared, on December 1, 1961, "I am a Marxist-Leninist," the first time that he publicly stated his allegiance to a communist doctrine.

With Castro's announced adherence to communism, Anibal Escalante, one of the earlier leaders of the PSP, organized the Integrated Revolutionary Organization (ORI) from the 26th of July Movement, the old PSP, and surviving members of the *Directorio*. Escalante went further, and within the ORI he tried to organize a group that would be dominated by old-line Communist loyalists. This was a serious miscalculation, for Fidel Castro, unwilling to allow competition for leadership, denounced Escalante on March 27, 1962, and thus destroyed his bid for power. Other potential sources of competition, including the University of Havana where both Communists and student leaders had independent political bases, were also purged.

In 1963 the United Party of the Socialist Revolution (PURS) was created, structured along the lines of the Communist party in the Soviet Union, with Fidel Castro as its first secretary. Under the PURS–run government, Castro was named prime minister, commander-in-chief of the armed forces, and director of the Institute of Agrarian Reform. His brother Raul was named second-in-command in all these posts. The Political Bureau of the party included, in addition to the two Castros, civilians Armando Hart, as party secretary, and President Osvaldo Dorticos, plus majors Juan Almeida, Ramiro Valdes, Guillermo Garcia, and Sergio del Valle, all long-time associates of Castro with strong personal loyalties to him. The party secretariat included former Popular Socialist Party leaders Carlos Rafael Rodriguez and Blas Roca, and Major Faure Chomon, earlier one of the leaders of the *Directorio*. The party's Central Committee had 100 members, more than 60 percent of whom were military men. Three women were included: Vilma Espin, Haydee Santamaria, and Celia Sanchez, who had been closely associated with Castro in the Sierra Maestra. In October 1965 the party was renamed the Communist Party of Cuba and reorganized to increase the size of the Central Committee. Anibal Escalante, who was in Eastern Europe after his earlier confrontation with Castro, returned to Cuba, made contacts with officials of Eastern European embassies, and began meeting with old PSP members critical of Castro's policies. In 1967 Escalante and persons associated with him were arrested and imprisoned.

As a part of Fidel Castro's vision and ambition, Cuba began to support other revolutions, especially in Latin America. The Andes were to be the Sierra Maestra of South America. An attempt to eliminate President Romalo Betancourt of Venezuela (in a car bombing that injured but failed to kill him), was blamed on revolutionaries connected to Cuba and resulted in the breaking of diplomatic relations between the two countries. Betancourt had been elected on a left-of-center platform, ending a tradition of military dictatorship in Venezuela, and the bombing turned many Latin American countries away from support for the Cuban revolution. In January 1962 Cuba was ousted from the

Organization of American States (OAS), which also recommended economic sanctions. In the following years all the other OAS members except Mexico broke economic and diplomatic ties with Cuba. The United States also banned the docking of any merchant ship that had entered Cuban ports, which further reduced Cuba's trade with the West.

Conflict intensified when Soviet missiles were sited in Cuba during the fall of 1962. The United States dealt only with the Soviet Union in deciding the outcome, without bringing Cuba into the negotiations. For the Cubans this reemphasized the fact that control of Cuba's destiny remained in the hands of the great powers, and especially the United States. Cuba also tried to balance Soviet power by improving relations with the People's Republic of China, then in the process of establishing its own independence from Moscow. The Chinese, limited in their resources and with no ability to project power outside the Asian land-mass, could not oust the Soviets. In 1968 the Cubans turned back to a position of full support for the Soviet Union, signified by Castro's defense of the Red Army's right to invade Czechoslovakia.

In 1970, at Castro's insistence, Cuba attempted to harvest 10 million tons of sugar. Although the 8.5 million-ton harvest was the greatest in Cuban history, it was short of the stated goal, and in the process the economy was disrupted. Castro accepted the blame and began a more rationalized planning of the Cuban economy, reducing the amount of ad hoc decision-making that had characterized his rule. Steps were taken to allow a very limited private economy. A number of observers believed that the Cuban revolution had begun to be institutionalized through the diffusion of the decision-making process. But after the 1986 Party Congress, Castro reversed this trend and reasserted the need to return to more centralized control. He closed the peasant markets and reduced the sale of private housing in a reemphasis of Marxist doctrine. To-day, Castro remains the ultimate decision-maker, albeit with advice.[16]

President Jimmy Carter initiated a U.S.–Cuban dialogue with the intention of normalizing relations.[17] In 1977 the United States lifted the ban on travel to Cuba, and some 250 major American corporations sent representatives to investigate the potential for trade. Tourists also began to visit the island, especially Cuban-Americans who used the occasion to become reacquainted with family members from whom they had been separated by political differences. The two countries signed an anti-hijacking treaty, and interest sections opened in the embassies of both capitals. But progress in the regularization of relations halted when the Cubans sent troops to Africa in 1978. Contact with the tourists, in particular those bringing gifts to family members still in Cuba, awakened in some Cubans a desire to emigrate. In April 1980 nearly 11,000 Cubans crowded into the ground of the Peruvian Embassy, demanding to leave the country.[18] The government opened the port of Mariel, a local bus ride from Havana, to small boats from the United States, which resulted in the emigration of some 125,000 Cubans. In the spring of 1982 the Reagan administration again restricted travel to Cuba, prohibiting business trips and tourism.[19]

Mythology of the Revolution

Governments need a national mythology to justify their existence and policies. In Cuba the mythology is omnipresent. Symbols focus on the elements of history that best legitimize the revolution. In downtown Havana, behind the old Presidential Palace, the refurbished yacht *Granma* sits on display in a glassed-in structure with special raised walkways, so tourists and school children can picture the realities of the landing in Oriente. Surrounding the *Granma* are relics of the weapons used by the invaders at the Bay of Pigs. The Presidential Palace, once occupied by Batista, has become a museum of the revolution.

Jose Marti is the martyr of Cuban independence and patron saint of the revolution. A monument to Marti in the center of Havana—a sculptured figure of Marti on one knee in front of a massive tower—dominates the Plaza of the Revolution, forming a backdrop to the speaker's platform for many of Castro's appearances. Marti looks out on huge portraits of Che Guevara and Camilo Cienfuegos painted on the wall of a building behind the plaza.[20] Small busts of Marti, apparently produced in some local factory, appear ubiquitously throughout the country. Everywhere the names of Julio Mella, Frank Pais, and Jose Antonio Echeverria appear on schools, parks, hospitals, and sports arenas. Even the calendar is given a slogan for each year: "1986: Year of the XXX anniversary of the landing of the *Granma*."

The greatest revolutionary symbol of all is Castro himself. His picture is not widely seen on walls and posters, but Castro appears in person in a guerrilla uniform of green fatigues and pistol belt, with his beard from anti-Batista days. His speeches are always printed verbatim in the official party newspaper, *Granma*, with a number of photos taken during the speech. Castro symbolizes the new Cuba, independent of the United States, constantly fighting for a revolution in a world society where man will not exploit man. Castro, the self-declared heir of Marti and Mella, the man who broke the grip of the United States, dominates Cuba.[21]

Cuba Today

Cuba today is different than the Cuba of the 1950s. For some, both inside and outside Cuba, the differences are good, while others regard the changes in Cuba in a negative light. Still, Cuba must be considered as it is today and not as its critics wish it to be. Both critics and supporters of present-day Cuba quote selectively from statistics about the pre-revolutionary period. On an average or per capita basis, Cuba was not a backward Latin American country before the revolution, but wealth, health, and education were seriously maldistributed and heavily concentrated in Havana. As a result, Havana was one of the most exciting cities in the Americas—close to the United States, pleasing to the eye and palate, and with every desire available for purchase.

Today's Cuba is a socialist state, allied with and subsidized by the Soviet Union. A large, recently constructed Soviet embassy dominates a major area of the Buenavista district of Havana. Its conference rooms, apartments for diplomats, and tower resembling a minaret are all surrounded by a wall. The Miramar district has a major office building, the Comecon offices in Cuba. News kiosks carry, in addition to Cuban government publications, Spanish editions of socialist magazines full of smiling children and triumphs of central planning. East European technicians, easily identified by their round, reddish faces and blond hair, ride the buses or visit the beaches frequented by governmental officials and their guests. Bookstores are well stocked with the collected works of Lenin, Engels, and Marx, along with the latest issues of Castro's speeches, the Family Code, or the latest Five-Year Plan. Novels by Alejo Carpentier and Gabriel Garcia Marquez are available, as are translations of Ernest Hemingway, a personal hero of Castro's, and books such as Mario Puzo's *The Godfather* (a novel containing gangsters who were intertwined with Cuban history). Children's books extol the virtues of socialism and the importance of the revolution. Russian-language engineering texts sell to an increasing group of Cuban technicians.

Havana itself shows the effects of studied neglect, since money has been shifted to the countryside. Few of the buildings have been painted recently, and whole structures have collapsed through lack of maintenance. Some of the older parts of the city are being refurbished through a UNESCO program to preserve the architectural past; and the beauty of the seafront highway, the Malecon, remains, although with much less traffic than in pre-revolutionary times. Plumbing, that North American measure of civilization, needs serious attention: water must sometimes be delivered by truck, and sewer lines often fail. Yet the Tropicana nightclub, a time warp of statuesque chorus girls with elaborate headdresses, provides well-paced evenings of entertainment to maximum capacity audiences. In downtown Havana, restaurants of every price and quality continue to serve a variety of dishes, from the swank but small 1830 club to Hemingway's favorites, La Bodeguita and Floridita. The transportation system includes taxis whose drivers reject fares they find awkward, and cheap but limited public transportation on municipal buses colloquially known as *quaquas.*

Many of the apartments and homes of the formerly exclusive Miramar residential district now house the less affluent and persons who previously would not have been there due to their mixed blood.[22] A former exclusive club on the waterfront is now the recreation center of the Tobacco Worker's Union. People can and do listen to most radio stations from the southern United States, and on many evenings atmospheric conditions make Miami television available in the homes. A lively trade of videotapes, brought in and copied by Cubans who have been out of the country, exists. Films from Mexico, Japan, France, and Eastern Europe, as well as Cuban productions, are shown in the theaters. Brazilian television, dubbed into Spanish, flavors the otherwise dull Cuban viewing fare.

The Cubans have invested heavily in tourism, and many tourists from Europe and Canada arrive to enjoy the beaches and see what a Marxist-run country is like. Regular flights to and from Mexico are often full. Tourists rent Volkswagens and are not restricted in travel around the country. In the major hotels are stores in which only foreign exchange can be used and in which most luxury items, from cosmetics to blue-jeans, are available. An illegal but not very closely regulated black market exchanges foreign currency at about six times the official rate.

Prices and wages are controlled, goods are in short supply, and there is a surplus of available personal funds. Savings banks have been established to siphon off some of the capital, and nightspots like the Tropicana cater not only to tourists but to many Cubans. Designer jeans for women are very popular and are often purchased with black market currency in the foreign exchange stores. Consumer products from Eastern Europe can be found even in the countryside, where even small farmhouses have refrigerators and washing machines. Cuban-made television sets are in most homes. Simple houses on a cooperative farm will have an automobile, perhaps a new Fiat-designed Lada or Polski, or perhaps an old Edsel, while Soviet-built tractors that look like Massey-Ferguson copies work in the fields.

Rural Cuba has been the greatest beneficiary of the Cuban revolution. Cane cutters, the backbone of the sugar economy, were employed less than half the year in the *zafra* (harvest). Now the cutting is 65 percent mechanized, and jobs have been organized to eliminate the months of unemployment. Rural areas now have highly improved medical services, as a result of distribution of public health personnel and the building of clinics in the countryside. Similarly, educational benefits have been extended to the agricultural population, with a ninth-grade education now approaching universal proportions and higher education available to those who qualify. Both education and health care are provided by the state without expense to the individual.

Despite a policy of industrialization and agricultural diversification, sugar remains the foundation of the Cuban economy. In the decade prior to the revolution, sugar supplied 84 percent of the export earnings; now it supplies 81 percent. As the demand for sugar falls in the world, Cuba plans to increase production. The 1984 harvest amounted to 8.2 million tons, Cuba's third largest. Projections call for eleven million tons by 1990, and eventually twelve.

The OAS boycott of Cuba no longer exists, and most of the Latin American countries now recognize the Havana government. Argentina annually promotes a trade fair in Cuba in which more than 150 firms exhibit, and Argentine exports to Cuba reached $250 million by 1985. As Uruguay, Ecuador, and Brazil moved back to civilian governments, relations with Cuba were restored.[23] Only Chile, Paraguay, and the United States, among the OAS nations, have no formal relations with Cuba.

Cuba remains one of the Americas, yet a different one. Culture is emphasized and subsidized. The Casa de las Americas publications center gives sought-after prizes for Latin American literature every year, and a significant film industry exists. A redistribution of wealth has taken place, and the grinding poverty of other countries in Latin America has been eliminated. Yet individual liberty and political expression are severely limited. Education is widely available, medical standards are high, and there is sufficient food, although greatly limited in variety. Housing remains a persistent problem, and its allocation is frequently criticized.

The rapid growth in population of earlier years has slowed, and the birthrate has fallen through a combination of factors: the availability of birth control and abortion, higher education, tight housing, and the greatly diminished influence of the Catholic church. Women often say "Two are enough." As a consequence the average population age is rising, which will increase the cost of medical services in the future.[24]

Fidel Castro remains firmly in power after almost thirty years, and could continue for fifteen or twenty years more. Now sixty, his health appears good, at least good enough to take U.S. congressmen scuba diving. Despite the emphasis on the creation of a "new type of man" who places the needs of the community above individual interests, Castro is a great individualist, larger than life — a Hemingway hero who refuses to be bound to the traditional role of a Latin American *caudillo*. He speaks brilliantly, using only a few notes of statistics, and crafts orations for two- or three-hour policy-making speeches. Castro has projected Cuba and himself onto the world scene to affect international politics as though he were the leader of a major world power. Despite links to the Soviet Union, Cuba has played an active part in the Organization of Non-Aligned Nations and hosted its 1979 meeting, with Castro subsequently serving as president of the group. Recently he has courted improved relations with the Catholic church, hosting American bishops, allowing his conversation about religion with a Brazilian priest to be published, and inviting Mother Theresa to open a chapter of her order in Cuba.[25]

Cuba and the United States

Debate continues in the United States as to its proper relationship with Cuba, one of several significant nations—the others being Vietnam, Albania, Iran, and North Korea—that Washington does not recognize. A number of factors influence the policy of non-recognition, including the question of compensation for nationalized properties, some $1.85 billion in claims plus interest. Yet relations have never reached a point where compensation questions have been seriously addressed.

A politically significant Cuban-American population, centered in Florida, for the most part strongly opposes any improvement in relations while Fidel Castro remains in power. Many, if not most, of the Cuban-American community lost property and sometimes a lifetime of achievement. Other Cuban-Americans had struggled against the Batista dictatorship and attempted to build a Cuba they envisioned, only to be displaced when they came into conflict with Castro's plans. Naturally allied with the anti-Castro exiles are the group of Americans who still view ideological conflict as a morality play, with Castro cast as one of the villains.

A large portion of the U.S. academic community disagrees with U.S. policy, pointing out that Cuba was, "and is perhaps better," than a number of Latin American nations, especially during the 1970s. Isolation of Cuba at best delays the inevitable and works against U.S. long-range interests. The State Department is not united in support of the isolationist policy. Wayne S. Smith, who served as chief of the U.S. Interests Section in Cuba from 1979 to 1982, stated that it is the United States, not Cuba, that will not negotiate a possible normalization of relations.[26] A growing number of Cuban-Americans also are reevaluating the traditional view of their community, and are calling for a more balanced policy.

Historically, the United States has been opposed by a Cuban anti-imperialist nationalism. This theme of Cuban culture extends from the 1868 anti-slavery movement of Cespedes, through the writings of Jose Marti, to the student organization of Julio Mella and the Generation of 1930, and finally to the establishment of the *fidelismo* of modern Cuba. Yet it is this nationalism, strongly evident in Cuba, that offers the possibility of reducing Cuban dependence on the Soviet Union.

Cuba is different, yet it remains a part of the Americas with a tradition that colors Cuban thought. It has continuing ties to all the other nations of the hemisphere, including the United States. What has happened in Cuba in the last thirty years is but one aspect of a change that is taking place in all of Latin America, as the old patterns of U.S. dominance are being supplanted by an emerging independence. As a result, new relationships must be built between the United States and the Latin American nations. Cuba represents the reality of a different America.

Notes

1. Wayne S. Smith, *The Closest of Enemies*, says (p. 144) that even if one disagrees with Castro, he remains "one of the most interesting political figures to stride about the world stage in the last half of the twentieth century."

2. For a good review of this period, see Patricia Weiss Fagen, "Antonio Maceo: Heroes, History, and Historiography," *Latin American Research Review* 11, no. 3 (Fall 1976): 69–93.

3. Duvon Clough Corbitt, "Cuban Revisionist Interpretations of Cuba's Struggle for Independence," *Hispanic American Historical Review* 43, no. 3 (August 1963): 395–404.

4. See C. Stanley Urban, "The Africanization of Cuba Scare, 1853–1855," *Hispanic American Historical Review* 37, no. 1 (February 1957): 29–45, for an example of one attempt by North Americans to annex Cuba. Also see Jaime Suchlicki, *Cuba: From Columbus to Castro*, 74–99.

5. For the text of the Platt Amendment, see Suchlicki, *Cuba*, 96–97.

6. For a background on University Reform, see *University Reform in Latin America.* (Leiden: COSEC, 1961). For its relation to Cuba and other countries, see Alistair Hennessy, "University Students in National Politics," in Claudio Veliz, ed., *The Politics of Conformity in Latin America.* (New York: Oxford Univ. Press, 1967), 119–57.

7. Erasmo Dumpiere, *Mella, esbozo biographico* (Havana: Instituto de la Historia, 1965). Also see *Julio Mella: Documentos para su vida.* (Havana: Comision Cubana de la UNESCO, 1964).

8. Ruiz, *Cuba*, 89, 158.

9. William S. Stokes, "The Cuban Revolution and the Presidential Elections of 1948," *Hispanic American Historical Review* 37, no. 1 (February 1951); Jose Alvarez Diaz, *Un Estudo sobre Cuba.* (Coral Gables: Univ. of Miami Press, 1963).

10. Tad Szulc, *Fidel: A Critical Portrait*, 211–459; Carlos Franqui, *Diary of the Cuban Revolution* (New York: Viking Press, 1980).

11. For the best discussion of the student movements, see Jaime Suchlicki, *University Students and Revolution in Cuba 1920–1968*, 58–86.

12. Franqui, *Diary*, 489.

13. Hugh Thomas, *Cuba: The Pursuit of Freedom*; Ramon L. Bonechea and Marta San Marin, *The Cuban Insurrection 1952–1959*; and Szulz, *Fidel*. For a Cuban chronology, see Antonio Nunez Jimenez, *En marcha con Fidel: 1959* (Havana: Letras Cubanas, 1982).

14. Szulz, *Fidel*, 463–520.

15. Suchlicki, *University Students*, 89–90.

16. *Granma*, February 5–8, 1986, reports the changes made by the 3rd Congress of the Communist Party of Cuba. A continuing series of shifts in policy were announced through the year, with the closing of the farmer's markets in April.

17. For a history of the attempts to regularize relations with Cuba during the Carter administration, see Smith, *Closest of Enemies*, 101–27.

18. Ibid., 198.

19. Harvey F. Kline, "Cuba: The Politics of Socialist Revolution," in 2nd Ed., Howard Wiarda and Harvey Kline, eds., *Latin America: Politics and Development*, (Boulder, Colo.: Westview Press, 1985), 446–487, gives an excellent political history of post-revolutionary Cuba.

20. Jose Marti represents the embodiment of Cuban nationalism and the struggle against U.S. domination. See Richard B. Gray, *Jose Marti, Cuban Patriot*; Jorge Manach, *Marti: Apostle of Freedom* (New York: Devin Adair 1950); and for his literary work, see Ivan A. Schulman, *Simbolo y color en la obra de Jose Marti* (Madrid: 1960).

21. See Edward Gonzalez, *Cuba under Castro: The Limits of Charisma* (Boston: Houghton Mifflin, 1974), especially chap. 9 (190–216). Smith, *Closest of Enemies*, 196, says that Castro could win an election in Cuba today.

22. For a background on race relations in Cuba, see Geoffrey E. Fox, "Cuban Racism," *Transaction* (September 1971); reprinted in Irving Louis Horowitz, ed., *Cuban Communism* (New Brunswick, N.J.: Transaction Books, 1972). For a view of race relations at an earlier time, see Foreign Policy Association, "Ethnic Composition of the Island's Population and Problems of Cultural Conflict," in Robert Freeman Smith, ed., *Background to Revolution* (New York: Alfred A. Knopf, 1966).

23. Argentina's president, Raul Alfonsin, made an official visit to Cuba in October 1986. A similar visit was made by Ecuador's president, Leon Febres Cordero.

24. Sergio Diaz-Briquets and Lisandro Perez, "Fertility Decline in Cuba: A Socioeconomic Interpretation," *Population and Development Review* 8, no. 3 (September 1982): 513–37.

25. Frei Betto, *Fidel Castro y religion. Granma: Weekly Review*, February 3, 1985, reported on the visit of five representatives of the National Conference of Catholic Bishops of the United States.

26. Wayne Smith, "Dateline Havana: Myopic Diplomacy," *Foreign Policy* 48 (Fall 1982): 157–74; Smith, "U.S.–Cuba Relations: Twenty-Five Years of Hostility," 333–51; Smith, *Closest of Enemies*. Also see the collection of letters to the editor arguing over U.S. policy toward Cuba in the same copy of *Foreign Policy*.

2

Poder Popular and the *Buro Politico:* Political Control in Cuba

Wilber A. Chaffee, Jr.

Cuba, the only one-party, Marxist-Leninist state in Latin America, is unique in having developed institutions for maintaining citizen participation. Only the Communist Party of Cuba is allowed to organize, and membership in the party is generally necessary for success in Cuban society. To run the government, a political structure, partly patterned on the Soviet Union, has evolved through trial and error into the present system. The only factor that has remained constant is the essential leadership, dominated by Fidel Castro and a loyal group who fought with him during the 1950s against the U.S.–backed dictatorship of General Fulgencio Batista. Fidel Castro maintains his general popularity in the country, and most observers believe that he could be elected in an honest competitive contest; no mean achievement for one who approaches thirty years in power.

Cuban politics, like most politics, has both a formal structure and an informal structure. An understanding of the formal structure is only the first step in an understanding of politics, since the internal workings of a nation are often better explained by its informal linkages. In Cuba all decision-making comes down from the top through a series of pyramidal structures that go from national to provincial and finally to municipal levels, and sometimes to zones of municipalities. For the purpose of administration, the country is divided into fourteen provinces (plus a special municipality, the Isle of Youth), and each of the provinces is divided into municipalities. Provinces are somewhat analogous to U.S. states, and the municipalities are similar to New England townships. Even though decisions on policy are made at the top of every pyramid, there is considerable autonomy in the day-to-day running of government and the economy at every level. Even at the local level are disagreement and alteration of specific policies.

Persons are integrated into the political system through a series of mass organizations that include most of the population. Ninety-nine percent of the grade-school children belong to the *Pioneros*; 99 percent of the workers are organized into official unions; 80 percent of Cuban women belong to the Federation of Cuban Women (FMC); small farmers are members of the National Association of Small Farmers (ANAP); and many young adults have membership in the Union of Young Communists (UJC).[1]

Formally, three major organizations reach into every area of national life and structure the politics and society of contemporary Cuba: the Committees for the Defense of the Revolution, the Assemblies of People's Power (*Poder Popular*), and the Communist Party of Cuba.

Committees for the Defense of the Revolution

The Committees for the Defense of the Revolution (CDRs) are structured like old-fashioned political wards, and for many of the same reasons; they directly link the political leadership with the population both in terms of the supply of social services and the expression of demands on the government. The committees have the role of maintaining local security and ideological enthusiasm for the government. Officially, 84 percent of the population over the age of fourteen are members of a CDR.

At the top, the CDRs are headed by a member of the Central Committee of the Communist Party of Cuba, Armando Acosta Cordero. Under him are two vice-presidents, a man and a woman. There are five levels of organization. A National Directorate of the Committees coordinates the work throughout the country. Under the National Directorate are the fourteen Provincial Directorates. These in turn direct the Municipal Directorates, which average about fifteen municipalities per province. The municipalities are broken down into zones, each with its Zonal Directorate overseeing the dozen or more local committees that have responsibility for a few blocks, in the cities, or larger areas in the rural communities.

Each local CDR has an elected chairman and vice-chairman, plus secretaries for Ideology, Armed Forces, Surveillance, Public Health, and Public Activities. Monthly the chairman of each local committee meets with the secretariat of his or her zone, where each CDR chairman receives a written memorandum noting the activities of the following month. The previous month is reviewed, goals are discussed, and persons and groups selected to be honored each December for outstanding service. The CDRs maintain a directory of all persons living in their area of responsibility, and register all newborn children.

The local Ideological Secretary meets regularly with the Ideological Secretary of the zone, who provides orientation and materials to be used in local meetings. The CDRs then organize seminars to discuss the material, which may include new policies from the government, speeches by the national leadership, or more mundane subjects such as family life, the bringing up of children, and other issues important to the smooth running of Cuban society. Proposed laws, including the new constitution, are examined in draft form and result in recommendations to higher levels of the government. The higher levels of government and the Party seriously consider CDR recommendations and sometimes alter proposals to conform with local concerns.

The Surveillance Secretary organizes night patrols around the committee's area not unlike the community watch groups that have developed in portions of the United States. The only differences are that they are organized on a national basis, and the definition of crimes includes activities considered suspicious in terms of state security. The CDRs are not armed and are not a police force, but if they find suspicious activities they notify the authorities. Suspicious activity could include individuals living beyond their legal means of income. Patrols are often carried out by middle-aged housewives or retired couples, to prevent interference with daily employment. As members of the community, the CDR activists know all the people who normally belong in the area and notice any out-of-the-ordinary activity or persons. At the time of the 1961 Bay of Pigs invasion by Cuban exiles, dissidents within Cuba were expected to rise up and support the invasion. The CDRs proudly claim that they knew the dissidents and had them placed in custody, which prevented their acting against the government.

The Armed Forces Secretary supports the work of the military and the government in its overseas work. When youths within a CDR district reach the age of sixteen, they are contacted to register for military service. When they are called into service, a going-away party is arranged, and a bigger celebration is organized for all who successfully complete their service. The CDR also looks after the families of "international workers," who are doctors, nurses, construction workers, and teachers sent overseas as a part of Cuban foreign aid. Although many of the CDR members are in the militia, and earlier the CDRs and the militias were interrelated, that relationship has been formally disbanded.

The CDRs are also responsible for general social work, such as identifying elderly persons no longer able to care for themselves, and for contacting the appropriate authorities in each case. They also encourage all students to stay in school at least through the ninth-grade level.

The ability of the CDRs to mobilize masses of people to demonstrate on behalf of the government is impressive. One of the greatest outpourings of mass support occurred during the Mariel exodus of dissidents during the Carter administration. The number of people who wanted to leave Cuba reflected badly on the country's image and undercut national self-esteem. The CDRs turned out half a million persons to march in support of the government. The CDRs are the mobilization arm of Cuba, enhancing nationalism through concern, contact, and information.

People's Power

People's Power is a unique institution among Communist countries, because its officials at the municipal level are elected by secret ballot of the electorate from a competitive slate of candidates. These officials in turn select deputies to provincial and national People's Power Assemblies in indirect elections.

People's Power was tried initially in 1974 as a one-year experiment in the province of Matanzas. It was then extended nationally following a December 1975 recommendation of the First Congress of the Communist Party of Cuba that the system be included in the new constitution. After six months of discussion throughout the country in the CDRs, the constitution with the People's Power provision was passed by 96 percent of the vote in a national referendum. The process included a new election law, a new political division of the country into the present organization of provinces and municipalities, and finally the creation of the National Assembly of People's Power in December 1977.

The highest organ of government is the 502-member National Assembly of People's Power that meets twice annually for two days. As the legislative body of Cuba, the Assembly passes the budget, confirms heads of ministries, makes laws, selects Supreme Court Justices, and sets five-year economic plans. The members of the Assembly, the *diputados* (deputies) are elected for five-year terms. Seventy percent of the deputies are either members of the Communist party or of the Union of Communist Youth.[2] The National Assembly also appoints a 31-member Council of State to run the government on a day-to-day basis between the Assembly sessions. The president of the Council, Fidel Castro, is both Head of State and Head of Government. This gives him the official power to name the first vice-president, five other vice-presidents, and the members of the Council of Ministers, all of whom are subject to confirmation by the National Assembly. In addition to its executive functions, the Council of State can legislate by issuing "decree-laws" when the Assembly is not in session. The Council of State also instructs the courts of Cuba.[3]

The election process in Cuba starts at the municipal level, where every 3500 people elect one representative to a Municipal Assembly of People's Power. In each of these constituent districts an electoral committee is appointed to oversee the nomination of candidates. The district is broken down into subdistricts of 300 to 400 persons, each of which can propose candidates, selection being through a show of hands. This process produces five or six candidates for each electoral district. The electoral committee investigates all candidates and publishes its findings about the qualifications of each. Candidates are not allowed to campaign; indeed, campaigning is a basis for disqualification. A secret ballot then selects among the candidates. Run-off elections are often necessary to obtain a majority vote. The winning candidate serves for two-and-a-half years in the Municipal Assembly. The oldest and the youngest elected deputies have the responsibility to open the debate of the new assembly, when the first order of business is the selection of the Executive Committee.

Municipal deputies must spend part of each week available to their constituents, to receive their complaints or opinions. Deputies are often given time off from their jobs. In many ways the municipal deputies operate as a county board of supervisors would in the United States, being responsible for the interpretation of state laws, limited in their own power, and the link to the citizenry. The deputies also are responsible for electing provincial and national deputies in indirect elections. They elect delegates from lists provided by a nominating committee headed by a representative of the Communist party and which is made up of representatives from the mass and political organizations.[4] The result is the concentration of Communist party officials at the higher levels of government, so much so that 70 percent of the members of the National Assembly are members of the party or of the Union of Young Communists. Twenty percent of the National Assembly are women.[5]

Provincial People's Power Assemblies can propose projects and can assign priorities to housing, hospitals, and other projects. The provincial assemblies with their executives act as an intermediary between national policy and its execution on the local level. As such, the provincial government allocates its budget, received from the national level, among the various municipal units. This is done by collecting requests and advice from the lower level and using the information for their own decisions. The assemblies are responsible for selecting the directors for industries, for moving personnel from one job to another to improve management, and for replacing persons who are removed or retire. State farms, industries, and agricultural cooperatives report at different levels, and in certain cases report only on the national level to appropriate ministries.[6]

The Communist Party of Cuba

The Communist Party of Cuba (PCC) is not legally an institution of the government, but in reality, as in most single-party states, it is the party leadership that runs the country. The Communist party is the creation and personal instrument of Fidel Castro, who is its first secretary. Originally organized in 1965 as the United Party of the Socialist Revolution, it later adopted its present name and expanded the leadership to include more of the old-line Communists who had not originally supported Castro's 26th of July Movement but had links to the Soviet Union.

Party membership is the goal of ambitious Cubans, since membership is the first and essential step of advancement in all areas of Cuban society. But membership is severely restricted, with priority given to members of unions, the working class. About 5 percent of the Cubans are members of the party, totaling about 500,000. Affiliation with a religious group disqualifies a person for membership, and at the present time members of the "inteligencia" are virtually excluded. The inteligencia are feared for the potential to take over or alter the leadership of the party. New members generally are selected from members of the Union of Young Communists who apply for consideration during their late twenties. Members of the union give enthusiastic support to the government and express considerable knowledge of Marxism. They also perform many voluntary duties to qualify for Party membership.

The direction of the Communist party officially lies in its National Congress, which meets every five years to adopt new national plans and to elect the Central Committee, the ongoing policy-making body of the party. The committee meets in plenary session at least once every year and officially is the highest body of the party between sessions of the party Congresses. Selection to the committee is prized, and the media normally cite a person's membership, a mark of honor and prestige. The Central Committee is more a club of the political elite, membership evidencing an individual's acceptance into the highest circles of Cuban society. It is curious that despite its importance, the average Cuban does not know who is on the committee, or even its size.

Policies and decisions are developed by the Central Committee of the Communist Party of Cuba through its own bureaucracy, housed in a building complex behind Havana's Plaza of the Revolution. The 225-member Central Committee works as a planning body and shadow government that oversees all actions of the official government. Every person of importance in Cuba is a member or alternate member of the Central Committee, from the generals and provincial heads to top medical men and administrators. These links, and the importance of being included at the top level for social and career reasons, cause a basic consensus of action throughout the country, since the "existence of factions" is decreed a "serious infraction" of party norms. As a consequence, the committee is the essential instrument of political control, for its members hold the basic executive positions of power in Cuba (see appendix).

The Secretariat, selected from the membership of the Central Committee, officially its executive body, is responsible for carrying out the committee's policies between the yearly meetings. To oversee the work of the Secretariat, a Political Bureau is elected from the committee to run the party. In the Political Bureau lies the political power of decision.

The Political Bureau's twenty-four members and alternates control both the party and the important posts in the government. Fidel Castro is not only the first secretary of the party, but also commander-in-chief, and president of the Council of State and Council of Ministers. His brother, Raul, is second secretary and minister of the Revolutionary Armed Forces. The third man on the bureau, Juan Almeida, oversees the party. Many members also hold positions in the Council of Ministers and in the Secretariat. The Political Bureau of the Communist party "recommends" to the National Assembly who should be elected to the leadership positions of the assembly.[7] Members and alternate members of the Political Bureau head the Communist party, the ministries of the Revolutionary Armed Forces and Culture, the secretariat of the Central Committee, the Council of State, the Committees for the Defense of the Revolution, the Women's Federation, the Confederation of Cuban Workers, and the Association of Small Farmers. In addition, governors of the two largest provinces and senior generals are included in the Political Bureau.

Even more important than the links of the Political Bureau into vital areas of Cuban life is the reality that the bureau is not the instrument of the Central Committee, but controls the committee and through it all of Cuba. The bureau can call the Central Committee into extraordinary session at any time. For example, on January 31, 1985, a Special Plenary Meeting of the Central Committee was called by the Political Bureau, which removed one of the alternate members of the Political Bureau and Secretariat (Antonio Perez Herrero) for "shortcomings and repeated errors," apparently for disagreeing with foreign policy initiatives of Fidel Castro.[8] Loyalty to Fidel Castro remains the most significant quality for leadership positions, with members of the M-26-July who fought in the insurrection dominating the armed forces, police (Interior), and the Communist party.

The use of competitive elections at the municipal level and the networks of control through the Political Bureau and Central Committee gives the polity a stable political system and, at the same time, the capability to make direct political demands. Supply and demand of political goods are thus carefully monitored, which is the essence of competent political leadership.

Unions

The unions, with a special place in Cuban politics, differ from other organizations and interest groups. The unions' secretary-general is a member of the Political Bureau, and the national committee of the Confederation of Cuban Workers (CTC) and its national directorate have the right to initiate laws, a power otherwise restricted to governmental organs. The secretary-general of the CTC has the right to participate in the sessions of the Council of Ministers and its Executive Committee. Normally the minister of labor is a member of the CTC, and the trade unions are guaranteed positions on the Central Committee and in the leadership of the provincial and municipal party organizations. A number of the ministries are headed by members of the CTC. Within the National Assembly and other governmental groups, the CTC acts as an interest group. The unions are the only institution that may act as an independent check on the power of Fidel Castro. There are several reasons for this special role.

Cuba calls itself a "worker society," a fact more of word than deed, since the workers do not control the factories. More important, the unions predate the revolution and have maintained an historical role of involvement in politics. This political tradition has never been totally broken. Further, the support of organized labor is vital to the Cuban economy. Even within Cuba's agricultural sector, important activities are carried out not by farmers, but by members of the sugar and tobacco workers' unions. In contrast to the fear of the inteligencia, workers are encouraged to become party members. For example, at the textile factory in Bauta, out of 4500 workers, 800 were party members. In theory the unions have the right to strike, but the right has never been exercised because Cuban society has "no class contradictions."[9] Yet a class conflict remains between the unions and the state-run management over wages and work rules. Management wants to keep wages low and to increase production quotas, while the unions express contrary interests. Such disagreements can be taken to municipal courts for resolution.[10]

The power of the unions is enhanced by the fact that much of their original organization was initiated by the Communists. Men such as Carlos Rafael Rodriguez and the late Blas Roca were incorporated into the Cuban government, including at the Political Bureau level, to accomplish the strategy of Fidel Castro to create a Marxist-Leninist state.

The position of these old Moscow-line Communists may have been negotiated by the Soviet Union in exchange for Soviet support to Cuba, a background that protects these men and gives them and their allies a somewhat independent power base within the government and the party. Their independence is limited, however. Anibal Escalante, another old-line Communist who was in the government, tried to establish a separate political bloc within the government and was imprisoned by Fidel Castro. Today old-line Communists are aging and will not last as long as the men of the July 26th Movement, who will eventually take over complete leadership of the unions. In the 1986 Communist Party Congress the late, old-line leader Blas Roca was removed from the Political Bureau and Carlos Rafael Rodriguez dropped from the eighth to the thirteenth position in the hierarchy. At the same time, Secretary General of the CTC Roberto Veiga Mendendez was elevated to full membership in the Political Bureau from his alternate member status.[11]

Although independent unions as an interest group are unlikely to challenge Fidel, there is the possibility that they will become a group outside the domination of Raul Castro or any other successor to Fidel. Even so, the unions have the biggest bloc of delegates in the Central Committee and the National Assembly, and their history of organization predates the revolution.

The Armed Forces

Some observers perceive a faction within the leadership headed by Raul Castro, second in the party and governmental hierarchy and designated successor to Fidel. Raul's strength lies in the armed forces and in the Federation of Cuban Women headed by his wife, Velma Espin.[12] His leadership of the armed forces is carefully controlled by the domination of loyalists in the officer corps. "More than 80 percent of the officer corps is drawn from militants of the PCC (Communist Party of Cuba) and the UJC (Union of Communist Youth)."[13] Many of the top officers of the armed forces are veterans of the 26th of July Movement who fought in the battle against Batista and are emotionally linked to Fidel Castro as fellow revolutionaries. One list of eighty-four M-26 July militants places twenty-four of them in various positions with the armed forces and a number of others in the leadership of the Ministry of Interior (police).[14] Most of these men are also members of the Central Committee. Many other officers hold position in the Central Committee.

Raul's major possible rival was Ramiro Valdes, formerly minister of the interior and number four in the hierarchy. A veteran of the Sierra

Maestra forces who holds the title of "comandante," Valdes, like Fidel, wears guerrilla fatigues and a small beard. The 1986 Communist Party Congress removed him from the Political Bureau and control of the interior ministry. He has been replaced by a General Abrantes Fernandez, who had been in the Directorio Estudiantil in the fight against Batista.[15] At the same time the budget of the interior ministry was cut.[16]

Future Leadership

In the early years of the Cuban revolution the support, both economic and political, of the Soviet Union was necessary for Cuba to break the political and economic domination of the United States over the island. At present the political system remains dependent on the support of the Soviet Union, a factor that limits the freedom of the Cuban leadership. Fidel Castro has been quoted as saying to Carlos Andres Perez, former president of Venezuela, "Carlos Andres, I am not an instrument of Moscow, I am a victim."[17] One of the most important considerations for Cuba's future is its relationship with the other Latin American nations and with the United States. Already Cuba has reestablished relations with almost all the other Latin American countries and has become a member of SELA (Economic System of Latin America) and the Caribbean Multinational Shipping Enterprise (NAMUCAR). Castro hopes for better relations with the United States, both to counterbalance the Soviet Union and for reasons of technology.

The Cuban leadership who took power almost thirty years ago are today in their late fifties. If they last another twenty years, they will provide great stability to the government but severely limit internal competition for positions. Fidel's domination of Cuba is complete. As a result, few substantive changes in Cuban policy or leadership can be expected in the foreseeable future. Fidel's brother, Raul, his designated successor, is only a few years younger and cannot be expected to outlast Fidel by many years. After Fidel and Raul a generational change in leadership is probable.

At the same time the ambitions of younger men could not possibly be fulfilled if the top positions remained closed. The Third Communist Party Congress, in February 1986, sought to solve this problem by extensive changes in the membership of the Political Bureau and the Central Committee. The 1980 Political Bureau had sixteen members, the 1986 bureau only fourteen. The new bureau carried over ten of its previous members and elevated to full membership three from the alternate list, including Vilma Espin and the head of the CTC. The governor of Santiago de Cuba Province was promoted from the alternate list of the Central Committee. An even more radical change took place in the list of Political Bureau alternates, with only two carry overs from 1980 and eight new members, most of them promoted from the list of the 1980 Central Committee. Almost a third of the 1980 Central Committee was replaced, mostly by alternates from the 1980 membership. The alternate membership of the 1986 Central Committee is almost entirely new. The general pattern of changes was either promotion or removal from the Central Committee. The new Central Committee, including alternates, has a significantly higher percentage of blacks and women, with blacks now making up 26.4 percent and women 18.2 percent. The new committee's average age of forty-seven is also younger than the previous committee's.[18] The new Central Committee represents a new generation of leadership in Cuba, and many of its members are too young to have participated in the revolution. If the pattern of change continues, the leadership of Cuba in ten years will be even more markedly different.

When the Castro brothers leave the political scene, the future of Cuba's political system will depend largely on the views of the new generation of leadership. Whatever the leadership, Cuba will remain a socialist state. In the People's Republic of China, the pulls of nationalism and the post-Mao leadership have wrought extensive changes. The same could occur in Cuba with her pull to accommodation with the other Latin American nations and her culturally unnatural links to Eastern Europe.

An often-forgotten factor is that Cuba's relationship to the Soviet Union is significantly different from that of the nations of Eastern Europe. The Warsaw Pact countries do not have a choice in their alliance with the USSR. Cuba's relationship is economic and can be changed any time Cuba wishes, provided that adequate economic alternatives are available.

Notes

1. William R. Long, "Unrivaled Style Is Key to Castro's Power," *Los Angeles Times*, June 17, 1986, 10.

2. Rene Gonzalez, "Que es la Asamblea Nacional del Poder Popular," *Granma*, August 5, 1984, 2.

3. *Granma*, November 24, 1985, 2.

4. Marta Harnecker, *Cuba: Dictatorship or Democracy?*, 86.

5. Interview with Jorge Hart Davalos, Executive Committee of the Provincial People's Power Assembly, Havana, July 13, 1984.

6. A good discussion of the possible evolution of the People's Power Assembly is in Archibald R.M. Ritter, "The Organs of People's Power and the Communist Party: The Nature of Cuban Democracy," in Halebsky and Kirk, eds., *Cuba: Twenty-Five Years of Revolution, 1959*–1984, 285–89.

7. *Granma,* February 10, 1985, 3.

8. Ibid.

9. Interview with Julio Reyes, secretary-general of the Education Workers and member of the National Directorate of the CTC, Havana, July 17, 1984.

10. Ibid.

11. *Granma,* February 8, 1986.

12. Eduardo Gonzalez, "Institutionalization, Political Elites, and Foreign Policies," in Cole Blasier and Carmelo Mesa-Lago, eds., *Cuba in the World* (Pittsburgh: University of Pittsburgh Press, 1979), 3–36.

13. *Direccion Politica,* (Havana, 1981), 125.

14. Ramon L. Bonachea and Marta San Martin, *The Cuban Insurrection, 1952–1959,* 332–33.

15. *Latin America Weekly Report* WR-85-49, December 13, 1985, 9.

16. *Latin America Weekly Report* WR-86-05, January 31, 1986, 3.

17. William R. Long, "Unrivaled Style Is Key to Castro's Power," *Los Angeles Times,* June 17, 1986, 10.

18. *Latin American Weeky Report* WR-86-07, February 14, 1986.

Appendix

Some Members of the Central Committee of the Communist Party

A complete list of the Central Committee as of the February 1986 Communist Party Congress can be found in the February 8, 1986, edition of *Granma.* This partial list provides a picture of the links between the Central Committee and the political control of Cuba.

All Political Bureau members and alternates are members of the Central Committee. Most of the members of the Committee were elected in February 1986. A designation of "M-26-July" indicates membership in the Movimiento 26 de julio, and "Directorio Revolucionario" indicates former participation in that organization.

Political Bureau (*Buro Politico*)

FIDEL CASTRO RUZ   First Secretary of the Party. Commander-in-Chief. President of the Councils of State and of Ministries. Secretariat.

RAUL CASTRO RUZ   Second Secretary of the Party. General of the Armies. Minister of the Armed Forces. First Vice-president of the Councils of State and of Ministries. Secretariat.

JUAN ALMEIDA BOSQUE   Vice-president of the Council of State. President, National Committee of Control and Revision. M-26-July.

JULIO CAMACHO AGUILERA   First Secretary of the Party, province of Santiago de Cuba. M-26-July.

OSMANY CIENFUEGOS GORRIARAN   Vice-president of the Council of

Ministers. Head of economic planning. M-26-July. (Brother of the late guerrilla hero, Camilo Cienfuegos.)

ABELARDO COLOME IBARRA   General of the Division, Army. Vice-minister of the Armed Forces. Member, Council of State. (Hero, Angolan campaign.)

VILMA ESPIN GUILLOYS   Chief of the Federation of Cuban Women (FMC). M-26-July. Wife of Raul Castro.

ARMANDO HART DAVALOS   Minister of Culture. M-26-July.

ESTABAN LAZO HERNANDEZ   First Secretary of the Party, province of Santiago de Cuba.

JOSE RAMON MACHADO VENTURA   Former Minister of Public Health. Secretariat. M-26-July.

PEDRO MIRET PRIETO   Vice-president of the Council of Ministers. Secretariat. M-26-July.

JORGE RISQUET VALDEZ   Secretariat. M-26-July.

CARLOS RAFAEL: RODRIQUEZ   Vice-president of the Councils of State and of Ministries. Former foreign minister. Former leader of the Popular Socialist Party.

ROBERTO VEIGA MENENDEZ   Secretary General of Confederation of Cuban Workers (CTC).

Alternate Members of the Political Bureau

LUIS ALVAREZ DE LA NUEZ   First Secretary of the Party, province of Matanzas.

SENEN CASAS REGUEIRO   General of the Division, Army. First Vice-minister of the Armed Forces. President, Association of Cuban-Polish Friendship. M-26-July.

JOSE RAMON FERNANDEZ ALVAREZ   Minister of Education. Vice-president of the Council of Ministers.

YOLANDA FERRER GOMEZ   Ideological Secretary of the Federation of Cuban Women.

RAUL MICHEL VARGAS   First Secretary of the Party, province of Guantanamo.

JOSE RAMIREZ CRUZ   President of the National Association of Small Farmers (ANAP). M-26-July.

JULIAN RIZO ALVAREZ   Secretariat. M-26-July.

ULISES ROSALES DEL TORO   General of a Division. First Deputy Minister of FAR.

DRA. ROSA ELENA SIMEON NEGRIN   President of the Cuban Academy of Sciences. Member, National Executive of the Federation of Cuban Women.

LAZARO VAZQUEZ GARCIA

The Secretariat

FIDEL CASTRO RUZ See *Buro Politico.*

RAUL CASTRO RUZ See *Buro Politico.*

JOSE R. MACHADO VENTURA See *Buro Politico.*

JORGE RISQUET VALDES-SALDANA See *Buro Politico.*

JULIAN RIZO ALVAREZ See *Buro Politico* alternates.

JOSE RAMON BALAGUER CABRERA First Secretary of the Party, province of Santiago de Cuba.

SIXTO BATISTA REGUEIRO General of the Division, Army. Chief of the Military Department of the Central Committee. Former alternate member of the *Buro Politico.*

JAIME CROMBET HERNANDEZ-BEQUERO

LIONEL SOTO PRIETO Ambassador to the USSR

The Central Committee of the Communist Party

JOSE ABRANTES FERNANDEZ Minister of Interior. Directorio Revolucionario.

ROGELIO ACEVEDO GONZALEZ General of the Division, Army. M-26-July.

ARMANDO ACOSTA CORDERO Former alternate member of the *Buro Politico.* National Coordinator of the Committees for the Defense of the Revolution.

SEVERO AGUIRRE DEL CRISTO Nominated by the Central Committee as Vice-president of the National Assembly of People's Power. Member, Council of State.

CARLOS ALDAMA ESCALANTE Head, Central Committee Department of Revolutionary Orientation.

ROBERTO DAMIAN ALFONSO GONZALEZ First Secretary of the Party, province of Granma.

DR. RODRIGO ALVAREZ CAMBRAS Specialist in orthopedic medicine. Director, Orthopedic Teaching Hospital.

JOAQUIN L. BENAVIDES RODRIQUEZ Minister of the National Commission for the Direction of the Economic System.

JOAQUIM BERNAL CAMERO First Secretary of the Party, province of Sancti Spiritus.

FLAVIO BRAVO PARDO   President of the National Assembly of *Poder Popular*.

MIGUEL CANO BLANCO   First Secretary of the Party, province of Holguin.

DORA CARCANO ARAUJO   Secretary-General of the Federation of Cuban Women (FMC).

JOSE FELIPE CARNEADO RODRIQUEZ   Head, Central Committee Office of Religious Affairs (was Chief of the Department of Science, Culture, and Teaching Centers)

JULIO CASAS REGUEIRO   General of Division, Army. M-26-July.

LEOPOLDO CINTRA FRIAS   M-26-July.

FAURE CHOMON MEDIAVILLA   Directorio Revolucionario

ASELA DE LOS SANTOS   Vice-minister of Education.

SERGIO DEL VALLE JIMENEZ   Former member of the *Buro Politico*. Minister of Public Health. Former Minister of Interior. M-26-July.

JOEL DOMENECH BENITEZ   President of the National Commission of Energy (CNE).

LUIS ORLANDO DOMINGUEZ MUNIZ

JUAN ESCALONA REGUERA   Minister of Justice.

RAMON ESPINOSA MARTIN   General of the Division. Chief of the Eastern Army.

ANTONIO ESQUIVEL YEDRA   Vice-president of the Council of Ministers.

PEDRO FERNANDEZ DIAZ   Secretary-General of the National Union of Construction Workers.

OSCAR FERNANDEZ MELL   President of the Executive Committee, Provincial Assembly of *Poder Popular*, City of Havana. M-26-July.

RIGOBERTO GARCIA FERNANDEZ   Revolutionary Armed Forces. M-26-July.

GUILLERMO GARCIA FRIAS   Former member of the *Buro Politico*. M-26-July.

FABIO GROBART   President of the Institute of the History of the Communist Movement and the Socialist Revolution.

PEDRO GUELMES   Minister of Communications.

NICOLAS GUILLEN BATISTA   President of the National Union of Writers and Artists of Cuba (UNEAC). (Poet.)

OMAR ISER MOJENA   M-26-July.

ALFREDO JORDAN MORALES   Former member, National Bureau of UJC and head of the Jose Marti Pioneer Organization.

CARLOS LAGE DAVILA   Works with the First Secretary of Central Committee of the Party.

JORGE LEZCANO PEREZ   First Secretary of the Party in the province of the City of Havana.

JOSE LOPEZ MORENO   Vice-president of the Council of Ministers.

ORLANDO LUGO FONTE   First Secretary of the Party in the province of Pinar del Rio.

ISODORO MALMIERCA PEOLI   Minister of Foreign Relations.

ARMANDO MANRESA GONZALEZ   First Secretary of the Party in the special municipality of Isla de la Juventude.

JORGE ENRIQUE MENDOZA REBOREDO   Director of *Granma*.

JOSE R. MIYAR BARRUECOS   Secretary of the Council of Ministers.

HUMBERTO M. MIGUEL FERNANDEZ   First Secretary of the Party in the province of Cienfuegos.

JESUS MONTANE OROPESA   Former member of the *Buro Politico* and the Secretariat. Chief of the Department of Foreign Relations of the Central Committee. M-26-July.

ARNALDO OCHOA SANCHEZ   General of a Division, Army. M-26-July.

HUMBERTO PEREZ GONZALES   Former alternate member of the *Buro Politico*. President of the Central Junta of Planning of the National Assembly of People's Power (JUCEPLAN). M-26-July.

FAUSTINO PEREZ HERNANDEZ   Ambassador to Bulgaria. M-26-July.

ANTONIO PEREZ HERRERO   Former alternate member of the *Buro Politic* and Secretariat (removed in a special session of the Central Committee on January 31, 1985, in dispute with Castro). M-26-July.

MANUEL PINEIRO LOSADA   Chief of the Department of the Americas of the Central Committee. M-26-July.

MARCOS J. PORTAL LEON   Minister of Basic Industries.

RODOLFO PUENTE FERRO   Ambassador to Angola.

FIDEL RAMOS PERERA   Vice-chief of the Department of Sugar of the Central Committee.

ROBERTO ROBIANA GONZALEZ   First Secretary of the Union de Jovenes Comunistas.

BLAS ROCA CALDERIO (deceased 1987)   Former member of the *Buro Politico*. President of the National Assembly of People's Power (1976). Former head of the Popular Socialist Party (Communist Party).

RENE RODRIGUEZ CRUZ   President of the Cuban Institute of Friendship with All Peoples. (ICAP)

HECTOR RODRIQUEZ LLOMPART   Minister-president of the State Committee of Economic Collaboration.

ANTONIO RODRIQUEZ MAURELL   Minister of the Sugar Industry.

JULIO TEJA PEREZ   Minister of Public Health.

DIOCLES TORRALBAS GONZALEZ   Minister of the Transport. Member of the Council of State. M-26-July.

RAMIRO VALDEZ MENENDEZ   Former Minister of the Interior and member of the *Buro Politico*. Comandante. M-26-July.

FERNANDO VECINO ALGRET   Minister of Higher Education, M-26-July.

NOEL Z. ZUBIAUR MIR   Secretary General of the CTC in the City of Havana.

Alternate Members of the Central Committee

RICARDO ALARCON DE QUESADA   Deputy Foreign Minister.

CARLOS LEZCANO PEREZ   General of the Brigade (brother is v-p of the Nat'l Assn & member CC).

DR. MANUEL DE J. LIMONTE VIDAL   Director, Center for Biological Research.

JULIAN LOPEZ DIAZ   Ambassador to Nicaragua.

MANUEL S. PEREZ HERNANDEZ   Ambassador to Bulgaria.

SAMUEL RODILES PLANES   General of the Brigade. Chief of the Western Army.

ARNOLDO TAMAYO MENDEZ   Colonel. Cosmonaut. President of the National Council of the Society for Patriotic and Military Education.

3

The Cuban Economy: Dilemmas of Socialist Construction

Nora Hamilton

T *he most difficult task was not the overthrow of Batista and the taking of revolutionary power. . . . The most difficult task is the one we are engaged in today: the building of a new country on the basis of an underdeveloped country, the creation of a new consciousness, a new man.*[1]

Contrary to the expectations of Karl Marx and other 19th-century political economists and philosophers, socialist revolutions have occurred not in advanced capitalist countries with fully developed agricultural and industrial bases, but in relatively underdeveloped countries in which economic development has been limited and highly uneven. Revolutionary movements that come to power in these countries thus confront a double challenge: to raise levels of production and productivity and at the same time to create a more just society in which scarce resources, and ultimately the benefits of growth, are equitably distributed.

When the revolutionary movement headed by Fidel Castro took power in Cuba in January 1959, it faced problems of long-term economic stagnation, vast disparities in wealth and income, excessive economic dependence on the United States, and an economic base strongly skewed to the production and export of a single product.[2]

In 1959, annual per capita income in Cuba was $200—the same as in 1902. Fifty percent of the population received 10.8 percent of the total income, while the top 10 percent of the population received 38.5 percent. Wealth was also concentrated geographically, with the prosperity of the capital city of Havana contrasting sharply with the relatively neglected provincial cities and rural areas.[3]

The further economic dislocations dated from the 19th century, when Cuba became the "sugar bowl" of Europe. By 1959 approximately three-fourths of Cuba's cultivable land was in sugar production; sugar provided one-third of Cuba's total income and 80 percent of its income from exports. Thus Cuba depended on sugar production and the price of sugar in the highly volatile export commodity markets for its income to import basic necessities, including other food needs. Because of the seasonal nature of sugar cane production, two-thirds of the field workers and 95 percent of the mill workers were unemployed or underemployed except during the sugar harvest. Total unemployment was 9 percent during the harvest but rose to 20 percent in the non-harvest period.[4]

In addition, much of Cuba's sugar production, as well as other sectors of the economy, were controlled by U.S. corporations. At the time of the revolution, the United States had $1 billion invested in Cuba; U.S. companies controlled 40 percent of the sugar crop and 55 percent of sugar mill capacity. More important, the United States was a major buyer of Cuban sugar; decisions by U.S. officials regarding its sugar quota affected the world market price and the Cuban economy. In return for preferential entry for a certain percentage of its sugar into U.S. markets, Cuba was required to open its market to U.S. manufactured goods, which undercut the development of its own industry. This situation resulted in numerous distortions: "An exporter of raw sugar, Cuba imported candy. Cuba exported tomatoes but imported virtually all its tomato paste. Cuba exported fresh fruit and imported canned fruit, exported rawhide but imported shoes. It produced vast quantities of tobacco but imported cigarettes. . . . To add insult to injury, even 'Havana' cigars were increasingly manufactured in the United States."[5]

There were also heavy investments in other sectors: U.S. companies controlled 90 percent of Cuba's telephone and electrical services and half of the railway system, and had important holdings in cattle and petroleum refining. In addition, U.S. citizens owned many of Cuba's tourist hotels. U.S. investment in tourism was concentrated in Havana and aggravated the historical centralization of the society. Havana became a center where U.S. consumption patterns—unavailable to the rest of the country and to the majority of the population—were emulated; it was also a center of corruption, drugs, prostitution, and gambling.

To what extent has post-revolutionary Cuba succeeded in overcoming the problems of underdevelopment and establishing the basis of a socialist economy? The development of Cuba's political economy can be divided into two periods: (a) a period of massive mobilization, change, and improvisation, encompassing roughly the first decade of the revolutionary government, typified by efforts to eliminate rapidly the legacy of underdevelopment and dependency; and (b) a period of economic consolidation and political institutionalization characterized by more stable economic policies and based on a more sober assessment of the time it would take to overcome the obstacles to economic growth and development and institute a transition to socialism.

This chapter will examine these two periods in the context of the following questions:

1. Can the goals of economic redistribution and egalitarianism be reconciled with the need to increase levels of production and productivity and raise the standard of living of the population?

2. To what extent has Cuba succeeded in eliminating monoculture and diversifying the economy?

3. Has Cuba exchanged economic dependence on the United States for economic dependence on the Soviet Union?

4. Can the tendencies toward bureaucratic centralism endemic to state-controlled economies be countered by tendencies toward decentralized management and democratization of decision-making at the workplace?

Revolutionary Mobilization: The First Ten Years

"I am not interested in dry economic socialism. We are fighting against misery, but we are also fighting against alienation. One of the fundamental objectives of Marxism is to remove interest, the factor of individual interest, and gain from men's psychological motivations. Marx was preoccupied both with economic factors and with their repercussions on the spirit. If communism isn't interested in this, too, it may be a method of distributing goods, but it will never be a revolutionary way of life."[6]

Less than three years after the revolutionary victory, the socialist direction of the economy had been firmly established, a process that had been accelerated by the growing U.S. hostility toward the Cuban experiment and by Cuba's increasing dependence on the Soviet Union. In the months following the Bay of Pigs invasion, the United States proclaimed an embargo on trade between the United States and Cuba, succeeded in having Cuba expelled from the Organization of American States, pressured NATO members to end all financial credit to Cuba, and declared that any ship trading with Cuba could not trade with the United States. Isolated in the Western Hemisphere and cut off from much of Western Europe's economic aid, Cuba had become dependent on the Soviet Union and other countries of Eastern Europe as a market for its sugar exports and for credit, oil imports, and technical and military aid.[7]

During this period the Cuban leadership enacted a series of measures to reduce the inequalities of pre-revolutionary Cuba and raise the standard of living of the poorer sectors of the population. Concentrations of wealth were attacked through the immediate confiscation of properties of former president Fulgencio Batista and his associates, through the agrarian reform law of May 1959, which expropriated properties of more than 955 acres, and through the expropriation of foreign companies as well as national firms accused of suspending production.

Other measures designed to raise the standard of living of the poorer sectors of the population included the extension of health services, the literacy crusade and the expansion of education, and the reduction of rents and utility rates in urban areas. The new jobs created in industry, agriculture, and construction virtually eliminated unemployment.[8] In order to curb rural-urban migration and decrease the domination by Havana over the rest of the country, investment in Havana was cut back and resources were concentrated instead on the development of provincial cities and the countryside.

Despite Cuba's economic (and military) dependence on the Soviet Union and the concentration of decision-making in a small leadership cadre, this period witnessed considerable economic experimentation and debate regarding economic goals and strategies. As a result, economic policy oscillated between adherence to Soviet or East European models and efforts to establish new directions, often opposed by Soviet advisors. Similarly, the tendency toward concentration of economic power in bureaucracy was mitigated to some extent by the charismatic leadership exercised by Castro and by mobilization campaigns and the establishment of mass organizations that enlisted vast sectors of the population in the implementation of policy. While these campaigns and organizations served primarily as a transmission belt for leadership direction and control of affected groups, they also enabled the latter to voice their demands, needs, and critiques to the leadership.

Two models guided economic planning in this first decade: the "balanced growth" model (1959–63) and the "turnpike model" (1963–70). The balanced growth model, as the name implies, focused on efforts to end Cuba's dependence on sugar and to diversify the economy. Initially this took the form of an attempt to apply the "guerrilla mentality"—the determination, enthusiasm, and effort that enabled a small band of guerrillas to defeat the army of Batista—to problems of government and economic development. Technical skill and expertise were downplayed, economists were dismissed from government, and planning was limited. Many Cuban professionals and technicians left the country as the revolution became radicalized. The determination to end dependence on sugar production took the extreme form of plowing over vast acreage of sugar lands and planting new crops, but inappropriate soil and climatic conditions, as well as the lack of qualified specialists in new crops, resulted in the failure of these experiments as well as a drastic decline in sugar production and exports.[9]

This failure, and the elimination of trade relations based on Western markets and supplies, resulted in a shift to an emphasis on planning through imitation of the economic system of the Soviet Union, focusing on a strategy of heavy industrialization and based on technical advice from the Soviet Union and Czechoslovakia. But this strategy also failed, in part due to the fact that it was applied mechanically, without taking the distinct conditions in Cuba sufficiently into account, and to the lack of adequate statistical data and trained personnel to make planning effective.[10]

During this period Cuba began to experience some of the basic dilemmas that would plague the economy in the following decades. On the one hand, the commitment to guaranteed employment meant that the average Cuban enjoyed a secure income and potentially greater access to goods and services, particularly since basic needs in education and health care were provided free of charge. On the other hand, the supply of goods and services was limited by a number of factors. Higher levels of consumption by previously impoverished peasants in the countryside curtailed the supply of agricultural goods available to the cities. The U.S. trade boycott stopped delivery of parts and supplies for industrial and agricultural machinery built by U.S. companies during the pre-revolutionary period, causing severe bottlenecks in both agricultural and industrial production. These production problems led to shortages in consumption goods produced domestically and to reduced exports, which in turn limited the ability of the government to import consumption goods and machinery.

The difficulties generated by the U.S. trade boycott were eventually overcome by the shift to machinery and supplies from the Soviet Union and East Europe, but this was a gradual and painful process. In the meantime, the lack of consumption goods limited the material incentives to work hard and to increase productivity, leading to problems of absenteeism and low productivity, which further aggravated the shortages of goods and supplies. Rationing was introduced to ensure an equitable distribution at reasonable prices of basic goods in short supply.[11]

These and other problems led to the most intensive period of debate and experimentation in Cuba's post-revolutionary history. The "balanced growth" model was discarded in favor of the "turnpike" model, based on the assumption that the best means to achieve a goal was not necessarily direct. Instead of seeking to diversify the economy immediately, Cuba would give priority to sugar production by increasing the area under cultivation and increasing mechanization; earnings from sugar export would be used to import machinery to diversify agricultural and industrial production on a sounder basis. The empasis given to sugar production did not mean that other sectors would be ignored; the production of cattle, fishing, and citrus fruit was developed, and that of cement, nickel, and electricity was expanded.[12] Also during this period, the nationalization of the Cuban economy was completed, by 1970 industry, finance, commerce, and all but 30 percent of agricultural land were controlled by the state.

The initial phase of this period was dominated by the "great debate" that took the form of a series of published articles by Cuban leaders and economists, with contributions by internationally known Marxist scholars such as Charles Bettelheim and Ernest Mandel. The issues involved are complex, but in general they revolve around the nature of the transition to socialism in a society in which the level of production is relatively low. The basic question was: Is it necessary to achieve a material base, a certain level of economic prosperity, before achieving equality and developing a social consciousness oriented to the good of society rather than to self-interest? Or can the drive to increase production be accompanied by the drive to egalitarianism, the elimination of self-interest in favor of collective interests and social goals? In other words, should the transition to socialism take place in stages, or is it possible to skip stages, aiming at achieving the highest level of socialism through concerted effort?[13]

The more orthodox argument, supported by French economist Charles Bettelheim and Cuban Communist leader Rafael Rodriguez, was that the form of economic organization and labor mobilization should reflect the level of productive forces in society. In Cuba, this meant that the basic unit of production should be the self-financing firm, with the market determining the allocation of resources to different units, as in capitalist societies (although private ownership was greatly reduced and central planning was an important component). At this level of development it was unrealistic to expect workers to have developed sufficient social consciousness to be motivated by such (moral) incentives as the greater good of society; to increase production and productivity it was necessary to reward them with material incentives, such as higher wages and bonuses for higher productivity. This meant increased inequality, at least in the short run, since the strongest enterprises would receive the most income, and the more productive workers would receive higher wages. The "market socialism" position was also advocated by Soviet and Czech advisors.[14]

The proponents of a more radical strategy, led by Che Guevara, argued that given the worldwide expansion of capitalism, the level of the productive forces in fact varies substantially even in underdeveloped countries like Cuba; both organizational forms and consciousness can reflect the highest level of productive forces worldwide. Thus economic organization can be totally centralized, with resources allocated to firms according to plan rather than through market forces.[15] A central element in this model is the development of the "socialist man" — egalitarian, self-sacrificing, and oriented to the collectivity rather than to self-interest. This model was based in part on the Chinese experience of intensive mobilization during the "Great Leap Forward."[16]

The debate was followed by experimentation that combined centralized planning and a mix of moral and collective material incentives in industry with relative decentralization and material incentives in agriculture. By 1966, however, Castro endorsed the "Sino-Guevarist" model, characterized by an empasis on moral incentives and the development of a socialist consciousness in all sectors, although economic decision-making was centralized in the leadership rather than in a planning apparatus. This orientation was influenced at least in part by pragmatic considerations: given the high level of income and potential demand relative to supply, the ability to provide material inducements was limited.[17]

This experimentation culminated in the "revolutionary offensive" of 1968–70, which focused on a large-scale increase in investment in sugar production with the aim of harvesting 10 million tons of sugar in 1970. The concentration of resources in investment in production entailed further curtailment of consumption, and people were asked to make severe sacrifices. One aim was to increase Cuba's ability to finance industrialization without increasing its debt; it was also hoped that sacrifices required for investment in production would pay off in raising levels of production throughout the economy.[18]

The 1970 sugar harvest was the focus of a massive campaign, with workers from industry, government, and other agricultural jobs mobilized to participate in cane cutting. Although the result was a record harvest of 8.5 million tons, it fell far short of the 10 million-ton goal, a failure that was all the more demoralizing since the 10 million-ton goal had been designated "a yardstick by which to judge the capacity of the revolution."[19] Further, the concentration of resources in sugar and the absence of workers from other sectors resulted in production declines in affected areas: milk, for example, dropped by 25 percent, and cement by 23 percent. The various reasons for the failure included waste by inexperienced cane cutters, poor coordination and planning by leadership and the bureaucracy, which resulted in the demoralization and cynicism of workers whose efforts were sabotaged by management inefficiency, and an unrealistic and therefore unattainable goal.

The failure of the revolutionary offensive led to a reassessment of the goals and strategies of the revolution in economic development, as well as in other areas. It was recognized that increasing the level of consumption could not be sacrificed indefinitely to raise levels of production: more attention would have to be paid to productivity, perhaps at the sacrifice of some egalitarian goals. And economic independence from the Soviet Union could not be achieved in the short run. It was also recognized that the intensive mobilization campaigns of the 1960s had too often been characterized by insufficient input from the mobilized sectors themselves. This had resulted not only in mistakes and waste that could have been avoided but also in limiting the enthusiasm of the population for projects in which they were required to make substantial sacrifices but had little initiative or decision-making control.[20]

It would be a mistake to interpret the setbacks experienced in the late 1960s as a total failure of the initiatives and experiments of the first decade. Production and productivity suffered in many areas, but the increased equality and improvements in the standard of living for the previously most deprived sectors of the population were undeniable. And if the experiments with moral incentives and the revolutionary offensive had assumed a higher level of social consciousness than was realistic, they undoubtedly contributed to the formation of consciousness in intangible but substantial ways. It would also be a mistake to interpret the changes of the 1970s as a retreat from the concerns and goals of the 1960s, although their expression and the strategies to achieve them were to undergo a substantial reorientation.

The Long Climb: 1970–1986

With the failure of the revolutionary offensive, the assumptions underlying Cuba's economic strategy shifted from the belief that socialist development could be achieved rapidly through a brief though strenuous effort, to recognition that it would be a gradual, long-term process. As expressed by one writer, formerly it had been considered a "great leap over a deep chasm"; now it was looked upon as "a long climb up a tall mountain."[21] In Fidel Castro's words, "The revolution is entering a new phase, a much more serious, mature, profound phase."[22]

Among the characteristics of the economic policies worked out over the 1970s were the following:

1. recognition that Cuba would remain economically dependent on the Soviet Union for a long time to come. This has resulted in a trend toward economic integration with the East European nations in the CMEA (or COMECON, the Council for Mutual Economic Assistance), increased Soviet influence, and a decline in economic experimentation and improvisation.

2. a shift in empasis from moral to material incentive and increased dependence on market mechanisms in an effort to raise levels of production and productivity.

3. a new emphasis on planning, involving the reactivation of the state Central Planning Board (JUCEPLAN) and the creation of several new state organizations to observe various aspects of planning. Prices and investment are centrally controlled; however, the new System of Economic Management and Planning (SDPE), introduced during the second half of the '70s, involved self-financing by enterprises and decentralized control of local firms by elected municipal or regional governments.[23] The responsibility for balancing supply and demand in the absence of determination of prices by the market is carried out by the Instituto Cubano de Investigaciones y Orientacion de la Demanda Interna (Cuban Institute for the Research and Orientation of Internal Demand), a market research agency of more than 100 research workers, mainly economists, sociologists, and psychologists, which attempts to balance production and consumption in areas as diverse as food, clothing and styles, recreation, and sociocultural activities.

4. continued reliance on the production and export of sugar, at the same time attempting to make Cuba self-sufficient in the production of food for domestic consumption and expanding production in other export crops and in industry.

Probably as important or more important than Cuba's economic measures were the economic implications of its political initiatives: the development and expansion of the Communist Party of Cuba, which is gradually taking over some of the functions traditionally exercised directly by the Cuban leadership; the reactivation of the Cuban trade union movement; and the creation of *poder popular*, a form of representative democracy, with direct elections for municipal government and indirect elections of provincial and national government. These measures had two basic thrusts: the institutionalization of the revolution, and the expansion of democratic participation.[24] It is notable that one of the first moves of the reactivated trade union movement was the endorsement of a wage structure linking wages to performance and productivity.[25]

According to some analysts, Cuba may be undergoing another major shift in its economic orientation. While Cuba retains the emphasis on productivity, elements of the market economy have been rejected as fostering capitalism, and there is a new focus on moral incentives. The extent and impact of these changes remain to be seen.

Growth Versus Equality: A Necessary Tradeoff?

Reagan sent a spy team to Cuba to gather facts for his anti-Cuba campaign. The team returned several months later with much data but no conclusions. The President, furious at the waste of time and money, asked why. "It's like this, Mr. President," explained the team leader. "In Cuba, there's no unemployment but nobody works. Nobody works but they always over-fulfilled their production goals. All the goals are overfulfilled but there's nothing to buy. There's nothing to buy but everybody has all they need. Everybody has everything, but everybody's always complaining. Everybody complains, but everybody goes to the square to pledge their lives for Cuba and Fidel, and then they go home and complain some more. So you see, Mr. President, we have lots of data but no conclusions."[26]

Even critics of the Cuban government recognize that Cuba has re-duced inequality and raised the standard of living of the poorest sec-tors of the population. The mechanisms for doing this include redistri-bution of wealth and income, through agrarian reform and expropria-tion of private enterprises, efforts to guarantee full employment, and social reforms that have made health services, education, and social security available to everyone. One observer notes that an estimated 20 percent of the income has been transferred from the wealthiest to the poorest sectors of the population.[27] The higher standards of liv-ing are reflected in greater literacy, increased proportion of school-age children in school, lower infant mortality and longer life span (see chapter 7, this volume).

Income inequality persists but has been greatly reduced. It is esti.mated that the wage comparison between a cabinet minister (the highest wage) and an agricultural worker (the lowest wage) is approx-imately ten to one (10:1), a substantial difference but much lower than in most developing countries (not to mention developed capitalist countries), even when the unemployed and underemployed are not in-cluded.[28] In Brazil, for example, the ratio between the *average* wage in the top class and that in the bottom class of the *urban* industrial sector ranged from 28.2:1 to 40.5:1 between 1968 and 1972.[29] Estimates of income distribution in Cuba between 1953 and 1978 indicate that the income of the lowest half of the population has increased from 6.2 percent to 32.8 percent, while that of the highest tenth has been re-duced from 38.5 percent to 21.1 percent. In Mexico, in contrast, the income of the lowest three-fifths declined from 30.6 percent to 20 per-cent between 1950 and 1975, whereas that of the top tenth increased from 38.6 percent to 43.5 percent.[30]

The Cuban government has also attempted to equalize investments in production and services among the different provinces. According to Castro's speech of July 26, 1984, each province had its own complete hospital center and higher education facilities, and new factories and plants were being constructed in every province.

While most observers agree that the Cuban revolution has reduced social and geographic inequality, they are not unanimous on the ex-

tent and nature of economic growth. Some observers also suggest that
the emaphasis on productivity in the 1970s has entailed sacrifices of
equality; that is, wage differentials have increased because of measures
tying wages to productivity, but these increases are small compared to
the vast inequalities of the pre-revolutionary period.[31]

Cuba's economic growth rate has fluctuated, and continues to parallel
earnings on sugar exports as well as natural conditions affecting agricultural production in general. After a brief period of accelerated
growth in the early 1970s, Cuba's growth declined in the late 1970s,
and the results of the first Five-Year Plan (1975–1980) fell far short of
anticipated goals. In the next decade, growth again increased, although
unevenly: total material production (including agriculture, forestry, and
fishing; mining, manufacturing, and electricity; and construction) increased by 16.9 percent in 1981, by 1.9 percent in 1982, and by 6.5 percent in 1983.[32] According to the report presented to the Communist
Party Congress in February 1986, GSP (gross social product) growth
had averaged a respectable 7.9 percent during the previous five years,
well over the 5 percent projected. Yet productivity continues to be a
problem, as indicated in Castro's report to the congress, which was
characteristically informative and self-critical with respect to Cuba's
problems.[33]

Cuba's growth does not always benefit consumers directly, since much
of it is oriented to increase productive capacity and exports; production of consumer goods is oriented at least in part to substitute imports
rather than simply to increase the quantity of goods available. But the
increase in quantity has been sufficient to reduce the number of products rationed. In 1970 practically all consumer goods were rationed;
by 1984 only 30 percent of income is spent on rationed goods. Aside
from the rationed market, which provided basic goods at frozen low
prices, nonrationed markets, including the government parallel market,
provided certain basic goods at higher prices as well as other specialties
not available in the rationed market, and there were private markets
for agricultural and artisan products.[34] The latter were eliminated in
1986, however, on the grounds that they were creating "capitalist en-
claves" and substantial income differentials.

Aside from the inconveniences of rationing and shortages, complaints
involve the lack of variety and quality of goods available. According
to an official from the Institute for Internal Demand, women make more
than 70 percent of their clothes, which reflects dissatisfaction with
manufactured clothing.[35] The contrast between the high quality of
shoes manufactured for export and the poor quality of shoes for the
domestic market was criticized at a meeting of manufacturers in Havana
in summer 1984. As noted by Benjamin et al. (in *No Free Lunch*), the
degree of dissatisfaction depends on the individual's situation prior

to the revolution. The fact that in Cuba no one suffers from hunger or malnutrition distinguishes it from the vast majority of Third World countries. Cuba's economic progress has fluctuated, but it has been sufficient to demonstrate that a commitment to equity can be combined with economic development and will benefit the entire population.

Monoculture Versus Diversification

At first glance, Cuba's efforts to diversify its economy appear to have been a resounding failure. Twenty-five years after the revolution, Cuban trade is as dependent as ever on sugar exports: in 1980 sugar accounted for 86 percent of total exports (compared to an average 84 percent between 1949 and 1958). Further, there is a strong correlation between the value of Cuba's sugar exports and its GSP. Cuba's foreign trade is characterized by a chronic deficit, due to dependence on sugar but also to the dependence on imported energy and the effects of worldwide inflation on the price of essential industrial imported equipment.[36]

But two factors modify this picture. First, all export sectors have grown, not only sugar production. Although the volume varies, Cuba now produces an annual average of 8 million tons of sugar, compared to an average of 6 million in the pre-revolutionary period. Citrus fruit production increased by 60 percent between 1975 and 1980 and is now a major export; there have also been dramatic gains in the fishing industry.[37]

Second, although Cuba continues to experience a trade deficit, it is less dependent upon exports to provide for basic needs than in the past. Sugar production had dropped from 22 percent of Cuba's goods and services to 6.1 percent by 1980. This reflects a dramatic increase in the production of agricultural goods (rice, poultry, beef, pork, milk, eggs, vegetables) for internal consumption, and in industrial production, including consumer durables such as refrigerators, stoves, radios and television sets, as well as in industries oriented to production, such as steel and cement.[38] Thus while Cuba continues to be dependent on sugar exports, it has made important gains in diversifying production for the internal market.

Economic Dependence or Socialist Integration?

The price of sugar has been reduced to 4.4 centavos . . . from an average last year of 8.58. . . . I would like our compatriots to think about what a price of 4.4 centavos means. . . . What would be the situation of our country without the revolution, without the socialist system, without equitable distribution, without the economic links our country has created with the socialist community? . . . So when the imperialists say that if we want to live in peace we must break our links with the socialist community, we tell them: these links will never be broken! Not only due to a question of principles, first of all, a question of elemental gratitude, but also because these links have been fundamental for our socio-economic development in these years and are essential for our future development.[39]

As indicated above, the optimistic expectations of rapidly obtaining self-sustaining growth in the 1960s were replaced in 1970 by recognition that economic independence was an unrealistic goal, at least in the short run, and that Cuba would have to continue to depend on support from the Soviet Union for a long time. In 1972, Cuba entered COMECON and signed a series of bilateral agreements with the Soviet Union. The thrust of these moves was that Cuba integrated its development plans with the plans of the COMECON countries and was integrated into the socialist "division of labor" as supplier of sugar. An agreement was worked out tying the price of Cuba's sugar to that of Soviet oil sales, and technical assistance would be provided from the Soviet Union and other East European countries to mechanize Cuba's cane cutting, develop the nickel industry, increase the output of electricity, modernize its oil industry, and reorganize planning. Cuba's debt with the Soviet Union was renegotiated.[40]

During the 1970s Cuba's economic interaction with Western countries increased, reflecting a general thawing of Cuba's relations. Hopes of reestablishing economic relations with the United States were eliminated, however, with the growing hostility between the two countries after 1979, and Cuba's current economic policy seems directed toward obtaining self-sufficiency in certain areas complemented by "socialist integration" — in essence a dependence on the socialist bloc countries for technical assistance and those materials it cannot provide itself.

Cuba's economic dependence on the Soviet Union is undeniable. In the 1970s Cuba's trade with the Soviet Union averaged 50 percent of Cuba's total foreign trade, but in 1978 it was 69 percent — the same level as trade between Cuba and the United States between 1946 and 1958. An additional 10 percent of Cuba's trade is with the Comecon (CMEA) countries. Cuba sells its sugar to the Soviet Union at prices above world market prices (although linked to these prices) and buys oil from the Soviet Union at prices below those of the world market (although this may be offset by higher prices for machinery and other capital and intermediate goods).[41] Cuba's trade deficit is financed by Soviet loans, which by 1976 totaled about $4.9 billion. These were rescheduled in 1972 with repayments to begin in 1986; they have since been postponed to 1990. Cuba also has a current debt of approximately $3.3 million with France, West Germany, Spain, Canada and Japan, with a good record of repayment.[42]

In general, socialist integration has worked well for Cuba. As indicated in Castro's speech of July 26, 1984, Cuba is cushioned against the massive economic dislocations that would result from the 50 percent drop in the sugar price if it were still tied to commodity export prices rather than receiving subsidized prices from the Soviet Union. The fact that the Cuban economy continued to expand in the early 1980s—a period in which most Latin American countries experienced negative growth—suggests that Soviet and East European technical and material assistance has been beneficial.

Cuba continues to aim at self-sufficiency in food production and other basic industries while importing those products it cannot efficiently produce itself. With the completion of several textile factories under construction in 1984, Cuba became self-sufficient in the production of textiles. Cotton used in the textile mills was imported, however, since the cost of importing inputs necessary for milling raw cotton would cost more than the cotton imports.

Economic dependence on the Soviet Union is not accompanied by the economic exploitation that accompanied Cuban dependence on the United States (the loss of resources entailed in profit repatriation resulting from direct investment by U.S. companies). Further, economic and technical assistance from the Soviet Union and Eastern Europe has been geared to Cuba's efforts to modernize and diversify its economy in its successive Five-Year Plans. It has been argued that the Soviet Union extracts political dependence, as shown by Cuba's foreign policy, but to what extent is debatable.[43] Given Cuba's size, limited resources, and the legacy of underdevelopment inherited by the revolution, a policy of aiming toward self-sufficiency in certain areas while increasing Cuba's integration in the CMEA appears to be a realistic one.

Democracy in the Workplace

"Why should a manager have to be absolutely in charge? Why shouldn't we begin to introduce representatives of the factory's workers into its management? Why not have confidence? Why not put our trust in that great proletarian spirit?"[44]

The lack of input from workers and other mobilized groups was recognized as an important factor in the economic problems of the 1960s, and particularly the failure of the revolutionary offensive of 1968 to 1970. In addition, the waste, inefficiency, and other problems resulting from overcentralization and administrative errors were factors in worker dissatisfaction that found expression in absenteeism (averaging 20 percent of the labor force in 1970) and low productivity on the job. The institutional changes in the 1970s—the reactivation of the unions, the development and expansion of the party, and the introduction of *poder popular*—were in part a response to the need to ensure input by workers into the decision-making process and specifically into economic decisions at the level of the workplace as well as at higher levels.[45]

Input from the workers is gained through a number of channels: (a) plans generated at the national level are discussed and refined at the provincial and local levels, with workers' assemblies in factories, state farms, and cooperatives having input in decisions regarding production norms and processes; (b) elected provincial and municipal assemblies have jurisdiction over firms and industries at their respective levels; and (c) the autonomy and scope of the unions have been expanded to make them forceful instruments of the rights and interests of workers.

Several factors may limit the effectiveness of these initiatives, however. One effect of the decentralization of economic control to the plant level has been contention between managers, who seek to promote efficiency and productivity, and workers who want to protect their rights against management infringement.[46] The ability of municipal and provincial assemblies to oversee the firms within their respective jurisdictions is limited by the many decisions made at the national level, over which they have no control.[47] And union leaders, accustomed to operating as transmission channels from the Cuban leadership to the workers and to working closely with management in the 1960s, in some cases have been slow to accept their new role as representatives of the workers, perhaps against the claims of management, although this appears to be changing.[48]

Two additional factors could inhibit workers' democracy: (a) Cuban dependence on Soviet models, which could lead to the creation of a bureaucratic caste, and (b) Cuban leadership's tendency toward paternalism to the population.[49] At the same time, any bureaucratic tendencies are countered by the fact that Cuba is a highly participatory society, as evidenced by the active involvement of the Cuban masses in various campaigns since the 1960s.[50]

Recent developments suggest a continued concern with broadening workers' control. The Third Congress of the Cuban Communist party (February 4–7, 1986) focused on the importance of workers' collectives in the development of plans. And there has been widespread experimentation with production brigades in which workers of a given firm, factory, or farm are given increased control over the entire production process, including management decisions.[51]

Conclusion

The answers to the four questions raised at the outset of this chapter reflect the complexity of the development process and the difficulties it has encountered. The Cuban leadership has been much more suc-

cessful in promoting equality than in promoting economic development, but there has been sufficient development to demonstrate that
these two goals are not incompatible. Sugar monoculture has continued
to dominate the export sector, although its importance has declined
within the overall economy, and the negative effects associated with
monoculture have been diminished by Cuba's relationship with the
Soviet Union. Economic dependence on the USSR is in some ways
similar to Cuba's pre-revolutionary dependence on the United States,
with the important qualification that the economic exploitation of
U.S.–Cuban relations prior to 1959 appears to have been replaced by
a more cooperative relationship with the Soviet Union. One example
is the contrast between the negative impact of U.S.–Cuban relations
on the development of Cuban manufacturing industry and the
economic and technical support Cuba currently receives from the Soviet
Union and the East European countries for industrialization. This support may have political costs, but the extent and nature of these costs
is subject to debate.

Perhaps the most important contradiction affecting Cuba's present
political economy is between the necessity to expand worker participation in economic decision-making, at both workplace and national
levels, and the tendency toward bureaucratic control generally charac-
teristic of a planned, state-controlled economy. In Cuba the importance
of workers' control is recognized at least in part, as evident in the creation of institutions designed to increase workers' participation in planning and the productive process as well as more general measures to
increase democratic representation. At the same time, bureaucratic
tendencies could be reinforced by the tradition of "benevolent paternalism" that appears to characterize the attitude of the Cuban leadership toward the population. According to Rabkin, "The problem of
Cuban politics is how to combine opportunities for mass participation
with a protracted process of elite-sponsored moral and social transformation."[52]

As the Cuban experience demonstrates, the construction of socialism
in an underdeveloped country is a long, difficult process. The flexibility
of the Cuban leadership, its ability to admit and learn from its past
mistakes, and the high level of involvement and commitment of the
population will undoubtedly continue to be assets in confronting the
economic challenges of the future.

Notes

1. Fidel Castro, speech of July 26, 1967.
2. For further information on the Cuban economy prior to the revolution,
see Donald W. Bray and Timothy F. Harding, "Cuba," in Ronald H. Chilcote
and Joel C. Edelstein, eds., *Latin America: The Struggle with Dependency and Beyond*

(New York: John Wiley & Sons, 1974; and James O'Conner, *The Origins of Socialism in Cuba.*

3. Carmelo Mesa Lago, *The Economy of Socialist Cuba,* 9–10; Claes Brundenius, "Cuba: Redistribution and Growth with Equity," 202.

4. Brundenius, "Cuba," 194.

5. Medea Benjamin, Joseph Collins, and Michael Scott, *No Free Lunch: Food and Revolution in Cuba Today.*

6. Ernesto "Che" Guevarra, cited in Bertram Silverman, ed., *Man and Socialism in Cuba: The Great Debate,* 5.

7. For information on U.S.–Cuban relations at the time of the boycott, see Bray and Harding, "Cuba," and Paul Hoeffel and Sandra Levinson, eds., *The U.S. Blockade: A Documentary History* (New York: Center for Cuban Studies, 1979).

8. Brundenius, "Cuba," 200–201.

9. Mesa Lago, *Socialist Cuba,* 11–12; Joel C. Edelstein, "Economic Policy and Development Models," 178.

10. Mesa Lago, *Socialist Cuba,* 14–16.

11. Frank T. Fitzgerald, "A Critique of the 'Sovietization of Cuba' Thesis," *Science and Society* 42, no. 1 (Spring 1978): 10–11.

12. Silverman, *Man and Socialism,* 9; Edelstein, "Economic Policy," 179.

13. For a discussion of the issues of the great debate as well as a selection of articles by the major protagonists, see Silverman, *Man and Socialism.*

14. Ibid.; Bray and Harding, "Cuba," 658–59.

15. According to Carmelo Mesa Lago, *Cuba in the 1970s,* 30, the highly centralized plan advocated by Guevara was similar to that supported by traditional planners in the Soviet Union, while the combination of planning and market mechanisms advocated by Rodriguez followed the economic reforms introduced in the Soviet Union in the 1963–65 period.

16. The Great Leap Forward was an experiment in China in 1958–60 based on the assumption that modernization should be accompanied by a growth in communist forms of social organization and the development of a popular communist consciousness. It was a response to the emergence of increasing inequality, particularly between the countryside and the city, as a result of the growth of the previous period, and an important feature was an effort to industrialize the countryside. See Maurice Meisner, *Mao's China: A History of the People's Republic* (New York: Free Press, 1977).

17. Mesa Lago, *Cuba in the 1970s,* 6–8; Bray and Harding, "Cuba,"660–62.

18. Edelstein, "Economic Policy," 183–86.

19. Ricardo Carciofi, "Cuba in the Seventies," in Gordon White, Robin Murray, and Christine White, eds., *Revolutionary Socialist Development in the Third World* London: Harvester Press, 1983), 199.

20. Archibald R. M. Ritter, 1985: "The Organs of People's Power and the Communist Party: The Nature of Cuban Democracy," in Halebsky and Kirk, eds., *Cuba,* 273.

21. Edelstein, "Economic Policy," 189.

22. *Granma,* August 30, 1970, cited in Mesa Lago, *Cuba in the 1970s,* 25.

23. Andrew Zimbalist, "Cuban Economic Planning: Organization and Performance," 224–25; and Arthur MacEwan, *Revolution and Economic Development in Cuba,* 181–84.

24. Edelstein, "Economic Policy," 188; Ritter, "People's Power," 273 ff.

25. Marifeli Perez-Stable, "Class, Organization and *Conciencia*: The Cuban Working Class after 1970," 297.

26. Cuban joke, quoted in Benjamin et al., *No Free Lunch*, 81.

27. Mesa Lago, *Economy of Socialist Cuba*, 191–95.

28. Ibid., 192.

29. Sylvia Ann Hewlett, "Poverty and Inequality in Brazil," in Hewlett and Richard S. Weinert, eds., *Brazil and Mexico* (Philadelphia: Institute for the Study of Human Issues, 1982), 321.

30. Brundenius, "Cuba," 202; and David Felix, 1982, "Income Distribution in Mexico and Kuznets Curves," in Hewlett and Weinert, eds., *Brazil and Mexico*, 268.

31. Mesa Lago, *The Economy of Socialist Cuba*, 197.

32. Brundenius, "Cuba," 209.

33. *Cuba Update* 6, no. 3 (Fall 1986).

34. Benjamin et al., *No Free Lunch*, 43–44, 60ff.

35. Eugenio D. Balari, address of July 14, 1984.

36. Jean Paul Beauvais, "Achievements and Contradictions of the Cuban Workers' State," 55; Mesa Lago, *The Economy of Socialist Cuba*, 183.

37. Beauvais, "Achievements," 51.

38. Ibid., 51–52.

39. Fidel Castro, speech of July 26, 1984, published in full in *Granma*, July 28.

40. Beauvais, "Achievements," 63.

41. Mesa Lago, *The Economy of Socialist Cuba*, 184.

42. *Cuba Update*, fall 1985.

43. See, for example, Mesa Lago, *The Economy of Socialist Cuba*, 187; Susan Eckstein, "Cuban Internationalism," 372–90; Wayne Smith, 1985, "U.S.–Cuba Relations: Twenty-five Years of Hostility," as well as other articles in the same volume.

44. Fidel Castro, speech of May 20, 1970, cited in Zimbalist, "Cuban Economic Planning."

45. Perez-Stable, "Class, Organization," 196; Linda Fuller, "Changes in the Relationship among the Unions, Administration, and the Party at the Cuban Workplace, 1959–1982," *Latin American Perspectives* 13, no. 2 (Spring 1986).

46. Perez-Stable, "Class, Organization," 299–303.

47. Rhoda Pearl Rabkin, "Cuban Political Structure: Vanguard Party and the Masses."

48. Ibid., 264; Fuller, "Changes."

49. Beauvais, "Achievements," 69. During our stay in Cuba, this paternalism was evident in the attitude of several officials with whom we spoke, although it was generally expressed in a genuine concern for the welfare of the population. Thus the president of Cuba's market research institute (Instituto de Investigaciones y Orientacion de la Demanda Interna) pointed out that its functions included efforts to raise levels of culture and knowledge; currently it was engaged in campaigns to reduce sugar consumption and cigarette smoking and to increase consumption of whole wheat bread.

50. Fuller, "Changes."

51. Mary Alice Waters, "Cuba: Economic Battle a 'People's War,'" *Intercontinental Press* 24, no. 5 (March 10, 1986).

52. Rabkin, "Cuban Political Structure," 267.

4

Cuban Unions and Workers' Control

Linda Fuller

In his closing address to the 1978 National Congress of the Cuban Union Confederation (CTC), Fidel Castro proclaimed: "There is no imagining the revolution without the role played by the unions. Regardless of what the administrators are able to do, the key, the decisive factor, is the worker . . . and it is the union movement that joins together all our workers. It is for this reason that the movement is of such importance. Without it the Party, the State would not be able to face up to their enormous task." The next year the union daily began a front-page editorial with the words "The unions are alive and active organisms in our society. They are not just ornamental organizations, as the enemies of socialism have claimed."[1]

Can we consider these pronouncements accurate descriptions of the current status of Cuban unions and their role in society? Or are they better described as polished examples of official rhetoric or perhaps wishful thinking? We will see from what follows that there is much truth in these two statements, for in comparison with the first decade following the victory against Batista, Cuban unions today are stronger, more influential, and more visible bodies. In other words, major changes have taken place in the workers' organizations as Cuban socialism has developed and matured.

Unions in Cuba are organized by economic sector. From 14 to 25 such sectoral unions, including ones in agriculture, industry, services, and administration, have existed in the post-revolutionary period. These sectoral unions are joined under one umbrella confederation, the CTC (*Central de Trabajadores de Cuba*), and the percentage of the work force now organized stands at around 97 percent. Currently unions are financially self-sufficient, supporting their activities through members' dues, collected from each worker every month. Base-level union officers are selected every two and one-half years in direct elections. Higher-level leaders of both the CTC and the sectoral unions are chosen indirectly by electors every five years.

The nature of the union movement is interesting for many reasons, including its relevance to the broader topic of workers' control. I will employ the term "workers' control" to refer to the *degree* to which workers themselves determine the character of production and their work.[2] Workers' control is not extensive in most societies and thus presents theoretical and practical problems for capitalist and socialist states alike. How can capitalism reconcile the pervasive and revered ideology of individual freedom and self-determination with what goes on in its factories? How can socialism claim the ascendance of the working class, if workers have little say over how they spend the major portion of their waking hours? And how much of the absenteeism, political apathy and discontent, cynicism and low productivity in both systems derives from the fact that workers have little power to decide what production should be like? While historically the response of unions themselves to demands for workers' control has been mixed, many observers who have studied the problem in a variety of settings have emphasized the importance of strong unions to the success of attempts to increase workers' control.[3] As we review the change that has occurred in Cuban unions with regard to one measure of the unions' strength, we shall see that Cuba is no exception: workers' control in this developing socialist country, as elsewhere, is enhanced by the presence of active workers' organizations.

Although a final determination of the strength of the Cuban unions can be made only after an investigation from several different perspectives, I will concentrate on but one of these: the relationship of workers' organizations to the two other major bodies that have a significant bearing on how work is controlled in Cuba—the workplace administration and the party nucleus. The changing relationship between the unions, the party, and the administration will be investigated in relation to four interconnected themes: (a) union *autonomy* vis-à-vis management and the party; (b) the extent to which the *interests* of the unions, management, and the party are considered parallel and harmonious or distinct and contradictory; (c) the degree to which the functions of the three entities are differentiated; and (d) what I will call *relative power*—the importance or weight of the unions in determining the nature of work and production at the Cuban workplace.

Together these four dimensions of the unions' relationship to other political and administrative entities can be taken as one important indicator of the vitality of the union movement. Thus, union strength will be greater when unions have some autonomy from management and political bodies, when they can define and pursue the specialized interests of their memberships, when their functions are different from those of the other bodies, and when they possess enough power to press successfully for the adoption of their agenda or point of view. But to the extent that a union's relationship to administrative and political bodies is characterized by the opposite kinds of qualities, the chances for the development of workers' control will suffer with the weakness of the union. In Cuba union strength, measured in terms of these four dimensions, has undergone important changes since 1959.[4]

Union Autonomy

The Cubans I interviewed who could remember the 1960s uniformly recalled them as a time when the unions were dormant.[5] Although there were variations among unions at different periods during the decade, in general the 1960s were a time when unions were heavily dependent on the state administration and the party. The job of the unions was to transmit directives and decisions from those two bodies to the rank and file, and to convince workers to carry out these directives and abide by these decisions without question or discussion. Unions were expected to behave as mouthpieces of administrators and party members, and to side with them in the event of any dispute or disagreement with the workers. The low level of union autonomy is well illustrated by the description of some workplaces early in the decade by Lazaro Pena, then secretary-general of the CTC: certain union leaders "back up their positions with threats because, instead of explaining the reasons for certain measures, they limit themselves to stating bureaucratically, and with a truculent air, that they must be accepted because the CTC or the Consolidate or such a [sic] Minister, orders it from above."

It is not surprising, given these circumstances, that many union leaders tended to be docile and nonassertive, further reinforcing union identification with the administration and the party, Again, in Pena's opinion: "There are other [union leaders] who more or less comply with the task assigned to them by management. They could be converted into administration employees and nothing would change or matter except that the payroll would reflect the true situation more clearly. There are committee members of union sections who act more like management than worker representatives."[6]

Pena's characterization is supported by Adolfo Gilly, who lived in Cuba in 1962 and 1963 and who described a few meetings he attended at Cuban worksites. Workers usually sat at one side of the room, and union leaders joined the administrators on the other. In one textile factory, although the physical space separating the two groups was not great, it seemed to Gilly that an "invisible wall" marked the boundary between them. In the ensuing discussion between an administrator and some workers, the union leader assumed a silent, decorative posture.[7] The visit of Jamaican writer Barry Reckord to a Cuban box factory at the end of the decade indicate little had changed. Reckord described a heated meeting called to discuss the case of a man who refused to work on a machine lacking a legally specified safety device; he had had his pay docked by the manager for the period when he did not work. What stands out in Reckord's report is the back-seat role assumed by the union representative. This individual's few interventions were characterized by attempts to avoid confrontation and to bolster management's position.[8]

About 1970 a shift started in Cuban perceptions of the proper role of the unions and in the behavior of the unions, as well. A central feature of this shift was an increased emphasis on union autonomy vis-à-vis administrators and the party. Public discussion of a more independent role for the unions surrounded the preparations for the 13th National CTC Congress, held in 1973. The theses eventually passed at this Congress dealt in several places with the topic of union autonomy. They stated explicitly that the unions were not state organizations and therefore were not dependent on, directed by, or controlled by any ministry or other state apparatus. Union independence from the party was likewise stressed. The common union practice of automatically supporting management actions and positions was soundly criticized in this document, as was the previously lopsided emphasis on conveying orders downward. To paraphrase one worker, the union's job would now be to serve as radar, to pick up the problems of the workers, as much as to tell them what the administrators thought their problems were.[9]

The basic formulations of union autonomy contained in the theses of the 13th CTC Congress were reiterated at the 14th CTC Congress (1978) and at the Second Party Congress (1980), and were underscored by Cubans I spoke with in 1982. For example, a national-level CTC official repeatedly stressed the obligation of the union and its leaders to communicate *whatever* opinions workers held, particularly a criticism or disagreement with the administration, and even if the issue seemed a minor one.[10] And the ideal union leader, in the view of many workers, was one who carried out this task firmly, independently, and with authority, and whose relationship with management was characterized by collegiality but not by cronyism.

The intent in the new stress on union autonomy, however, was not to forestall cooperation between the workers' organizations, administrators, and the party. Unions are expected to work with administrators and the party without totally identifying with them. Complete "dependence" or "independence" are not viewed as the only two possibilities;

rather, autonomy is a matter of degree. This perspective is worth stress-ing because it differs from the common notion in capitalist countries of how unions should function. In a capitalist context, supposedly, unions are fully independent of management, who are their adversaries, and the state acts as a neutral umpire whenever conflicts arise between the other two groups. Even though this conception does not corre-spond to contemporary reality, unacknowledged adherence to its tenets could lead one to interpret any mention of union cooperation with administrators or the party—let alone any concrete example of it—as evidence that nothing has changed in Cuba, that the unions remain as dependent as ever. The important strides workers' organizations have made in the direction of increased autonomy since 1970 would then be minimized, if not overlooked entirely.

Although union and party pronouncements and workers' reports all prove that union autonomy did begin to increase after 1970, this kind of evidence would be less convincing had it not been accompanied by the development and systematization of a series of workplace mecha-nisms through which unions could ascertain, organize, and report members' opinions, suggestions, and demands. Although various meet-ings and assemblies had been held during the 1960s to gather input from the rank and file, they did not occur regularly everywhere and were often organized on an ad hoc, topical basis.

Beginning in the 1970s, however, the unions' potential to act as an independent representative of Cuban workers was bolstered by their regular participation in three workplace bodies: the production and service assemblies (*asambleas de produccion y servicios*), the management councils (*consejos de direcction*), and the planning assemblies. Production and service assemblies are held on a monthly basis at individual work centers. Unions lead the assemblies, at which any issue relating to pro-duction can be broached; they participate in their preparation, and it is their responsibility to see that workers' suggestions are acted on. The union is also a permanently invited member of the enterprise man-agement council, which meets more often and assumes the responsibil-ity for direction of day-to-day operations. Finally, the unions perform their task of gathering and channeling worker input in assemblies held in conjunction with the formulation of the enterprise's technical-economic plan. The first Cuban workers had input into their work centers' plans through this method in 1974. By now these planning assemblies occur yearly in the majority of enterprises, and the unions play a central role in organizing, soliciting, and defending the view-points of the workers in this critical forum.

Despite the gains made in union autonomy since 1970, there are in-dications from the highest levels of the party, the government, and the union, down to the direct producers themselves, that many are still not satisfied with the amount of autonomy the unions have or with the balance that prevails in some workplaces between transmitting guidelines downward versus opinions and criticisms upward. In 1980, for instance, Carlos Rafael Rodriguez, a high-ranking government and party official, acknowledged that "Our unions are much better at transmitting the party's orientations to the working class than they are at gathering from the working class the desires, the criticisms, the suggestions to which the leadership has to be alert." Similarly, Roberto Veiga, current secretary-general of the CTC, has criticized workplaces where unions and management act like "one big happy family."[11] In the union press and in interviews, individual workers have also complained about the unions' lack of independence, and about union leaders who are too timid or deferent in their dealings with administrators to serve as effective worker representatives. In Cuba, as elsewhere, without the organizational backing of an autonomous union to represent the producers' viewpoints, workers' interests are likely to be disregarded.

The story related to me by one woman worker illustrates this point. She had asked for a transfer, but the administration at her work center kept stalling, neither refusing nor granting her request. Eventually she approached her union, which she said she had not done earlier because the union officers were intimidated by management and had a long history of backing them on everything. As she had expected, the union sidestepped the issue, claiming there was nothing they could do until the administration actually refused her request. The resolution of her problem (and other analogous ones at this work center) came only after the boss was removed.[12] Other workers with similar complaints referred to a vicious circle that becomes common in such workplaces: workers stop expressing their concerns to the union leadership when they realize the leaders are unlikely to be firm or to persist in presenting them to the administration. As a result, the union leadership loses the backing of its membership; once management realizes that the union has lost influence with the workers it is even less likely to take union demands seriously, and the authority of the union is further undermined. For the union to be effective, the administration must view it as having the respect and support of the rank-and-file, and their respect and support depend, at least in part, on the union's reputation for independent action in its day-to-day encounters with management.

Converging and Conflicting Interests

The unions' lack of independence in the pre-1970 years corresponds to a time when their interests and those of administrators and the party were assumed to be identical. This idea served as an important justification for the dependent character, and eventual near disintegration, of the Cuban unions. Why should the unions behave autonomously if their interests were precisely those held by the party and workcenter management? Indeed, as this concept of harmony did not admit the possibility of antagonisms or contradictions between the unions and other groups in Cuban society, what was the need for special organizations to defend workers from their own state and party representatives? Such an ideology, however, proved far too simplistic. It did not describe adequately the reality of socialist construction in Cuba, nor was it a helpful guide for the women and men who were attempting the transformation. In retrospect, protracted adherence to this doctrine slowed down the process. Despite the theory, conflicts between workers, administrators, and party functionaries existed from the beginning. And as the workers' organizations deteriorated, the direct producers were the ones left without influence. At the time, some Cubans foresaw the *Movimiento de Trabajadores de Avanzada* (Advanced Workers' Movement) as the socialist replacement for the unions.[13] But, as one worker recalled, this movement could not possibly have filled the growing gap between those who held decision-making power and those who did not, precisely because its interests were too close, too consistent with those of the administrators.[14]

As the Cuban unions began to function more independently after 1970, the previously held assumption of a complete correspondence of interests between the unions, the administration, and the party also began to change. As the second revolutionary decade unfolded, it became increasingly inaccurate to argue that no room was allowed for conflict or differences between labor and the state.[15] In 1970 the minister of labor, in a well-known speech, conceded that the belief that workers, peasants, and administrators always shared the same goals did not fit Cuban reality. The following year he went on to argue that contradictions not only existed between union and administrations, but should be welcomed: "The development of the constant contradictions that must necessarily turn up between the trade union organizations and the administration will strengthen the Revolution every day. . . . We must not fear contradictions. Rather, we must welcome them. They must be viewed as a positive element."[16]

Even though the role of unions vis-à-vis administrators and the party is now characterized by greater independence within a framework of cooperation, it would be absolutely wrong to think the interests of unions versus these other entities are now completely contradictory. Consensus on the broader goal of constructing and strengthening socialism prevails, yet there is now a recognition, an acceptance, sometimes an encouragement of a diversity of interest. Answers to important questions (such as how much a production or service delivery unit can turn out in one year, or how much emphasis should be placed on boosting output versus worker health and safety), are now expected to, and do, vary, and it is the proper role of the union to advance its members' positions when disagreements on such questions arise. Many Cubans used the phrase "non-antagonistic contradictions" to refer to such disagreements, implying the existence of conflicts and at the same time assuming that they can be resolved within the parameters of socialism.[17] One administrator warned me this would be the hardest thing to try to explain about union-management relations in Cuba: how contradictions can exist between two groups that are not fundamentally antagonistic.[18]

While describing them as "non-antagonistic," most workers with whom I spoke readily acknowledged the existence of differing, sometimes discordant, interests between the union and the administration. It is reasonable to surmise that workers' current widespread recognition of a divergence between their own interests and those of management can be linked to the implementation of a new economic management and planning system, *Sistema de Direccion y Planificacion de la Economia* (SDPE), which began in the latter half of the 1970s. Decades ago Lenin foresaw the growth of tensions between the two groups resulting from the necessity to expand society's material base by reorganizing the socialist firm to maximize both output and efficiency. The SDPE was instituted in Cuba for precisely these reasons, and to accomplish its ends the decision-making authority of the firm regarding planning, production, and the disbursement of earnings was increased. Nonetheless, heightened autonomy has been accompanied by the requirement that enterprises cover their expenditures with their income. Increasing output and decreasing costs has thus become the focal point of enterprise operations to an extent unprecedented in socialist Cuba. In other words, individual production units must now attempt to operate according to certain ground rules that, in some respects, are not unlike those governing the operation of the capitalist firm. The result is not hard to predict. Conflict between the interests of workers and managers will increase insofar as administrators, in an effort to cut costs and boost output, overlook or violate legislation or custom regarding health and safety, remuneration, quotas, quality standards, and so forth. In his main address to the 14th National CTC Congress, Veiga referred to the potential for an increase in worker-management tensions as a result of the changes instituted by the SDPE, and reported that in meetings held in workplaces all over the country in which the theses of the Congress were discussed, two suggestions aimed at smoothing relations at the workplace arose. The first was to formalize into law the rights of the enterprise-level union structures, and the second was to elaborate a unified work code that would govern labor relations under the new planning and management system, a task that has since been completed.[19]

Differentiation of Functions

Accounts of union activity in Cuba prior to 1970 indicate that the functions of the workers' organizations during this period were unclear.[20] According to Lazaro Pena, some union leaders in the 1960s wandered aimlessly through offices and plants, giving the appearance of activity but doing nothing.[21] Although Pena suggested more political education as a remedy, the reason why some leaders at this time may not have known what they were supposed to do was more complicated than his solution implied. In part, this situation stemmed from a lack of differentiation between the functions of the union and those of the party, the administration, and other organizations, particularly the Advanced Workers' Movement. As one would expect, given the emphasis on the harmony of interests in society and the dependent posture of the unions that then prevailed, lines of authority and responsibility were badly blurred. What in later periods came to be considered specific and legitimate union tasks were then absorbed by these other bodies—if not given up entirely. By the end of the decade unions retained few if any areas of exclusive authority, and in most workcenters they settled into a subordinate role of backing up the party's administrators and Advanced Workers' projects. Under such circumstances it is not surprising that in the late 1960s there was talk of eliminating unions entirely as relics of Cuba's capitalist past.

It was logical that the post-1970 emphasis on union autonomy and the acceptance of the specificity of workers' interests should be coupled with an attempt to distinguish union functions from those of other political and administrative groups with responsibility for production and service delivery. Attention turned from questioning the necessity of unions, to recognizing their importance as distinct entities, to trying to figure out how their activities should be separated from those of the party and the administration. This process began with general union pronouncements regarding separate spheres of union action and distinctive methods of union work.[22] In addition, attention was directed toward minimizing the prevalent practice of uniting party, administration, and union leadership in the same individual. High-level administrators were thus expressly prohibited from running for union office. Likewise, party members were encouraged to minimize their candidacy in local union elections after 1970, and 1975 figures showed that only about 5 percent of the local union leadership belonged to the party.[23]

The policy of encouraging a separation of union, party, and administrative leadership continues to be stressed at the workplace, a point mentioned by a number of workers in response to my queries concerning the roles played by the union, the administration, and the party at their worksites. One worker reported that even in musical groups she knew, an effort was made to divide authority deriving from these three sources among different individuals.[24] Some I spoke with argued that the important point was that the *leadership* rather than *membership* of the three groups remain distinct—that the same person not occupy "multiple commands," one worker put it.[25] Yet no one felt that administrators or union leaders should never be party *members*, though some definitely preferred that the number of party members among these groups be minimized.

To understand the change that has taken place since the 1960s, when union, party, and administrative functions were largely undifferentiated, it is helpful to examine how Cubans currently distinguish between the proper workplace responsibilities of the three groups, and also how they understand them to overlap. Expanding production and service delivery at the worksite level is a major purpose of all three. Within that framework, the unions have three major tasks: to organize and systematize workers' input into decision-making about production, to educate and prepare workers to participate in this fashion, and to defend workers' rights. The administration facilitates the union's discharge of its primary responsibilities by helping prepare and conduct production and service assemblies, by aiding in the implementation of health and safety legislation, and by making scheduling adjustments, for example, to allow workers to participate in educational activities. The primary responsibility of management is to *administer* production according to the firm's technical-economic plan. Here again, the union is expected to work with management in the performance of its main task, for instance through participation in the management council, through involvement in the determination and execution of the enterprise plan and, more recently, by overseeing and evaluating management's performance. But if something goes wrong at the point of production, management shoulders the ultimate responsibility.

The worksite party nucleus has no analogue under capitalism, and therefore its functions in relation to those of the union and the administration may be unfamiliar to readers. The party nucleus is increasingly a force to be reckoned with at the Cuban workplace. Yet, although it is integrated into decision-making at the level of production through its participation on some regularly functioning bodies (for example, party representatives attend management council meetings), its importance stems less from any formal authority at the workplace than from the ideological and political influence it exercises throughout Cuban society.

The major role of the party is neither to look out for workers' interests, nor to organize worker input into decision-making, nor to manage. In fact, it is expressly prohibited from becoming involved in this last area. The party is supposed to harbor a broader perspective of the entire revolutionary process, as opposed to the narrower viewpoints held by administrators and workers. As such its main job is to help guide the activities of both the union and the administration — regardless of whether the leaders of either are party members — to ensure that the production process runs efficiently, smoothly, and according to the social, economic, and political guidelines set forth in the party's development program for the country. Yet the party is supposed to guide only in a general fashion. Thus, as one union officer said, the fact that the unions accept the guidance of the party does not mean that they are "going every day to the party to ask what has to be done."[26] Party members are expected to make sure that *everyone* does his job, one worker explained. They must be aware of what goes on throughout the workcenter, she continued, and added that for this reason it is very important that party membership accurately mirror the composition of the entire population.[27]

In discussions regarding the relationship between the functions performed by the unions, the administration, and the party, my interviewers offered a number of examples that help clarify the roles of these three workcenter bodies. In one, the administration of a large factory sanctioned some workers for being absent too often and slowing production. The union, however, argued that the sanctions were not just, because the real cause of absenteeism at the plant was the administration's decision to institute rotating shifts. Here the party backed the administration's imposition of the sanctions. Its job, as a result, was to try to explain to the workers why the administration — despite union objections — was not only correct in sanctioning the absentees, but obligated to do so: the product of this factory was judged essential to the welfare of the entire economy, so the plant had to operate 24 hours a day, and the institution of rotating shifts was seen as the only fair way to meet this demanding schedule.[28]

A second case concerned a supervisor who made advances to a woman working under him and was rejected. As a result, the supervisor gossiped disparagingly about the woman around the workcenter. The union defended the woman publicly, and the party supported the union. The party's stance in this case was instrumental in ensuring that the woman was protected from reprisals and that the supervisor's behavior was altered. It was clear from what a number of others said that party backing can be a great help to the union in getting action on workers' demands, or to support the workers' positions when complex, delicate, or confusing problems occur at the worksite.[29]

A final example, which helps to convey a sense of the proper functions of the party, the union, and the administration, describes a situation in which the roles of the three became badly confused. The trouble involved the allocation of apartments to workers, a decision which the entire collective was involved in making. (The division among the workers was not uncommon, since the scarcity of housing means that allocating units is often a trying business.) The difficulties really began when the union held several meetings to try to resolve the disagreement, during which both the administration and the party intervened inappropriately. The party overstepped its authority by taking over the task of chairing one of the union meetings and then by delivering a report that presented the party's position on who was right and who was wrong. With these actions the party merely added fuel to the fire, instead of assuming its proper function to help workers clarify and analyze the issues involved and to guide them toward an amicable solution.

Management, for its part, further complicated the situation by bringing up administrative information about individual work records at one of the union meetings, when it should have stayed out of the matter altogether because the dispute did not involve them. This series of meetings was described to me as "wild and ugly." The matter was not solved until the municipal and provincial branches of the CTC became involved and an outside party leader acted as arbitrator, as the members of the party nucleus at the workcenter should have done. The whole affair had gotten out of hand because everyone was busy doing someone else's job, turning what could have remained a disagreement within the union into a "crisis" at the workplace.[30]

Relative Power

Despite their lack of independence, without clear functions, and operating under the assumption there could be no important conflicts between workers and those segments of society directing the socialist construction on the workers' behalf, unions survived the first decade of the revolution, albeit as subordinate and relatively powerless bodies. At first, their relative powerlessness may have been overshadowed by an exuberant egalitarianism that infused social relations, not just at the workplace but elsewhere in the new post-revolutionary society. In the absence of any structural underpinnings, however, the ideological trappings of equality became tattered by the end of the decade. At many production units relations between administrators, political cadres, and unions revealed themselves as little more than a benevolent form of socialist paternalism: workers could only assume that those in charge knew what they felt and needed, and hope that their interests would be served in the end. Yet direct producers lacked power at the point of production, and the best indication was the sorry condition of the unions. As one woman recalled, "A big gap developed between the administration and the workers. The administration was too all-powerful.

The workers had no control over anything."[31] A member of the Young Communists interviewed in 1969 was less circumspect: "The worker hates the power situation in the factory. The manager uses power all the time; enjoys beating people down. That's authoritarianism."[32]

The power situation at the Cuban workplace started to change after 1970 as the unions gained autonomy, took on the primary responsibility for a number of important tasks, and began to recognize that in the course of carrying out their functions they would come into conflict with the administration and the party. The shift was typified by the use of the word *contrapartida* (counterpart) to describe the relationship of the union to the workplace administration. The term appeared in a 1971 speech by the minister of labor and took on a more active, combative connotation as the decade progressed.[33] It is used to refer to the unions' role as management overseer: in fulfilling its counterpart role the union is to keep an eye on administrators' performance, inform them of any deficiencies or errors, and help them make any necessary improvements. Yet it is not considered sufficient for unions just to respond to the actions of management after the fact. Instead they are expected to assume a more offensive posture, confronting management firmly and authoritatively whenever they feel that management are acting incorrectly, unjustly, or inappropriately in the decision-making process. Irresponsibility, laziness, cronyism, bureaucratism, dishonesty, and poor production and service delivery are some of the behaviors most commonly mentioned in the union press that call for a counterpart response from the workers' organizations. One woman cited an example of how the union's assumption of the counterpart role can be important in protecting producers from the effects of these management behaviors. By law, job openings at workcenters must be open to internal applicants, even if they require further training, before others can be considered. Making sure this happens, she said, is really up to the union in its role as management counterpart. The union must oversee the whole procedure of filling job openings in order to avoid the kinds of irregularities she said were commonplace "before," when bosses just hired someone from their families or even off the street without ever giving workers at the center a chance to apply. This couldn't happen anymore at her workplace, she concluded, because the union wouldn't let it.[34]

As one might imagine, Cuban unions have encountered difficulties when trying to exercise their counterpart role. Some union leaders, for example, are not prepared to exercise their counterpart function because they lack knowledge and information. Yet to be an effective counterpart, according to one worker, union leaders really have to know "as much as the enterprise director."[35] Otherwise they tend to accept whatever the administration says, and are unable to adopt or defend a strong position in the face of management error or intransigence. Specifically, some Cuban leaders need to become better versed on all aspects of labor legislation, as well as on topics of management and planning. They must know enough about the principles on which their economy operates, argued Roberto Veiga, to recognize deficiencies *and* to understand what might be causing them.[36] If leaders and members are not sufficiently knowledgeable in these areas, for unions acting as management counterparts would have little practical impact on the balance of power at the Cuban workplace.

But the lack of adequate knowledge is not the only thing that has interfered with the unions' ability to exercise fully their role as management counterparts. Workers complained that some managers have thwarted union attempts to perform this role, because they did not understand or chose to ignore the unions' legitimate counterpart activities. Managers at some worksites have continued to do things as they please, despite union objections. This is bound to occur sometimes at every workcenter, but what about the workplaces where it becomes endemic? What about the case of a manager who in the workers' evaluation performs poorly, yet consistently refuses to recognize the right of the union to intervene where it has authority? Posed another way, do the unions have any power to get rid of a bad boss? What the workers' organizations can or cannot do in this situation is a good test of their power at the worksite.

During no period since the revolution have Cuban workers had the formal authority to select or to remove their managers. Top administrators have always been chosen by the state agency responsible for production or service delivery in a given sector of the economy, and *only* by decision of this same agency can an administrator be removed from her/his post. Evidence suggests, however, that even though workers have never had the final say when it came to getting rid of an administrator, they have always, even in the early years of the revolution, had a certain informal influence in matters of this sort. Yet their influence was limited by the weakness of the unions at the time. Workers lacked a strong organizational base of their own from which to counter ineffective or unjust managers. "A worker could always confront a manager at the production assembly," one man recalled. "But the person had to do it individually, without union support. The assembly might even have backed the worker, but that's not enough. You need a structure—like a strong union provides—to be effective."[37]

Even though the formal authority to fire a bad manager continues to reside with the state, workers today, as a result of the increase in union power at the worksite, generally have more influence over the removal of superiors than in the past. Workers expressed confidence they could have a decisive hand in the dismissal of an administrator, and I learned of three cases (two in one workplace) in which the situation had actually come up. According to one national CTC official, "The workers' opinion that a boss should be gotten rid of carries a lot of weight with those who actually have the power to fire him or her."[38]

Cuban workers mentioned a number of routes they might pursue if they were intent on removing a manager. The fact that responses to my inquiries on this subject varied indicates there is no firmly established procedure to follow in such cases. The method chosen probably differs according to the type of workplace, the position of the disputed administrator, and the nature of the complaint against her/him. Some informants said the issue might first be broached in a union meeting or even a production assembly. Many workers, however, preferred not to go before an assembly or a meeting as a first step. Instead they could approach the leadership of the base-level union organization, either personally or with a written complaint. If they were not satisfied with his response, they could go to the next highest level of union organization. Most workers also said they could go directly to their local party nucleus with complaints, agreeing it would be inconceivable for the party not to be involved in a matter as serious as this. After their case had been presented, workers said some investigation would have to be carried out, generally by the union or the party, to verify their charges against the boss and to determine whether the allegations were supported by facts. If the results of this inquiry corroborated the workers' complaints, the case would be presented to the administrator's superiors, possibly through the party or a higher union body. No one seemed to doubt that if the charges were serious and could be supported, "the workers with the union can move the manager out!"[39]

Conclusion

Finally I will address two questions: first, if the relationship among the union, the party, and the administration at the Cuban worksite has indeed changed in the ways I have described, how can we explain why this happened; and second, what does this mean in terms of workers' control in post-revolutionary Cuba?

An immediate, if oversimplified, response to the first question might be that the relationship between the union, the party, and the administration at the workcenter changed as a result of decisions taken by high-level political leaders in Cuba. This response is true, as far as it goes, but we need to probe further to determine why the leadership decided to make these particular kinds of changes, and why it decided to make them when it did. We will examine the unions' subordinate position vis-à-vis the other bodies *before* 1970, and second why the situation began to look different after that.[40]

A large part of the explanation for the Cuban unions' minor role in the early years stems from the relationships between the unions and the July 26th Movement *before* the victory against Batista, and between powerful sectors of the union leadership and the political leaders of Cuba *after* Batista's defeat. Both relationships were characterized by a good deal of enmity and distrust. During the war to oust Batista, the CTC organization—long characterized by economism, reformism, corruption, and bureaucratization—was the dictator's most faithful, and by the end, almost his only political ally. Under the notorious Eusebio Mujal, it suppressed strikes, mobilized workers for pro-government demonstrations, and even applauded government repression of July 26th supporters within union ranks. After Batista, while most *mujalistas* went into exile or were removed from their leadership posts, the loyalties of their replacements were divided and uncertain. Their wavering support for the increasingly radical approach to development by the new government became obvious when, for example, important union leaders opposed elements of Cuba's new nationalization and agrarian reform programs. It is not surprising that Cuba's political leadership, despite enthusiastic mass support, was loath to encourage the growth of autonomous and active unions, because leaders of these unions would likely have opposed the direction the revolution was taking.[41]

By 1962 or 1963, however, the revolution was fairly secure on all social fronts, and the union leadership, after some bitter and tumultuous confrontations with the government, had come out solidly for the construction of socialism. The reason for the unions' continued deterioration for the remainder of the decade is, therefore, somewhat of a puzzle. Perhaps part of the reason was the dearth of good models of powerful unions in other socialist countries for Cuba to emulate.

To some extent the decline of the unions can also be viewed as part of a zealous effort to replace all remnants of old capitalist patterns and habits with a new set of social relations among society's members. Moreover, the development of strong and autonomous unions was further inhibited by the fact that during the previously mentioned political struggles over control of the post-revolutionary unions, the government was forced to throw its support behind the Communist unionists, surely with some misgivings, since the party's relationship with the July 26th Movement has been, and continued to be, characterized by considerable tension. And finally, the unions, like nearly every other institution in Cuba, suffered in the last part of the decade because the whole country was focused on one overriding task: to produce 10 million tons of sugar in 1970.

The turnaround in the status of the unions began to occur after the negative results of certain policies pursued in the late 1960s began to assume distressing proportions. Highly centralized economic and political decision-making resulted in a host of operating difficulties, unworkable decisions, and increased power inequalities. At the same time, egalitarianism was being emphasized, particularly through the drive to uncouple the link between work effort and remuneration. Independently, and because the two policies were in many ways contradictory, overcentralization and egalitarianism both contributed to very poor economic performance. In addition, the disappointing overall performance of the economy was exacerbated by the unpopular decision to reduce production of many consumer items in order to maximize capital investment. The inconsistencies, inefficiencies, and injustices that resulted from all these actions were reflected in extreme dissatisfaction in the workplace: absenteeism swelled, productivity dropped, and quality suffered, depressing the economy's performance even further.[42] Although these symptoms of discontent were economic, they had clear political implications; and under these circumstances a change was made — a change prompted in large part by the actions of Cuban workers to which the country's political leadership was compelled to respond.

But why this kind of response? History is replete with examples of repression and militarization as antidotes for disquiet among society's producers. An additional reaction might have been a further narrowing of the already small circle of citizens who made major decisions in Cuba. The unions, for example, might have been abolished rather than strengthened (by all accounts, they were almost dead anyway). Some indications suggest there may have been some disagreement within the country's top leadership over exactly how to respond to the urgent situation before them. We know little of the character of what may have been such a split. We only know that a defining feature of the post-1970 period in Cuba has been a systematic devolution of political and economic authority to groups in society who had previously had much less. The changes in the workers' organizations are but one example.[43]

For an explanation of why certain choices were made at this juncture, we must look to the history of the institution and consolidation of socialism in Cuba. The differences in this regard between Cuba and much of Eastern Europe are suggestive. First, the seizure of power by the July 26th Movement was a purely indigenous affair. It involved far greater participation from the Cuban population than did the institution of socialism in many parts of Eastern Europe, even though, in comparison with countries like Nicaragua and Vietnam, great numbers of Cubans were never deeply involved in the overthrow of the old regime. But the subsequent consolidation of socialism, more than the actual seizure of power, illustrates the real contrast in terms of mass participation between Cuba and much of Eastern Europe. From the very begining, socialism in Cuba was either kept alive or considerably strengthened through the widespread participation and involvement of large numbers of Cubans. The Bay of Pigs invasion, for instance, was repelled by the swift response of hundreds of thousands of members of the citizens' militias and the Committees to Defend the Revolution, whose birth can be traced to this U.S. debacle. And many harvests, both of sugar as well as of crops destined mainly for Cuban consumption, were successful only because scores of Cubans responded to the call to put aside their ordinary duties and go to the countryside throughout the 1960s. Finally, the literacy campaign — the most successful of its day and the model for others that followed in the developing world — could have been successful only with the active participation of well over a million Cuban citizens.

The point is that for a full decade before the country's political leadership assumed the direction it did in the early 1970s, it had had a history of calling for base-level participation and involvement and, even more significant, of receiving an enthusiastic and widespread response to those calls. This kind of history is not one Cuban socialism shares with many countries in Eastern Europe. Perhaps this history can help explain why increased participation in political and economic decision-making became a central tenet of the leadership's response to the crisis of the late 1960s, even though such a response would not have been workable elsewhere given the very different processes through which socialism was instituted and consolidated.

We also need to consider what this new workplace relationship between the unions, the party, and management means in terms of workers' control in Cuba. But a full appraisal of the strength of workers' organizations cannot be made on the basis of this relationship alone. Such a judgment involves knowing the content of union functions, and how these have changed over time. Here there are some encouraging signs. The unions' main task in the 1960s was to mobilize workers to produce more, better, and faster, according to the dictates of Cuba's political leadership. Since 1970, however, the unions have begun to organize, systematize, and coordinate workers' input into decision-making about production, both in worksite-level forums and, which is very important, in the wider national arena. In the early period unions were not much concerned with the defense of workers' rights. Contemporary Cuban unions, however, actively engage in the defense of workers' rights and the advocacy of their interests, albeit with varying results.

Besides understanding what kinds of activities unions are involved in, to appraise their status it is also important to know something about their organizational capacity for carrying out the tasks they are supposed to perform. Here too are some indications of increased union strength. For example, in the 1970s the unions' structure was expanded

72 *Linda Fuller*

and reorganized, allowing workers' organizations to participate more effectively in economic planning. The unions now organize virtually all working Cubans, compared to only about 60 percent of the labor force in the 1960s. Further, the unions are now financially self-sufficient; previously part of their activities had been financed out of state coffers.[44] Finally, all union leaders are now chosen through regularized electoral procedures. Two changes in the overall context in which unions operate also hold promise for the expansion of workers' control. First, the SPDE has meant an increase in autonomy to individual production units, which is a necessary but not a sufficient prerequisite for meaningful democratization at the work site, and second the growth of workers' influence within and on the Cuban Communist Party.[45]

The picture that has emerged from this discussion of the changing relationship between unions, management, and the party is one of more autonomous unions with a more powerful presence in worksite decision-making, and with particular areas of primary authority. Conflicts between the interests of union members, the party, and management are expected to arise and to be resolved in the daily course of production. Considered in organizational capacity and operating environment which have been discussed briefly above, this changed relationship is a positive sign for the growth of workers' control in Cuba.[46] Far from frustrating or opposing workers' control, as in some capitalist countries, and far from fading into obscurity with the appearance of socialism, unions in Cuba have proven essential to producers' efforts to expand their control over production. Despite certain difficulties, unions have been important for workers' control because they have provided the vehicle through which individual workers have been united to create a collective force capable of exerting an influence on the course or production at the workplace and beyond.

Notes

1. Castro's quote was reprinted in *Trabajadores*, February 6, 1979, p. 2. The editorial appeared in *Trabajadores* August 7, 1979, on p. 1.

2. Although the primary focus here is workers' control in the micro arena or at the worksite, it is important to recognize that producers' involvement in the macro-level political arena is an integral determinant of workers' control as well.

3. See, for example, Evelyne Stephens, *The Politics of Workers' Participation: The Peruvian Approach in Comparative Perspective* (New York: Academic Press, 1980); John Witte, *Democracy, Authority, and Alienation in Work: Workers' Participation in an American Corporation* (Chicago: University of Chicago Press, 1980); and Carmen Sirianni, *Workers' Control and Socialist Democracy: The Soviet Experience.*

4. This work is part of a larger study entitled "The Politics of Workers' Control in Cuba, 1959–1983: The Work Center and the National Arena." Primary

data for the study include government, union, and party publications and documents and interviews and visits to worksites that took place during three trips to the island in 1982 and 1983. Most interviews took place in the Havana vicinity.

5. Their comments jibe with a variety of published accounts describing the progressive deterioration of the unions during the first decade of the revolution. See Martin Lionel, "Reestructuración sindical en Cuba," *Cuba internacional* (April 1974):30; Marifeli Pérez-Stable, "Whither the Cuban Working Class?," 66; idem, "Institutionalism and Workers' Response," 32; Carmelo Mesa-Lago, *Cuba in the 1970s*, 3; and Arthur MacEwan, *Revolution and Economic Development in Cuba*, 152.

6. CERP (Cuban Economic Research Project), *Labor Conditions in Communist Cuba* (Miami: University of Miami Press, 1963), 101.

7. Adolfo Gilly, *Cuba: Coexistencia o revolución*, 21–22.

8. Barry Reckord, *Does Fidel Eat More Than Your Father?*, 101–6.

9. Juan Lopez, "Cuba's Workers Steeled in Struggle," *People's World* (June 17, 1972):6.

10. Interview, September 9, 1982.

11. Roberto Veiga, "Informe central at XIV Congreso Nacional de la CTC," *Trabajadores* (supplement, November 29, 1978): 25; and Marta Harnecker, "A Cuban Leader Answers Some Tough Questions," *Cubatimes* 2 (Spring 1981):33.

12. Interview with a member of the Public Administration Workers' Union, September 13, 1982.

13. This movement was composed of an elite of Cuba's best workers, who were elected in workcenter assemblies. In 1969 they numbered around 235,000, or approximately 12 percent of the employed labor force.

14. Interview with a member of the Health Workers' Union, September 27, 1982.

15. This was the argument made by Bonachea and Valdés in 1972. See Rolando Bonachea and Nelson Valdes, "Labor and Revolution: Introduction," 382.

16. *Granma Weekly Review*, October 24, 1971, 4–5.

17. The phrase is borrowed from Mao Zedong.

18. Interview in a steel factory, October 1, 1982.

19. Although some provisions of the SDPE have increased conflict between workers and management, other stipulations of the new management and planning system appear to mitigate these conflicts or relocate them. For example, workers and managers share in the firm's "profits" under the SDPE, thereby giving both an interest in lowering costs and increasing output. Moreover, under the SDPE, enterprises are beginning to contract directly with other enterprises for their raw materials and supplies. In an economy in which the supply of production inputs is consistently much lower than the demand for them, interfirm contracts tend to heighten conflict between the workers and managers in one enterprise and the workers and managers in another.

20. See, for example Bertram Silverman, "Organización económica y conciencia social: Algunos dilemas"; and Terry Karl, "Work Incentives in Cuba," 36.

21. CERP (Cuban Economic Research Project), *Labor Conditions in Communist Cuba*, 101.

22. *Granma Weekly Review*, September 21, 1973, 7–12.

23. Jorge Domínguez, *Cuba: Order and Revolution*, p. 319, also reports that approximately another 8 percent of the local union leaders in 1975 were members of the Young Communists. An alternative interpretation of attempts to separate union and party leadership would be that it is a way to weaken unions by isolating their leaders from the "true" locus of power and authority

(the party). I do not find this interpretation very plausible: first because an important prerequisite of union strength in a socialist setting is that there be a clear distinction between union and party leadership; and second, because my reading of the post-1970 evidence strongly indicates that unions have not decreased, but rather increased their power and authority during this period.

24. Interview with a member of the Cultural Workers' Union, September 21, 1982.

25. Interview with a member of the Health Workers' Union, September 27, 1982.

26. Marifeli Pérez-Stable, "Whither the Cuban Working Class?," 70.

27. This last point about party composition was mentioned to me on a number of occasions. Cuban workers felt that given the "watch dog" role played by the party, it was imperative that all strata, especially ordinary workers, were members. If the party came to represent only the most educated or the highest status groups, they reasoned, the party would lack familiarity, knowledge, and understanding of the workers' points of view, and the balance of power would shift to the side of management.

28. Interview in a steel factory, October 1, 1982.

29. Interviews in a steel factory, same date, with a member of the Education and Science Workers' union, and with a CTC official September 29, 1982.

30. Interview with a member of the Cultural Workers' Unions, September 21. 1982.

31. Interview with a member of the Cultural Workers' Union, September 25, 1982.

32. Reckord, *Does Fidel Eat More Than Your Father?*, 96.

33. *Granma Weekly Review*, October 24, 1971, 4.

34. Interview with a member of the Cultural Workers' Union, September 25, 1982. See also *Trabajadores* (Nov. 9, 1978, 3) for a report of how a union played its counterpart role after an administration blamed a worker's own negligence for an accident that caused his death.

35. *Trabajadores*, June 19, 1979, 1.

36. *Trabajadores*, June 14, 1979, 2.

37. Interview with a member of the Health Workers' Union, September 27, 1982.

38. Interview, September 29, 1982.

39. Interview with a member of the Education and Science Workers' Union, October 3, 1982.

40. In considering these questions I will emphasize "internal" rather than "external" explanatory factors. A more complete answer would also have to examine "external" factors in some detail, especially the relationship between Cuba and other socialist nations and the fact that Cuba, a developing socialist country, must exist within the context of a pervasive capitalist world market.

41. For more information on this period, see Hobart Spalding Jr., *Labor in Latin America*; Ramón Ruiz, *Cuba: The Making of a Revolution*; Lionel Martin, "Reestructuración sindical en Cuba," *Cuba Internacional* (April 1974):28–30; Pérez-Stable, "Whither the Cuban Working Class?," 60–77; Grupo Cubano, *Un estudio sobre Cuba*; O'Connor, *The Origins of Socialism in Cuba*; J.P. Morray, *The Second Revolution in Cuba*; and Ralph Woodward Jr., "Union Labor and Communism: Cuba," 3 (October 1963):17–50.

42. Mesa-Lago, *Cuba in the 1970s*; idem, *The Economic Development of Revolutionary Cuba*; Bonachea and Valdés, "Labor and Revolution: Introduction," 357–83; and Archibald Ritter, *The Economic Development of Revolutionary Cuba* (New York: Praeger, 1974), all present data on these measures of dissatisfaction.

43. A more widely known example was the institution of elected municipal, provincial and national assemblies known as the Organos del Poder Popular (Organs of Popular Power, or OPP).

44. See Roberto Hernández and Carmelo Mesa-Lago, "Labor Organization and Wages," 215; Cuban Communist Party, *Second Congress of the Communist Party of Cuba: Documents and Speeches* (Havana: Political Publishers, 1981) 60; and interview with a national CTC official September 29, 1982.

45. For more information on these last two topics, see Linda Fuller, "The Politics of Workers' Control in Cuba, 1959–1983: The Work Center and the National Arena," chaps. 6 and 7.

46. My conclusions are in apparent opposition to some other recent and diverse pieces on Cuba, which see few signs of any increase in the power of direct producers on the island. See, for example, Jean-Pierre Beauvais, "Achievements and Contradictions of the Cuban Workers' State," 49–71; Ronaldo Munck, *Politics and Dependency in the Third World*; and Jorge Domínguez, "Revolutionary Politics: The New Demands of Orderliness," 19–70.

5

Architecture and the Building Industry in Contemporary Cuba

Howard Glazer

O_{ut} *to lunch. It's noon time.*

The story is told that this was the answer to Fidel Castro as he scanned the all-but-empty drafting room of the architectural office that he, Che Guevara, and a small group of government officials had come to visit, unannounced. The office had been given the job of designing multistoried apartment buildings for a new housing project.

The year was 1959, soon after the fall of the Bastista dictatorship. Optimism and idealism had not yet confronted the realities of deep-rooted economic underdevelopment. Cuba's construction industry was in a state of virtual stagnation after many private builders and architects had fled (with other wealthy Cubans) to Miami. Unemployment in the building trades was especially high. To give employment to the hundreds of idle construction workers, to counter the chronic housing shortage, and to show Cubans the kind of housing they could expect from the revolutionary government, the new government had directed some of the still-functioning architectural offices to design a new housing project.

Castro's response to the empty office: "We don't have time to waste with lunch hours. Workers need jobs and people need housing. From now on have food brought in so everyone can continue working through their lunchtime." Fidel and Che Guevara pored over plans for the multistoried apartment buildings. Che argued that Cuba simply could not afford the proposed buildings, which would contain spacious, if not elegant, apartments not unlike those of Havana's middle class before 1959. Castro's response was, "But that's *why* we had a revolution — so every Cuban can have such a place to live!"

76

Much has happened in Cuba since those early days of boundless optimism. The huge cost of industrial development, of economic diversification, of the commitment to provide free education and health care, of Cuba's willingness to assist other fledgling revolutionary governments, and of continuing U.S. hostility and economic blockade has postponed indefinitely the hope that the government could provide free quality housing for every Cuban. Yet from a beginning of thatch-roofed and mud-floored *bohios* in the countryside and slums and shantytowns in the cities, a transformation has taken place. Housing itself has been dramatically improved. But there also has been the simultaneous construction of hundreds of schools, clinics, hospitals, resort facilities, new towns, industrial complexes, and even a delightful zoological park in Havana, all part of the contribution of planners, architects, and builders to this physical/social metamorphosis.

Housing in Cuba prior to 1959 followed a typical Third World pattern, with an extreme qualitative difference between urban and rural homes. In the countryside more than four-fifths of the dwellings were *bohios*, and only 10 percent had even the most primitive electricity or plumbing. Although most urban dwellings had electricity, fewer than half had complete sanitary facilities, and fewer than half of those were of even acceptable quality. By the time of the revolution, about half of the total inventory of 1.4 million dwellings was considered substandard.[1] Following the overthrow of the Bastista dictatorship, the new government took the critical first steps to deal with the grave problems of housing. These steps were intended to be an integral part of other basic policy changes, including urban reform and nationalization of banks, of many industries and of the educational system.

The 1959 Housing Law

The first housing law, decreed within weeks after the January 1, 1959, victory, halted evictions. Within months, most rents were reduced by 30 to 50 percent, with the greatest reductions for the lowest rents. But the law also protected small landlords and provided for ten-year tax exemptions for owner-occupied houses built in the following two years, which was an attempt to discourage rental construction and to encourage home-ownership. In October 1960, the Urban Reform Law established the concept of housing as a public service, with the stated future goal of providing housing at no cost to all citizens. This revolutionary ideal was to influence Cuba's housing policy for years to come, and it reflected the early post-revolutionary optimism about the possibilities for rapid economic development and a smoother transition to socialism. Only in recent years, confronted by the reality of economic limitations and the difficulty of changing human behavior in a single generation, has this ideal been abandoned.

The first stage of the Urban Reform Law, in addition to dealing with

the issues of evictions and rents, required that landlords, who were permitted to retain their own homes and a vacation home, sell all investment property. The speculators, large landlords, and private mortgage
lenders were thus hurt by the Urban Reform Law, but the majority of
small owners, who had invested in property for old-age security,
benefited by receiving an assured lifetime income from the sale of their
private holdings. Former small landlords also benefited because these
payments were guaranteed, in contrast to the past problems of widespread rent delinquency. Current tenants were given first priority to
buy. Tenants would amortize the price of their dwellings, paying a
regular rent (already reduced in 1959) for a specified length of time —
between five and twenty years. The state collected amortization
payments from the tenants and, in turn, paid the former landlords in-
stallments of up to 600 pesos a month. This was a comfortable income
when the average monthly income in Cuba was about 100 pesos.

The second stage of the Urban Reform Law began a program of
government-constructed housing to be leased with lifetime occupancy
rights at a maximum rent of 10 percent of the family income. It was
anticipated that a third stage would begin within a decade when the
government would provide housing free of charge. The Urban Reform
Law also established two basic urban tenure forms. The majority of
tenants became homeowners, joining the one-third of urban families
who already owned their homes before the revolution. Long-term
leaseholding under the legal concept of "usufruct" (an ancient legal concept resembling a life-long lease) controlled the new or existing gov-
ernment-owned dwellings. Other forms of renting were totally prohibited, except for short stays in such transient facilities as hotels, vacation houses, or apartments.

Families who thus became homeowners were required to pay only
until the official established price was amortized. Rents for long-term
leaseholders, however, were based on ability to pay, not to exceed 10
percent of annual income, without regard to the size, quality, or location of the dwelling. Leaseholders, however, were obligated to continue
these payments indefinitely, without accruing any equity. All residents
were responsible for arranging and paying for normal maintenance
and repairs within their own houses and apartments, regardless of
tenure status. In multifamily buildings of four or more units, local
government agencies assumed the responsibility of common area
maintenance and major repairs. But in the turmoil of such major social
adjustment, only minimum materials and human resources were
devoted to maintenance and repair. The result was a severe deterioration of much of the housing stock.

This distribution of support resources for maintenance was not due
solely to indifference of neglect, although it might have been short-

sighted. Two issues of major importance influenced this practice. The first was to ensure that the countryside and small cities, which had historically been neglected in favor of the larger cities, would have priority of material and labor resources. The second was to diminish the allure of Havana, to make it unattractive to those Cubans thinking of moving from the countryside to the glamor of the largest city. Mass migration out of the countryside had been a serious social problem of pre-revolutionary Cuba. Indeed, of all Latin American and Caribbean countries, Cuba is the only example of success in stemming the flow of rural people into large cities and of equalizing the quality of housing, health care, educational facilities, and social services between rural and urban populations. Consequently, by 1985 this dual policy could be relaxed. The result is that, now, large sections of Havana are beginning to be repaired, repainted, and restored.

The new government housing policy from the beginning was directed essentially at these issues:

1. clearing the worst squatter settlements and relocating their residents,
2. concentrating resources for construction activity in the countryside,
3. establishing and developing a large public housing sector,
4. upgrading urban and rural infrastructure, and
5. providing technical assistance and credit mechanisms for private, self-built housing.

In the first attempt to eradicate urban slums, the government briefly experimented with an organized "self-help" initiative. Each household was committed to no less than twenty-four hours of work per week. During 1960 and 1961, approximately 3500 homes were constructed by former residents of squatter settlements through this "self-help" initiative. Each new community contained 100 to 150 dwellings, accompanied by some community facilities such as schools and clinics. But the combination of unskilled labor, high absenteeism, and labor-force instability resulted in low productivity and poor-quality construction. The concept of self-help housing was quietly dropped. Yet it would remain dormant as an official policy for twenty years, although unofficially it continued to produce thousands of new dwellings. Despite all the problems of the early program, the dramatic result was the elimination of almost fifty squatter settlements from city fringes.

A major thrust of the early post-revolution housing program was new construction. Most new units were single-family detached residences and low-rise (four-story) walk-up apartment buildings. *Habana del Este*, however, was an exception. This ambitious 2300-unit development was built mostly on vacant land that had been assembled by speculators before the revolution. The plan was centered around the neighborhood unit and the superblock, and combined high-rise and walk-up residential buidings with the attendant community facilities and commercial areas. Here, in *Habana del Este*, one can find the spacious apartments that Fidel and Che had disagreed about during that noon-hour visit in 1959. The neighborhood unit and the superblock concept survived and became the design foundation for new urban developments. The generous apartment sizes, however, were not to be duplicated. Economic reality had overtaken idealism, and the direction now was toward more efficient, minimal-space standards.

Rural Housing

Rural areas were even more affected by state-sponsored housing programs. The agrarian reform laws had converted large plantations and ranches into state farms and had distributed land to thousands of landless peasants. Small farmers were guaranteed that their property would not be expropriated, but they were encouraged to sell their land voluntarily to state farms. An important incentive to do so was the provision, for life, of rent-free, fully furnished dwellings located in rural new towns that provided schools, clinics, libraries, and commercial services. This method of urbanization of the countryside was to play a key role in implementing Cuba's fundamental goal, that of minimizing the differences between rural and urban living. To provide modern services to rural areas, it was essential to concentrate residents in communities large enough to make such services viable. In the small dairy community of Jibacoa, for instance, where the residents enjoy a bookstore, a barber shop, and a medical clinic, every apartment balcony boasts a rocking chair, a house-warming gift from the local administration.

During the first five years of the program, some 26,000 units were built in rural areas. The resulting 150 settlements ranged in size from several dozen houses to several thousand. By then, 70 percent of the agricultural laborers were salaried workers with stable and adequate income. During these first years, 1959 to 1964, the government sponsored or directly built almost 55,000 new dwellings in both urban and rural areas, including the above-mentioned 26,000 rural dwellings, a dramatic contrast to the pre-revolutionary period when almost all new standard housing was built in urban areas, particularly Havana. Private construction, with some government supervision, financing, or technical assistance, added an additional 30,000 units. The combined total of 17,000 standard units per year was significantly higher than the pre-revolutionary average of 10,200 in the years 1945 to 1958. Tens of thousands of additional units were also constructed without any governmental assistance. While many were of better quality than those found in pre-revolutionary shantytowns, by government criteria they were often substandard.

The first Housing Conference to evaluate past performance and develop future policy was held in 1964. This conference recommended a program for preventive maintenance, repairs, and rehabilitation of existing housing. There was also a renewal of government-assisted self-help housing in rural areas and recommendations for establishing savings and loan cooperatives. Although conference participants concluded that only industrialized construction could rapidly expand housing production, they cautioned against the indiscriminate use of imported systems without careful evaluation. Nevertheless, the results of the conference were not encouraging since housing production, in general, was forced to become subordinate to more urgent needs of the national economy. Early economic development strategy had emphasized basic industry and central control of economic planning and administration. By the time of the conference the limitations of this strategy became apparent. Consequently, much more emphasis would now be directed to agriculture and related industries. Cuba simply did not yet possess sufficient skilled labor, industrial infrastructure, or the financial ability to import factories, machinery, and raw materials in large quantities. Sugar was Cuba's only export capable of earning substantial foreign exchange. The emphasis, therefore, was to expand, modernize, and mechanize the agriculture sector. Here the goal of a 10 million-ton sugar harvest originated, resulting in severe disruption in almost all other sectors of the economy. Although the harvest was the largest in Cuba's history—8.5 millions tons—it still fell short of the target and triggered a fundamental reevaluation of Cuba's economic program.

Throughout the late 1960s, because resources were devoted to developing infrastructure and production investments, the government allocated only minimal resources to housing. Only a total of 44,000 dwellings was built in the years 1964 to 1970. In fact, from 1968 through 1971, government production of housing dropped to an average of only 5000 units a year.[3] These were concentrated in small rural towns near state farms and high-priority industrial settlements in the interior. The larger urban areas, particularly Havana, were virtually ignored. Because of the low priority given to new housing construction and housing maintenance and the economic disruptions during the late 1960s, the national housing shortage became acute. By 1970 it was estimated that there was a shortage of at least a million units.[4]

Skilled labor was especially scarce as more workers found higher paying jobs in other sectors of the economy. In an attempt to counteract the severe shortages of materials and labor, new emphasis was again put on industrialized, prefabricated systems. A lightweight, prefabricated building system, originally developed in Cuba before 1959, was

Figure 5.1 Housing, Habana del Este, Havana. One of the first major projects built after the revolution. The apartments were of generous size and were never duplicated because of financial constraints.

Figure 5.2 Historic restoration, La Plaza Vieja, Havana. Front facade of the Casa de los Condes de San Juan de Jaruco, built between 1733 and 1737. Restored in 1984, it is now used for exhibitions, small musical performances, special meetings, and receptions.

Figure 5.3 Restaurant "Las Ruinas," Havana. Exceptionally dramatic integration of 19th-century stone walls into a prefabricated concrete structural system.

Figure 5.4 El Palacio de las Convenciones, Havana. The Palace of Conventions was built and inaugurated in 1979 when Cuba was host for the summit conference of the Movement of Nonaligned Countries. It incorporates extensive use of prefabricated concrete structural members.

Figure 5.5 Experimental concrete prefabrication plant, Havana. Center for the development of new panel designs, panel systems, and prefabricated baths and kitchen assemblies.

Figure 5.6 Hotel Marazul. Architect Mario Girona has designed numerous hotels, airports, and other special purpose buildings making use of prefabricated concrete structural systems.

Figure 5.7 "Jose Marti" housing project, Santiago de Cuba, 1962, illustrates the adaptation of prefabricated concrete building systems to the tropical climate. Note the sheltered balconies.

Figure 5.8 Agricultural cooperative housing, Jibacoa, a new community for agricultural families near Havana. Facilities include shops, library, and day-care center.

85

used for one- and two-story construction, especially in small towns and rural areas.

After five years of declining housing starts, there was pressure to increase building in urban areas. Although construction materials in general were in short supply, production of cement and other building products had improved in the previous decade. The biggest obstacle to expanding housing production appeared to be an acute labor shortage. During the previous decade, however, citizens had shown their ability to participate actively in solving their housing problems by constructing more than 300,000 self-built housing units. Voluntary work on agricultural and construction projects, including housing, had been successfully organized through the Committees for the Defense of the Revolution (CDRs). The next logical step was the concept of the "microbrigade" system.

Microbrigades

Cuba's approach to self-help housing in the early 1970s was unique. Responding to the intense demand for housing, combined with low productivity in the general economy, Cuba created the microbrigade system. Instead of using regular construction labor, or depending on each individual to solve his own problems, workers from existing workplaces formed brigades that worked under the supervision of experienced technicians and skilled craftsmen provided by the Ministry of Construction. The ministry also furnished land and equipment. Plans and materials to construct four- and five-story buildings containing twenty to thirty apartments were provided by the government. Usually a semi-prefabricated system was used that combined masonry block walls and prefab concrete floor and roof slabs. This effectively utilized semi- and unskilled labor that was available.

Upon completion, these apartments were distributed to workers from the same workplace, but not necessarily to those who had actually participated in the construction: priority was given to those with greatest need and the most outstanding job performance. New residents paid a maximum of 6 percent of family income, rather than the regular 10 percent, in acknowledgment of the "surplus work" contributed either as microbrigade members or by working more on their regular jobs. Since the remaining workers had previously agreed, even without the brigade members who had been released from their normal jobs, to achieve at least the same levels of production, the result was higher overall productivity. Ordinarily the microbrigade consisted of 10 percent of the total work force. This resulted in a very significant increase in total economic output. While the most obvious purpose of the microbrigades was to tap a new source of labor for housing construction, the goal to foster higher workplace productivity was an important consideration in the early 1970s prior to reorganizing economic planning and management mechanisms. The microbrigade system also tended to reduce job turnover, since most government-built urban housing was being distributed through workplaces, rather than through block-level CDRs.

Of the more than 200,000 houses and apartments created in the years 1971 to 1975, only two-fifths were government-built. As in the previous decade, the majority of new dwellings continued to be self-built with little or no direct government aid.[5] Beginning in 1972, government housing construction increased to an annual average of nearly 19,000 units during the years 1972 to 1975. More than 50 percent of these units were built by the microbrigades, and the balance by regular government construction workers. Havana and other large cities received a disproportionately large share of this construction to redress their neglect during the previous period.

The microbrigades continued to grow rapidly until 1975, then leveled off, largely because limited resources did not allow the establishment of a microbrigade for every workplace desiring to create one. In 1978, government officials proposed changing or phasing out the program. One major criticism of the microbrigade housing was its generally lower quality and higher cost, compared to equivalent buildings erected by regular state brigades. Most microbrigade workers, who came from a variety of job classifications, continued to receive regular wages (often higher) from their own workplaces. As a result, they often earned higher wages than unskilled construction workers. Compounding the problem, most microbrigade members were assigned to work on labor-intensive, traditional and semi-prefabricated construction, since they lacked sufficient skills for the more complex industrialized systems. On the other hand, microbrigade members who had acquired building craft skills began to receive regular wages directly from the Ministry of Construction.

An additional doubt about continuing or expanding the microbrigade system concerned the subsequent inequity. Most government-sponsored housing in urban areas was distributed only through workplaces utilizing microbrigades, so many people with similar or greater need had no access to new housing. Others effectively excluded from the fruits of the microbrigade system were employees in workplaces not conducive to forming microbrigades, families housed in temporary shelters created by natural disasters or dangerous conditions in their previous dwellings, or people in severely overcrowded housing.

What to do with microbrigades was considered and debated at the 1978 convention of Cuba's Central Union Federation. One proposal was to convert most or all of the microbrigades into state construction brigades. Another was to phase out the microbrigades. The labor federation opposed workplaces losing their role in distributing housing but agreed that there should be a uniform system of payment for housing. The unions also argued to protect the wage levels of microbrigade workers, no matter what alternative was selected. There was universal agreement that the microbrigades had represented a vital response during a period of acute labor shortage and continued to be a well-organized, dedicated labor force that should not be lost. The convention recommended, therefore, that workplaces continue to distribute a certain portion of all new housing, and opened the possibility of some of the microbrigades being organized into state brigades, without affecting the workers' salary levels or seniority.

By 1980, the overall labor situation had changed. Economic productivity was increasing at a steady rate, and it became difficult to remove workers without affecting production. The 1970s also had seen a significant growth in the construction sector that resulted in state brigades of skilled workers able to construct the new, more technically advanced, prefabricated construction systems. These changes would prove inadequate to satisfy the huge demand for housing, in part because of the expense and inefficiency of an overly mechanized system. The Cuban people's eagerness to lend direct assistance to obtaining their own housing was also becoming increasingly apparent. An intensive two-year study of housing problems eventually forged the new General Housing Law, ratified in late 1984.

Yet, despite the problems of inefficiency and inconsistent quality, microbrigades by 1983 had completed 100,000 units, nearly half of all government-built housing in the late 1970s and early 1980s. The number of microbrigades has remained constant, although microbrigade housing represents a declining portion of total new construction. It appears likely that the attention the new law gives to other forms of self-built housing will provide outlets for voluntary labor, both individual and collective, and will ultimately end the uniquely Cuban experiment with microbrigades.

For the moment, however, microbrigades continue to function, even though they constitute an ever smaller percentage of total government-sponsored construction. This has also resulted in workplaces controlling the distribution of a small proportion of new housing, and it should gradually solve the growing problem of equitable access to housing.

Project-Housing

The microbrigades fostered a building boom in the early 1970s, which produced large-scale housing projects on the outskirts of most Cuban cities. The endless rows of four- and five-story walk-ups in enormous superblocks were occasionally punctuated by a high-rise prefabricated building. When, in the early 1970s, attention was turned again to inner-urban slum areas, the already dilapidated inner city had deteriorated even further. This led to Cuba's first major urban redevelopment project in *Cayo Hueso*, a neighborhood bordering on Havana's downtown commercial area. Because these old, rundown buildings were not the historically valuable areas of colonial Old Havana, a clearance project was chosen. Since demolition could not begin until families had been relocated, this process was slow, for few relocation units were available when emigration from Cuba all but ceased after 1972.

The first buildings constructed were five-story walk-ups. In the second phase, several twelve- and eighteen-story towers were constructed. High-rise construction, it was argued, was necessary to maintain the area's previous high density while providing larger units for each family and additional open space and essential community facilities. The rapid growth of high-rise apartment buildings was particularly prevalent in a number of provincial capitals and in both central and suburban Havana. Over the objections of numerous architects and planners, such site planning and design was championed by engineers and construction agencies who claimed greater efficiency and economy, despite the argument that costs had not been correctly calculated. One glaring discrepancy was the tying-up of giant cranes, often for years, at a construction site while waiting for delivery of imported elevators, pumps, and other essential equipment. The opponents of high-rise buildings point out that the actual "down-time" cost of these cranes is rarely calculated into the final cost of construction.

The argument of land-use efficiency had been coupled with an unshakable faith in mechanization, a faith that may be undermined as the new Housing Law becomes effective. Moreover, the enthusiasm for high-rise construction among housing engineers and builders is not necessarily shared by those who live in the buildings. This lack of enthusiasm for high-rise living was summed up by the superintendent of construction at a large development in Camaguay. The project contained a number of buildings, both four- and five-story walk-ups and a few high-rises. When asked which Cubans prefer, he replied, "Well, we like to build the big ones," pause, then a smile, "but the people like the low ones better to live in."

In recent years, more and more Cuban architects and planners are attempting to reverse this trend toward high-rise apartments, not only because of the preference for low-rise housing, but because of the serious problems that high-rise housing imposes on the cityscape, on city services, and on the expense of maintenance. A not-unrelated issue involves the use of existing housing in Havana. Early in the revolution, when new government agencies were being organized, houses in upper-middle-class and wealthy neighborhoods were taken over by various newly formed bureaus. Many of the owners had fled to Miami, and the houses were often large enough to accommodate office use with only minimal remodeling. As the agencies grew they took over adjacent houses, until eventually some ministries occupied scores of adjacent houses. Meanwhile, the government began building high-rise apartment buildings. Recently, a number of influential Cuban architects and planners have recommended that high-rise office buildings be built and that the houses, often with beautiful surrounding gardens, be returned to housing families.

A possible impediment to implementing this proposal may be the historic reluctance of some agencies to project an image of governmental power and authority. The use of houses as offices is certainly less overbearing than the use of conspicuous high-rise office buildings. The challenge to Cuban architects is to design appropriately scaled office buildings that would combine the desired efficiency with the equally desirable qualities of human scale and beauty. Judging from many of the schools, clinics, recreation buildings, museums, resorts, and so forth, designed by contemporary Cuban architects, the challenge can be met.

Other Contemporary Challenges

By 1980 it was clear that planners of housing policy, who had expected to reach annual construction of 100,000 units, were overly optimistic. The magic formula was to have been an expansion of prefabrication.[6] Central government production actually declined in the late 1970s; from 1976 to 1980, approximately 250,000 houses and apartments were created, an average of about 50,000 a year. Of these, only 16,500 were constructed directly by the government. The balance, two-thirds of the total, were built privately. Government-built housing was also concentrated in areas where priority was given to attracting and retaining population, such as on the Isle of Youth and in the central provinces. Havana and other large cities also received a disproportionate share of state construction. The scarcity of land discouraged extensive private building, and the government, during these years, to promote high densities, assumed major responsibility for providing housing.[7]

Understaffed local government agencies often found it next to impossible to regulate, let alone count, most of these units. Consequently, they did not appear in annual official construction statistics. Not until statistics from the 1970 and 1981 censuses became available did the extent of nongovernment construction become known. From 1959 to 1970, 416,000 houses and apartments were created, averaging 24,700 annually. But only 100,000 were built directly by the government, and another 30,000 with some public involvement.

Renewed interest in self-built housing came from several directions. Housing analysts noted, in the late 1970s, that the majority of new units continued to be built privately. Rather than considering this a problem, it was acknowledged that other socialist countries, at a similar stage of development, also had built a majority of their new housing privately, especially in small towns and rural areas. Recommendations were made to tap this potential officially by organizing local and national government agencies to assist and facilitate private construction.[8]

Although, in the current five-year plan, the government is still taking primary responsibility for housing construction, inexpensive one- and two-story self-built housing will be encouraged in rural communities, small towns, state-owned farms, small cities, and even in the outskirts of larger cities. Government-sponsored, prefabricated, four- and five-story walk-ups and high-rise elevator buildings will still continue to predominate in larger urban areas. Because of criticism of high-rise apartment buildings by architects and planners as well as by Cubans in general, the likelihood is growing that there will soon be new plans for high-density but low-rise developments.

The 1976 United Nations–sponsored "Habitat" conference, confronting the worldwide issues of housing, urbanization, and community development, gave particular attention to the issue of self-help housing—a process extremely common in developing countries but also actively promoted by a number of Western industrial nations. The English delegation, led by John F.C. Turner, was an especially vocal advocate of the self-help idea.[9]

At one plenary session devoted exclusively to the self-help housing concept, the leader of the Cuban delegation spoke in opposition to the whole idea. Cuba believed, she told the delegates, that full-time workers should not have to spend their time building their dwelling, that housing should be a basic social service comparable to education and health care—free to everyone. Self-help housing might be appropriate, she conceded, in countries where underemployment was common, but not where there was full employment. Advocates of self-help housing at the conference argued with equal vigor that no developing country can possibly afford the enormous cost of providing decent housing to everyone, that some method of direct involvement from the final occupant is essential. Cuba's unique microbrigade system was one way to obtain this direct involvement but, despite its accomplishments, it has had serious limitations.

The 1981 census showed that less than a third of the houses and apartments constructed in Cuba after 1959 were built by the central government agencies. The balance were constructed privately on a self-help basis, usually by a combination of family labor, neighborhood assistance, and some purchased work usually requiring special skills. It is unfortunate that because of the severe shortage of construction materials and inadequate government regulation, many of these new dwellings were of substandard construction and poorly located. The 1984 Housing Law proposes to aid in upgrading and, where necessary, replacing existing substandard self-built housing. Most important, the new law establishes programs to provide qualified labor for both maintenance and new construction, including the licensing of contractors. Architects' and engineers' professional associations are also beginning to provide low-cost architectural services and model plans for various housing styles, sizes, and materials.

The 1984 Housing Law

Perhaps the most significant single act, after the original Urban Reform Law of 1959 that totally altered the practices of pre-revolutionary Cuba, is the new Housing Law of 1984, which reverses many existing policies and provides new opportunities for diversity.

Since the early 1960s, housing has frequently been a neglected part of Cuba's investment policy. Good housing, no matter how important, was an economic luxury difficult for a developing country to afford. But for the first time since the halcyon days when Fidel Castro talked of every Cuban having quality free housing, a far-reaching, comprehensive analysis of housing policy has been undertaken by the National Assembly, Cuba's parliament. New attention is paid to self-built housing, which was virtually ignored officially by the government from the early 1960s to the late 1970s. Maintenance and repair of existing buildings is emphasized, and deteriorated urban areas are scheduled to be rehabilitated or completely redeveloped. Rural housing and new towns' policies and changed in response to the growth of agricultural cooperatives.

Cuba's new General Housing Law confronts one of the major issues of a country that has set high goals in providing every citizen social services that are often beyond the country's immediate economic capabilities. The law resulted from more than two years' work by a number of agencies, including the National Assembly's Commission on Construction and Housing, the Council of Minister's Secretariat, the Construction Ministry and its Technical Center for Housing, the Ministry of Justice, the Revolutionary Armed Forces Ministry, the Central Planning Board and its Institute of Physical Planning, the People's Savings Bank, the State Committees for Prices and Finance, and the Office for Service to the Organs of People's Organization of Cuban Trade Unions (CTC), and the Federation of Cuban Women (FMC).[10] The new law covers a number of basic policies:

1. *Conversion to ownership.* Cuba's 460,000 rent-paying families, representing one-fifth of all households, will become homeowners by

amortizing the price of their dwellings. Purchase price is established as the total of the household's monthly rents — based on the October 1984, payment — to be paid over a twenty-year period. All payments from previous years are credited toward this total price, but a minimum number of years must still be paid. This will range from five years for dwellings built before 1940, to thirteen years for those erected after 1971. A family can decide to pay more rapidly; conversely, if household income falls so that amortization payments would exceed 10 percent of income, the term can be extended. Households also have the option of setting the total price to be amortized by using a method based on the type of construction, usable floor area, location, extra yard space, and depreciation. This alternative will benefit higher-income households living in small or poorly located dwellings. This method of calculating purchase price is called the "legal price," to distinguish it from prices on the unregulated "free market," or those derived from income-based rent.

An additional 740,000 households, or almost one-third of the total population, are considered neither owners nor rent-paying tenants. Many of these will acquire title to their homes without paying any amortization. These include most residents of self-built housing and rural new towns. Certain leaseholders, however, will not become homeowners. These residents — who will continue with rent-free leases — include those living in single rooms with shared services, in structures beyond repair, or in units built with scavenged materials.

2. *Housing distributed by the government.* New government-built housing will be sold to high-priority families, who will pay off the "legal price" of their dwellings with low-interest loans over a period of twenty years, in high-rise structures, and fifteen years in all others. Few families are likely to pay the full price, since they will receive credit for payment in their prior residences. The new law also provides for stretching out payments over a longer period of time if the household cannot afford the regular payments. Most publicly built new housing will be distributed by the local government agencies rather than by workplaces. Exceptions include dwellings "linked" to, or owned by, workplaces and those financed out of "social and cultural funds" created out of workplaces' profits.

3. *Sales exchanges and inheritance.* The new law permits free market sales of land and housing, and the right to build on the roofs of single and multifamily housing. Yet the "free market" will not operate without controls. A "real estate sales tax" will be levied and, in addition, the state reserves the right to step in and exercise its option to purchase the property at its "legal price." When households exchange dwellings they will normally take their mortgage debt with them, but the new law provides for the parties involved to exchange the debt or to assume

payment of the debt on both dwellings. The new law will now permit the inheritance of a dwelling that becomes vacant after the death of its owner, even if the heir did not previously reside there. The law also updates regulations on the fate of dwellings owned by people who emigrate, an important item given the 1984 agreement between Cuba and the United States that permitted renewed migration of at least 20,000 Cubans annually to the United States.

4. *Self-help housing.* The new law provides for active government involvement in fostering a variety of forms of self-help construction. These include building by individual households and by cooperatives. Cooperatives are established only on a temporary basis for the purpose of building multifamily housing. Once completed, the apartments are owned as condominiums. Trade unions and other organizations are encouraged to promote such cooperatives among their members. Land, or the right to build on roofs, can be purchased from private parties, as can surface rights in perpetuity on state-owned land. Priority for state land will go first to cooperatives formed by trade unions seeking to build near their workplaces, then to other cooperatives, and finally to individual builders who fulfill certain criteria. Union-sponsored cooperatives will probably carry on the work of the microbrigades, which began to be phased out in early 1980s. Low-interest loans are available to cover a wide range of building costs: materials and construction or repairs, land, architectural and other technical assistance, rental of tools and equipment, and contracted labor from self-employed licensed tradespeople, specialized government tradespeople, or specialized government enterprises.

5. *Short-term rental.* Owners are permitted to rent rooms—with or without separate sanitary facilities—to no more than two households at any one time. Leases can be for a minimum of one week or a maximum of six months and are renewable. There are no restrictions on the amount of rent charged. If the homeowner chooses not to renew the lease or there has been a breach of contract, and the renter refuses to leave, the owner can then request the government to attach 50 percent of the renter's income. If, after three months, the renter household still refuses to leave, its members can be evicted.

Permitting short-term renting is seen as a transitional measure to make space available, on a voluntary basis, in existing housing. This policy is expected to provide more options for recently divorced couples, married couples living apart for lack of housing, people doubling-up with relatives, and workers and technicians temporarily transferred to other parts of the country.

6. *Management, maintenance, and repairs.* Normal maintenance and repairs will continue to be the responsibility of individual owners, but the government will contribute to costly major repairs of structural

elements and common areas of deteriorated multifamily buildings. The draft housing law proposed that public agencies contribute to paying for costly repairs for both single-family and multifamily units, whether with common areas or not. This was rejected in the National Assembly on the grounds that the government should not promise what it realistically cannot provide.

Low-rise multifamily housing will be "self-managed" by a council of all residents (in practice not unlike cooperative boards in the United States). Residents are responsible for paying "common costs" of maintenance and repairs. High-rise structures will be managed by local government agencies, which will subsidize part of the maintenance costs.

7. *Non-payment, unwelcome household members and illegal occupants.* All amortization payments—whether for existing, new state-built, or self-built dwellings—will be withheld from salaries in the same way consumer loan payments have been for many years. Only self-employed workers will pay directly, and if they fall more than three months in arrears they can be declared "illegal occupants" and risk eventual eviction. Any member of a household who is not linearly related (that is, parents, grandparents, and children) can be asked to leave by the owner(s). Special provisions are made in the case of former spouses. Occupants who are held to be "illegal" under the new law, including squatters occupying state or private housing or land without permission, must return to their legal residences. If that is not feasible, the government will assign them a room or a housing unit. If the illegal occupant still refuses to move, 30 percent of his or her salary will be attached for three months. As a last resort, the police can remove the recalcitrant party.

8. *Workplace-"linked" and -owned housing.* To assure a stable work force, a limited number of housing developments will be designated as either "linked" or owned by specific workplaces, military institutions, or other political or social organizations. The National Assembly debated about what to do with the thousands of families without members employed in the workplaces to which their housing is linked. Unable to reach a consensus, the matter was sent to the National Housing Institute for further study, leaving only the broadest provisions on workplace-linked or -owned housing in the new law.

The new law's radical departure from Cuba's recent past reflects two realities. The first is that a culture with a long history of private ownership continues to be influenced by the concept of "ownership"—that better care will be given a dwelling that is "owned." This was probably a difficult conclusion to reach because the revolutionary government began with a determination to reshape Cuban values and principles—to make a "new Cuban man." One of the sought-after changes was the merging of private interests with the common good, an equal respect for public as well as one's own private property. That this process will take more than a single generation seems, now, to be acknowledged.

A second important conceptual change is that housing should not be considered a capital investment, but rather a consumer product. Historically, housing in pre-revolutionary Cuba was often the source of investment income, and consequently was considered a capital investment. But after 1959, when renting, speculation, and income production ceased, housing could more logically be considered simply one more consumer product.

In his closing speech on the new Housing Law at the National Energy Forum, President Castro made this distinction:

> The law passed in the early years of the Revolution affected landlords — they were the property owners. In the present case the law will affect the state, but the state won't go bankrupt. Let me point out here that the state's revenue is not high, really, given the low rents that are paid here and we are laying the foundations so that everybody will have their home which they will maintain and take care of.
>
> Housing is not a means of production — that was made clear by the founders of socialism. It's not a factory or a work tool. It is an article for family use. The fact that a family owns its property does not contradict the principles of Marxism-Leninism in the least; on the contrary, they are enriched by that fact and under our conditions the law is perfect . . . if the law passed, it will be authorized for homeowners to rent one or two rooms if they want to. That will help solve our problems at present. Once a citizen can have his own apartment, he will no longer live in a rented room; the law is a transitory need.

The new law reflects the reality of history. In 1984, only 40 percent of all new dwellings had been built by either the Ministry of Construction or by quasi-governmental agencies; 60 percent were built by the owner/occupant. By 1985, these percentages had changed to 30 percent government-built, 70 percent private. But the vast majority of private building was taking place in the countryside, especially where cooperatives were active. Now private construction will be encouraged in urban areas as well, with the emphasis on the construction of additions and the remodeling of already existing housing. In Havana, within a few months after the passage of the law, the change was noticeable.

Ernesto Cardenal wrote in the early 1970s, "Havana is a city that has been heavily punished by the Revolution." The policy of neglecting Havana resulted from consciously directing limited resources into the countryside, where historically all public service and facilities, including housing, had been much poorer than in urban areas. The revolutionary government in Cuba was also determined to halt the endemic problem in all Third-World countries: mass migration from the countryside to cities. In 1980, Havana could not even obtain paint to improve the appearance of the old, neglected buildings. The government, it seemed, would even welcome migration from Havana into the countryside.

But by 1985 the pattern of ignoring Havana had begun to change. Not only was there a very successful start on the restoration of Old Havana, but neighborhoods throughout the city showed the results of painting, repairing and, frequently, major rehabilitation.

Undoubtedly the most influential public involvement in this process came with the establishment of local units of "People's Power." These units, constituting the most powerful voice of local government, were given the task of distributing construction materials allocated by the central government. People were also encouraged to produce materials locally. Very quickly, throughout Cuba the government undertook not only to provide materials and technical assistance, but also to regulate private construction more closely through building permits, licensing self-employed contractors, and direct supervision and review.

The budget for maintenance and repair of housing and community facilities also increased significantly. The complaints expressed in meetings between the local People's Power delegates and their constituents reinforced government studies spearheaded by the construction committee of the National Assembly, Cuba's parliament. Between 1977 and 1983, local agencies increased their maintenance budgets fivefold. During the same period, the value of materials sold directly to consumers for maintenance, repairs, and new construction grew almost tenfold.

In early 1985, a number of Cuban architects who had been working with the problems of housing for many years were very enthusiastic about the potential benefits the law offered. It was not that they believed the concepts of private ownership and the new emphasis on self-help housing would solve all problems, but rather that the broad diversity the new law provided would result in both more, as well as better quality, housing. Even as quickly as early 1985, although the mechanics of implementing the new housing law were still being organized, hundreds of small self-help projects were begun throughout Havana. New second-floor additions, handsome (and occasionally not so handsome) restorations of run-down houses, and hundreds of minor improvements, for example, exterior paint and stucco, were transforming the city.

Cuba's approach to producing housing has fluctuated between a recognition that traditional materials and techniques can be mastered by unskilled and semiskilled labor—resulting in increasing the potential work force available to build housing—and an almost reverential conviction that prefabrication and advanced technology could provide the potential for greater production. It was logical for Cuba, following the traditional Marxist emphasis on science and technology as the prime generator of economic development, to embrace wholeheartedly the concept of industrialized construction.

Cuba, however, lacks some of the raw materials, sources of energy, and the strong industrial base and skilled labor to use prefabrication technology exclusively. Cuban planners and architects face an additional dilemma. Prefabrication for housing, as it has been practiced, requires clearing a site of all trees and leveling grades to facilitate standardized panel construction. This inflexibility often destroys a potentially beautiful site that needs instead a design that pays strict attention to topography, existing landscaping, and solar orientation. Cuba's tropical climate demands that prevailing breezes, shade, and protected outdoor spaces be used to lessen dependence on costly mechanical cooling. This is extremely difficult to accomplish with building systems that cannot be modified to suit the size.

It is ironic that Cuba has mastered the creative and flexible use of prefabricated concrete construction in other types of buildings. In Havana, a number of buildings using precast concrete construction are outstanding examples of creativity. One is *El Palacio de las Convenciones de Cuba*, completed in 1979, and inaugurated with the Summit Conference of the Non-Aligned Movement (NAM). Lenin Park contains museums, exhibition buildings, and specialized schools, all well designed and all using prefabricated concrete systems. Possibly one of the most striking buildings is *Las Ruinas*, a plush restaurant on the outskirts of Havana that encompasses old stone walls into a contemporary structure built of prefabricated concrete.

It is clear that Cuba does not lack architectural talent and that prefabrication need not be sterile, cold, or inflexible. Rather, Cuba's architectural skills need to be directed toward creating housing that better reflects Cuba's unique needs. Proven concepts, such as sheltered open spaces, arcades, and other sun protection, and careful orientation of sun and air can all be integrated into prefabricated systems where such technology may be economical and efficient. But Cuba's architects can also tap the potential of traditional materials, design principles, and simple construction techniques that facilitate the full participation of all Cubans in creating their own housing.

Even before the changes implemented by the new housing law, the increasing tempo in government and private construction had opened intense discussions about future housing policies. The issues of site planning, building design, rehabilitation, conservation, waste management, urban renewal, and the desirability of resident participation had received keen attention.

Beginning in 1980, the government began giving highest priority to "nonproductive" investments, while reducing resources invested in educational and health facilities to accomplish this balance. Coupled with greater availability of materials and labor, government housing output nearly doubled in the first half of the 1980 decade. Overall pro-

duction exceeded eight units per one thousand population, compar-
ing favorably with recent production levels in Western Europe. In a
move to protect historic districts and other deteriorating neighborhoods, the government established specific programs for rehabilitation.
In the late 1970s, Old Havana was designated a national landmark to
prevent further indiscriminate demolition.

Meanwhile, a comprehensive plan was completed, and greater
resources were designated for restoring the main squares and their con-
necting streets. In late 1982, UNESCO granted Old Havana "world
cultural heritage" status. While UNESCO provides no funding for actual construction, they have provided important expert assistance. Architects have searched to find new ways to preserve Old Havana's hundreds of landmark buildings and thousands of other structures in the
historic districts. They have also become interested in preserving other
older areas for conservation, whether of historic value or not. A number
of historic buildings have been restored for use as small galleries, restaurants, and shops. The quality of restoration has been exceptionally high
and with Havana's rich heritage of 17th-, 18th-, and 19th-century architecture, it could become an historical treasure, celebrating the trade-
wind charm of climate and the succeeding surges of colonial overlay.

The concern for conservation and renovation has often met with opposition. Construction agencies in Cuba, as in many other countries,
always seem to prefer total clearance and new construction to the in-
fill of buildings and restoration, the usual argument being that new
construction is less costly than rehabilitation. Some of the general public
also criticized the program, probably reflecting the historic discontent
with dilapidated buildings. But as more rehabilitation has been completed and the public has seen tangible results, the early doubts have
begun to change. Architects have shifted emphasis to moderate rehabilitation with ample resident participation instead of the more costly total
rehabilitation, thereby keeping per-unit costs below those of new construction. By carefully programming rehabilitation, it also is possible
for the majority of current residents to remain in their neighborhood.

Housing density, as it relates to site planning and building design,
has become another issue of disagreement among planners, architects,
builders, and housing officials. While there is general agreement on the
need for higher densities to preserve valuable land and minimize infrastructure costs, the debate centers on the best strategies to achieve
these goals. The apparent contradiction on density policies that encourage building four- and five-story structures in rural new towns,
while unplanned and uncontrolled growth continues in the cities, has
not been ignored. Recent studies for the new Havana Master Plan show
that even buildings in Cuba's largest city average only one and a half
stories. In an attempt to achieve higher densities, the plan proposes

high-rise buildings in the central city. But the dependency on twelve- and eighteen-story structures has been severely criticized. And, ironically, it has been found that high overall neighborhood densities have not actually been achieved with high-rise housing because of the substantial amounts of land occupied by low-rise community facilities and the virtually useless open space required between high-rise buildings.

As is happening worldwide, low-rise, high-density buildings, are being studied as a desirable alternative. Higher densities are also planned in existing neighborhoods by constructing "in-full" building on small vacant lots and on the roofs of existing single-family and multifamily structures. Many Cuban architects and planners contend that a combination of historic preservation, urban renewal projects, and incorporating the desirable design features of traditional Cuban housing can all be constructively applied in newly developing areas. Buildings that combine mixed uses, using existing street patterns as the focus for pedestrian activity (in contrast to the superblock) and the use of interior courtyards and covered sidewalk arcades (extremely appropriate in a tropical climate), are a few examples that are being discussed.

The ultimate goal is to overcome the monotony in current housing design and to respond better to the climatic and cultural conditions unique to Cuba. Because much of the building technology came essentially from cold European climates, the planning and building design is ill-adapted to a tropical region. In tropical conditions where shade is of great importance, large unprotected open areas, frequently found in new developments, are especially undesirable. And Cubans, like most other people, seem to prefer more central urban locations. Not infrequently they are willing to trade units in suburban developments for inner-city housing, even though it might be in poorer condition.

For the time being, traditional superblock site planning in suburban areas and high-rise structures in many downtown areas will probably continue in government housing. The future, however, is more likely to see more experimental designs, much more high-density/low-rise construction, and a return to some traditional Cuban planning and design principles. Housing design is maturing, just as the whole nation is gaining confidence, and the result is the ability to change without defensiveness, to utilize tradition where it serves the country's goals, and increasingly to create new concepts and practices that are uniquely Cuban.

Because the need for new strategies to solve the problem of decent housing is worldwide, how well Cuba succeeds in its efforts can prove valuable to the dozens of other nations facing a similar challenge.

Cuba has already made enormous progress in providing housing for its people. If it is not what Fidel Castro envisioned as he reviewed the plans of *Habana del Este*, it stands in remarkable contrast to every other

Latin American country where tens of millions continue to live in shantytowns and slums, often without even the most minimal public services.

Given peace, the normalization of relations with the United States, and the opportunity to devote more resources to the problem, Cuba may well demonstrate that the universal problem of housing can be solved in a Third World country.

Notes

1. Jill Hamberg, "The Dynamics of Cuban Housing Policy," 588.

2. Ibid., 594.

3. Jose Manuel Fernandez Nunez, "La Vivienda in Cuba," quoted in Hamberg, "Cuban Housing Policy," 594.

4. "La Situacion de la Vivienda en Cuba y su Evolucion Perspectiva," quoted in Hamberg, 597.

5. Hamberg, "Cuban Housing Policy," 600.

6. Ibid., 603.

7. Ibid.

8. Ibid., 608.

9. John F.C. Turner, *Housing by People: Towards Autonomy in Building Environments* (New York: Pantheon Books, 1977).

10. "Cuba's New Housing Law: Tenants to Own the Dwellings," *Cuba Update* (Winter–Spring 1985), 12–13.

6

Women in the Workplace

Dawn Keremitsis

The Tropicana nightclub has never closed; the gorgeous Cuban woman is on display nightly for the foreign visitor or the local resident. At the same time, the stores in Havana contain more uniforms than elegant dresses, and many of those who arrive to enjoy the Tropicana spectacle come in work clothes, perhaps at the end of their day in the plant. The average woman in Cuba today is a combination of the nightclub beauty and the factory worker, for music and dance and the cane cutters in the sugar fields are part of the Cuban identity. Government attempts to move women out of the house and into the work force come into conflict with the traditional capitalist image of the dependent woman supported by her husband. Even women who labor for wages in the public workplace come home to complete their double day by preparing meals and cleaning house. The Cuban wage-earning woman must thus be viewed from many perspectives if we are to evaluate the impact of the changes introduced with the overthrow of the Batista regime.

Women Wage Earners Prior to the Revolution

Before the revolution, the U.S. businessman brought to Cuba his concepts of the role of women, which were reenforced by the Spanish heritage. During the male workday, middle- and upper-class women remained in the house as an indication that their husbands were financially successful. In the evenings, these wives further demonstrated the male's wealth and status by displaying their beauty in elegant fashions and jewelry. Women worked for wages only if their husbands could not support them, so paid labor became an indicator of class and usually race as well.

In 1958 paid working women occupied only 9.8 percent of the total registered workers, many of whom had recently migrated to the city from impoverished rural centers. Professional gamblers, many from the United States, recruited young women to serve as prostitutes, which would further encourage wealthy tourists to visit their nightclubs in glamorous Havana. Frequent ads appeared in the local press for young women of "good appearance" to work for salaries, commissions, and tips in Havana nightclubs.[1] While 1,563,000 women listed themselves (in a survey of Cuban women) as housewives, an additional 25,064 were classified as beggars. By the time Fidel Castro arrived in power in 1959, almost half a million women (464,000) were unemployed, unable to secure even marginal jobs.[2]

Margaret Randall, in two books on Cuban women after the revolution, says that today's Cuban woman sets her hair, manicures her nails, and dresses up in order to model herself after the fashion of the rich or the elite class before the revolution. At the same time, she tries to fit the image of the new wage-earner. She drives a tractor while wearing her hair in curlers, and her manicured fingernails remain covered by gloves when she works in the fields, so that she will appear attractive and "feminine" that evening.[3]

Actually, few women appear in the streets in skirts, and shorts can be found only in resorts, as most women wear trousers more suitable to their work. The major travel guide to Cuba mentions that women can wear pants, skirts, and sports clothes, but that the long dresses that characterized the pre-revolutionary era appear only rarely, except at diplomatic functions.[4] The Cubans who attend the Tropicana come in a variety of outfits ranging from work clothing to elegant gowns, and all are apparently considered acceptable.

During the revolutionary fighting, women did leave the home to give medical aid, sew uniforms, and cook and care for troops, and they probably made no attempt to appear elegant. They also did not fit the pre-revolutionary image of the dependent woman supported by her husband. Many taught peasants in the countryside to read and write, especially during the early literacy campaigns. In 1961 they helped reduce the national rate of illiteracy from 23 percent to 3.7 percent. In the late 1960s, Cuban men and women, aided by volunteers of both sexes from overseas, harvested the sugar.[5] Although these women had worked outside the house to aid the revolution, however, their position in society in relation to men had changed little. One Cuban (male) has suggested that a more effective method altering woman's position would be to say that "man must be woman's comrade" instead of "woman must be man's comrade."[6]

Women's Labor Force Participation

As the revolutionary government tried to become self-sufficient in production, the administration made major efforts to expand the labor force, especially after many professionals and skilled technicians left

Cuba. First they recruited men and then women and youths, hoping
to reach a national goal of one million female entrants into the paid
work force by 1975. By 1974, 688,000 women had become paid laborers,
and by 1980 they reached 1,108,000.[7] For a variety of reasons, many
women had left home.

The 282,069 women who participated in the Cuban labor force in
1964 had increased to 371,069 by 1968, but then the number leveled
off. It has been suggested that in the 1960s the lack of durable consumer goods gave women little incentive to earn money, since 76 percent of the women who joined the labor force in 1969 left before the
end of the year. In 1973 another 115,960 women started to work for
wages for the first time, and by 1979 women comprised 30 percent of
the total work force.[8] Women had been educated, had learned new
trades, had taken advantage of additional daycare centers for their
children, and the stores had merchandise they wanted to buy.

The government attempted to reserve certain jobs for women in its
effort to bring more into the labor force. In 1968 the Labor Ministry
listed thirty different types of jobs, such as librarians, archivists, and
telephone operators, that had to be filled exclusively with women. Many
women did not apply for these "frozen jobs," as they did not feel that
they had the required skills; the administration has had difficulty finding women to fill them.[9] Women also had to deal with the contradiction of the government requesting, but not insisting, that they enter
the work force, along with society's continued preference that they stay
in the home.

The national administration suggested that one step to avoid a shortage of female workers could be taken before a new factory opened:
managers should decide which jobs could be done by women so they
could be recruited and trained in advance. As the regime moved away
from utilizing women in traditional social services and employed more
of them in factories, qualified female applicants had to be recruited.
It is estimated that of 671,000 new jobs created by the administration
since the 1970 industrialization, 70 percent, or 470,000, have been for
women.[10]

The problems that women have encountered in adjusting to the contradiction between aiding the revolution, by being productive workers,
and in adjusting to society's continuing ideal of women's place in the
home is exemplified by the success of the government's campaign to
utilize women as volunteers. A volunteer does not have to worry about
possible incompetence, and receives only praise for her efforts. As many
as 500,000 women work as neighborhood guards, and by 1970 the
Women's Federation had started 3403 Mutual Aid Brigades staffed with
volunteers to work with peasant farm women. That same year, women
gave 20.1 million hours of volunteer labor in harvesting sugar cane

alone.[11] Although feminists in the capitalist world see the use of volunteers as exploitation of women, some Cuban women may need this experience to gain the confidence that will prepare them for paid employment. In addition, socialism emphasizes the need of loyal citizens to contribute their labor to the transformation of Cuban society. To volunteer is a patriotic duty!

Legal Changes in Occupations

A dramatic change in the work force occurred after the 1959 revolution, when female prostitutes and domestic servants became illegal under the new administration. Although the Batista census figures had listed only 1500 female prostitutes, after the revolution thousands went to New York and Miami along with their pimps. Those who stayed had to find another line of work, although some say prostitution (but not street walkers) continued into the 1970s.[12] Since the revolution, an estimated 90,000 former prostitutes in Cuba have enrolled in courses to learn other occupations.

Private domestic servants also sought other work, as one out of every five women employed in the Batista years had worked in this occupation.[14] Some had sufficient education and skills to take over jobs in banks when the middle-class male workers left the country. Another 20,000 enrolled in schools for the "advancement of domestic servants" in Havana. The national government hired former domestics to work in hotels, schools, hospitals, or protocol houses maintained for foreign guests, doing essentially the same work as formerly but with improved status and wages. Many more worked in the expanding numbers of daycare centers, the lowest-paying occupation in Cuba. A four-year training school for nursery school teachers enrolled 500 students the first year. Public nurseries have started for children aged four to six, and their numbers continue to grow to comply with working women's demands.[15]

Women Professionals

The greatest increase in women's employment has been in professional services, which by 1979 employed 521,200, about two-thirds of all women wage-earners.[16] Even prior to the revolution, 57 percent of those in education and 60 percent in health had been women, and the numerical increase is undoubtedly due to the expansion in these fields.[17] Women (and the government) apparently find it easier to accept (female) employment in traditional occupations outside the home.

In the 1970s a woman headed the Department of Health and Ecology, but in the Department of Public Health, only 13 percent of the administrators (twenty-three) were women. Women also comprised about one-third of the overall management in the department. The emphasis on health services is evident, and in 1979 a conference recommended an increase in facilities, suggesting 49 new hospitals, 110 polyclinics, 19 dental clinics, 51 homes for the aged, and 16 homes for the disabled, all of which would create more need for workers in fields dominated by women. Hospitals and medical aid are available to everyone without charge, which creates a large demand for trained assistance. Although half of Cuba's 6000 doctors left after the revolution, Cuba now has 9000 licensed doctors and 6000 more in medical school.[18] But when women filled 60 percent of the medical college admissions, the Cuban administration decided to limit the percentage of women students to 55 percent. The leaders felt that the Cuban people would not accept a situation similar to that in the Soviet Union, where women almost completely dominate the profession.

Few women administer the hospitals, about 16.5 percent of the total, but professional women do run maternity homes and childbirth clinics.[19] A 1984 article in *Granma* (August 4) showed a large photograph of two women, one an MD and the other a microbiology technician, doing research on gonorrhea. The accompanying article commented only on their findings, an indication that it is no longer unusual that women provide major contributions to the health field.

In both the national archive and the state library, men direct the institutions and women serve the public. Even so, several women historians do work on equal footings with their male counterparts at both establishments. One Cuban historian, affiliated with the national university, spends much of her time in the archive and maintains professional ties with her male associates. She frequently participates in foreign conferences and has published widely, both articles and books. By living alone and eating out much of the time, she has been free to write. If she had accepted the traditional role of women in society, she probably could not have achieved her reputation and assignments.

Another highly qualified woman historian originally came from Britain to write on the tobacco industry. She married a Cuban, has a son and daughter, and now lives in Havana. She is active in the academic world and Cuban organizations and is helpful to visiting scholars. She and her husband apparently work together as equals and appear happy and well adjusted to life in Cuba.

A married couple, both historians, are employed by the Cuban government as college professors. She came from Argentina and her husband from the United States. Together they publish works on women, among other subjects, both in Cuba and abroad; their publications carry both their names.

An important woman in the arts is Alicia Alonso, who heads the National Ballet, which has an international reputation for quality. Alonso started working in Cuban ballet in 1948, but left Cuba in 1956 in opposition to the dictatorial regime of Fulgencio Batista. Since the revolution in 1959 she has worked hard to produce a trained dance group. The company has 156 dancers who perform in theaters, work-centers, and factories. Alonso also runs a national ballet school for both men and women, which has helped make the Cuban national ballet an international favorite.

Industrial Trades

The second-largest field for women is industry which, in the early 1980s, utilized 16 percent of the female work force, 181,200, a 76 percent increase from 1970. Claes Brundenius has noted that female workers tend to be substantially better educated for a job than their male companions, especially when they enter new fields.[20] Undoubtedly, a factory manager would prefer a man if they were otherwise equal!

One reason for the change is the expansion of vocational schools teaching marketable trades. Forty thousand women have taken courses in dressmaking, still a typical female occupation. The Ana Betancourt School for Peasant Girls brought 14,000 young women into Havana to learn dressmaking and to finish sixth-grade schooling. In the 2654 functioning academies of the government, dressmaking schools teach useful skills and also transmit ideological training. Studies include political and cultural subjects as well as sewing instruction, and women students do volunteer work on the side. Beginning courses in shop and home economics are taught to both boys and girls, and there is a school for cooks and waitresses. Either sex can take courses in cattle raising, tractor driving, electrical work, and crane operation. Technical training always includes a general sixth-grade education.[21]

Textile production is a major industry in which women can always be utilized, and their proportion varies. When one mill outside Havana opened in 1931, women comprised 31 percent of the workers and helped run the 1500 looms that produce manta, the rough cotton cloth. (Because of the ease with which women learn to run looms, this is one of the jobs often filled by females in cotton textile mills.) The workers now in charge have brought in power-operated spindles and 4500 modern looms, so the factory can produce its own thread and yarn instead of importing these products. Even though operations remain simple, production has tripled. Each worker today operates 30, instead of 70, looms on one of the three eight-hour shifts. To maintain a high level of output, workers themselves award prizes to the persons who achieve the highest rate of production. The factory also has a daycare center to encourage women to leave home for paid employment. The government continues to push for an increase of women in textile production—perhaps to keep down costs, as women still average lower wages than men.

Many older women have become skilled artisans, some assembling violins in factories that started after the revolution. Additional women work in the cigar and cigarette industry, an activity common to women in many nations. One of the major jobs held by women in cigar factories is as a stemmer, one who removes the central stem from tobacco leaves. One 43-year-old stemmer had spent twenty-seven years in the industry, first in a small shop outside Havana (for five years) and then in the General Cigar Company, which employed more than 600 workers. When that company laid her off, she was an experienced worker and was able to find work in her hometown, normally difficult at that time because family relatives controlled the labor force in the provinces. After again being discharged, she rolled cigars in her own home before returning to Havana to a major factory. Before the arrival of the present administration, Havana controlled most of the jobs, and it was not easy to work in one's own town.

Another woman worked 40 years in the trade. Still another stemmer, who was 61, had spent forty-five years in the industry. She married a cigar-maker and worked with him at the large Rey del Mundo factory until, in 1949, the plant laid off nearly all its women workers.[22] Evidently family connections made a major difference in finding work, but not enough for a firm to keep women over men as paid employees.

Today a much higher proportion of women work in the cigar factories. In a cigar plant in Havana, the manager informed me that women composed at least half the work force. He proudly claimed responsibility for the changes he said he had made to comply with government directives encouraging the employment of women.

Women's Traditional Duties

Whether or not women leave the house for paid jobs, they are expected to maintain the home and care for the children; men only occasionally help in household functions. In the first decade after the change to a socialist government, fathers, brothers, husbands, and even young fiancés continued to insist that women remain in the home to make the male life pleasanter by providing domestic tasks ranging from cooking and cleaning to sex. One example is 19-year-old Iris who, with her eight brothers and sisters, remained at home supported by her father's earnings. She said that she wanted to go out and work but her fiancé, a Cuban soldier, would not "permit" her to do so. Only when convinced that it was his revolutionary duty did he consent to have Iris seek the employment that interested her.[23] Iris's case illustrates the problems for a woman who has to deal with the conflict between family expectations and support for the socialist program. It must be assumed that since 1970 fewer cases such as Iris's exist, since the socialist ideology has become more firmly implanted.

Childcare creates another major problem for women who want to reconcile this conflict. Women assume that a socialist government should provide childcare if their paid employment is needed. Daycare centers are expensive and must be constructed as well as staffed. In 1974 women asked that a capacity for 50,000 children be raised to 150,000, undoubtedly still far below that sufficient for all working women with children. Although the government provided daycare free for wage earners until 1977, since then it has charged three to forty pesos a month (a peso being closely equivalent to a dollar), depending on the worker's income, probably in an attempt to lessen the demand. After a million women entered the labor force in 1980 and unemployment became another issue, officials preparing the 1981–1984 project for Cuba assumed that no more women would enter the paid labor force, so they listed a lower goal for construction of additional daycare centers than in 1980. The provision of daycare centers can be used by the government to control the number of women who enter the labor force. There is no evidence that husbands of the wage-earners accept the responsibility for caring for their young children.

Political Support for Women Wage-earners

The Federation of Cuban Women was organized in 1960 for the express purpose of incorporating women into the social, political, and economic life of the country and to provide them with an official link with the national government. It, too, is staffed primarily with volunteers (99.3 percent), with a few paid administrators.[24] Headed by Vilma Espin, the federation organized women from the base up, starting in delegations, then in blocks, regional boards, provincial boards, and the national executive council. In 1962, when the first FMC congress was held, 9012 delegates represented 376,571 women participants. By 1969, three-quarters of all the adult women in Cuba, 1,132,000, belonged.[25] According to the 1980 official figures, FMC had a membership of 2,312,471, or 81 percent of all Cuban women over fourteen years of age, less than half of them wage-earners.

When the Second National Congress of the Federation of Cuban Women met for five days in 1974, Fidel Castro sat in on every session, listening to discussions of issues ranging from the problems of working mothers who tried to share household duties with husbands, to the need for more education for women who wished to obtain gainful employment. Workers clamored for more daycare centers, laundries, and workers' dining rooms. As mentioned above, they voted to demand the tripling of the daycare centers. Despite the fact that the Family Code (which made women and men equal under the law) was made official the following year, little change came about in family practice.[26]

The members of the federation participated in the formulation of the Family Code, organizing discussions on the local level to discover social problems that could be corrected by setting new national standards. On Women's Day, March 8, 1975, Fidel Castro accepted for the government the final version of the Family Code, handing the document to Vilma Espin.

Under the code, a pregnant woman has paid leave from her job for six weeks before childbirth and for three months after. Up to one year's leave is also possible. The code covers many aspects of family life other than working conditions. Child support, for example, can be the responsibility of either the man or the woman, which does not change in the case of divorce. Vilma Espin commented that the new Family Code needed to be applied even when women did not leave the house, to break old taboos and to help women break away from their mother's experiences and adjust to a changing society. She obviously was aware of the conflict experienced by women who decided to enter the public work force.

The federation also promoted many activities of women, including the planting of several miles of new forest, hardly a traditional female assignment. The federation started training schools for peasant girls and domestic servants in such fields as law enforcement and civil defense. In the first decade of the revolution, the federation organized the sewing classes as early as 1960, and by 1970 had 94,786 graduates.[27] It also worked actively to promote the position of women in society and has tried (unsuccessfully) to repeal Resolution 48 of the Cuban labor code which terms certain jobs, such as railway conductor, cemetery worker, and house painter, unsuitable for all women solely because the jobs are considered a "threat to [women's] reproductive capability." The FMC has represented women in the trade union movement, and even forced the dismissal of a factory director after he made derogatory remarks in front of paid members of their group.

Representation of women in the Communist party grew from 5.4 percent in 1980 to 12.79 percent in 1983. In the Council of State, twenty men and one woman participate. In 1975 women held five of the twelve alternate posts for the Party's Central Committee, and in 1980 women represented 12.1 percent of the committed members and 14.3 percent of the alternative representatives.[28] In 1983 the percentage had decreased to 11 percent, consisting of sixteen of the 150 members. Twelve women were chosen among the eighty two alternates.[29] The official party supports the administration efforts to improve women's working conditions, and in July 1984 the daily newspaper, *La Prensa*, interviewed Réne Peñalver, an official of the Communist party Central Committee concerning their problems. She had headed a session on women's issues in a national meeting that year in which they discussed the continuing need for daycare centers, laundries, and public dining rooms, which would shorten the length of the woman's "double day." Peñalver hoped that the interchange between workers and leaders of the ruling party would contribute to future developments, but offered nothing specific.

Women Workers in Political and Government Offices

Vilma Espin has become one of the fourteen members of the Politburo as well as head of the Federation of Women. Other women holding national political office have included Marta Deprés of the state council, Libia de Moya, who headed the production section of the national women's committee, and Digna Cires, chief of the department of women's issues of the national administration.[30] How much impact these women have had on government decisions is difficult to determine, but they do represent a change in government attitude.

Women have filled some top government administrative posts. They directed offices in the Foreign Relations Commision, Constitutional and Judicial Affairs, Economic, Scientific and Technological Collaboration, Commission of Industry and Building and Building Materials. They also continued in their traditional areas of health and ecology, culture and art, education and science, labor and social security, domestic commerce and foodstuffs. Vilma Espin heads Children and Woman's Equality. Nora Frometa, the first woman minister appointed by the new government,[31] headed the Food Ministry. When the Labor Courts first started, seventy-one female labor judges handled women's cases.

The Education Department, which has worked hard to indoctrinate Cuba's young citizens as well as to make them literate, in the early 1980s employed the highest percentage of women public officials, 26 percent. The Department of Higher Education, oriented toward the technologists and managers in society, employed more administrators (1231, only 13 percent women) than did the agency charged with educating the mass of the population.[32] As already mentioned, the government also employed many women as elementary school teachers, librarians, and archivists, all traditional female fields.

The Foreign Relations Department employed eighty-five women, 21 percent of the total office workers, but primarily in minor office positions. Only three women have been appointed ambassadors. In important posts such as officials in the Cuban embassy within the Soviet Union, only two of the seventy-two were women, and in posts representing their country in the United States, two out of twenty-four. Although many women worked in foreign service, few were in a position to formulate decisions.

The military tended to exclude women from official positions, although they do take military training. Only twenty-one women 3 percent of the total, held high ranks in the Cuban army. The highest post was that of a woman major who commanded regular troops, and women did head the all-female antiaircraft artillery regiment. In 1980 the government recruited new reserves, especially women and students, for a territorial militia that would construct military bases, maintain a rear guard, protect factories and farms, but not defend frontier areas. Although women must recognize that supervisory military positions still may not be considered for them in society, they now are able to enlist in officer training in the university.[33]

Office Workers

Women also have held professional and clerical jobs not directly connected with the government. Of seventeen newspaper editors in Cuba in the 1970s, two were women, and five of Cuba's 26 magazines had women editors. When Margaret Randall arrived in Cuba from the United States in 1969, she became a member of a writing collective, 58 percent of whose members were housewives. Women worked as office clerks, telephone operators, and bank clerks and comprised 43.8 percent of the second tier of directors in the Banco Nacional in Havana, which supposedly provided one of the best opportunities for women to advance with the least discrimination. A survey undertaken in Cuban companies in 1974 noted that 38 percent of work centers questioned did not promote women, primarily because managers felt more responsibility brought conflict with family duties. Again, society expected women to accept home obligations first and paid employment second.

Impact of Education

One of the major emphases of the Castro government has been to expand educational facilities. Even though Cuba had a relatively high literacy rate before the revolution compared to other Latin American nations, when the new educational program began with the change in government, many men and women in their thirties learned for the first time to write their names. At first few went beyond grade school, which stops at the end of the sixth year. Later more students wished to continue their education and advance into more specialized fields, which required more facilities. In the 1970s the government constructed 180 high schools yearly, each to hold 500 students. Although schooling is supposedly the same for both sexes, military service is obligatory for boys. The specialized military academy, however, had 300 women students in 1973. Women comprised 55 percent of all students in junior high in the 1970s and provided the majority of the instructors. Of those enrolled in schools of higher education, women composed 40.6 percent. Of the adult women enrolled, 24.9 percent in 1970 and almost 48% in 1980 had to earn wages in order to attend classes. To be educated, one had to become a wage earner.

Dr. Lazara Penones headed the School of Journalism at the University of Havana, where 49 percent of the 66 students were women in the early 1980s. In the early 1980s women made up 90 percent of those majoring in psychology, and about 60 percent of those in biochemistry and biology. Men dominated other sciences and mathematics. More women than men majored in education and literature, as is true in most societies.

Unemployment

There is considerable controversy over the apparent unemployment that in the late 1970s overtook Cuba, as it has in so many socialist nations. Some believe that the "baby boom" of the 1959–1965 period and the introduction of youths into the labor market by 1976 brought a large surplus. Others argue that it was the large numbers of women who entered the work force rather than the young which caused the rise of unemployment. The growing scarcity of jobs did effect women wage-earners more than it did men. Between 1970 and 1979 male unemployment increased from 1.3 percent to 2.5 percent, while the female percentage went from 1.2 percent to 12 percent. In 1976, 13.6 percent of all women seeking work could not find it, and 74.2 percent of all those unemployed that year were women. It is claimed that in 1980 unemployment is one reason for the voluntary exodus of approximately 140,000 Cubans to the United States, which did help relieve Cuba's problem at the time. The excess of workers is also seen as a reason for the deploying of many to aid the socialist governments in Algeria, Libya, and Nicaragua through service contracts.[34] Although in 1980 Fidel still aimed for 33 percent of all adult women to enter the labor force and 31.4 percent had done so, 7.8 percent of women in the labor market classified themselves as unemployed, compared to 2.5 percent of the men.[35] Women had been educated, had learned new trades, and had taken advantage of additional daycare centers for their children; the stores had durable goods they wanted to buy; but the women had trouble finding jobs. Apparently at this stage in Cuba's development, the administration sees no need for additional women in the paid work force.

Summary

Although progress has been made for the wage earner in Cuba, women still have not found equality with men in society or the workplace, in spite of efforts by the national administration. Cuban society still faces the contradiction of the elegant woman who remains in the home and the woman in the labor market who contributes to modern Cuba. It is not easy for most Cubans to adjust to a world whose women complete equally with men at home and in the public workplace. The Family Code tried to make such equality legal, but only a few husbands considered domestic duties their personal responsibility. It is primarily the women who take care of the children, cook the meals, and clean the home, often in addition to earning wages. In twenty-five years, the position of the woman wage earner has changed considerably, and she has many more opportunities to enter public life. But she still must deal with this continuing duality of social desirability and government expectations. Has the situation of rising unemployment made it easier for her?

Notes

1. Tomas Fernandez Robaina, *Recuerdos Secretos de Mujeres Publicas*.
2. All data in this paragraph may be found in Carmelo Mesa-Lago, *The Economy of Socialist Cuba*, 118; Muriel Nassari, "The 'Woman Question' in Cuba: An Analysis of Material Constraints on Its Solution," *Signs* (Winter 1983); Chris Camarano, "On Cuban Women," *Science and Society* 25, no. 1 (Spring 1971): 48.
3. Margaret Randall, *Cuban Women Now: Women in Cuba Twenty Years Later*.
4. Paula DiPerna, *The Complete Travel Guide to Cuba*, 14.
5. *Cuba Review*, September 1974, 5.
6. Robaina, *Recuerdos Secretos*, 22.
7. Claes Brundenius, *Revolutionary Cuba: The Challenge of Economic Growth with Equity*, 730.
8. Mesa-Lago, *Socialist Cuba*, 118; Brundenius, *Revolutionary Cuba*, 73, 134.
9. *Latin American Times*, June 6, 1973.
10. Ibid.
11. Jorge Domínguez, *Cuba: Order and Revolution*, 493.
12. Ibid., 498.
13. Randall, *Cuban Women Now*, 17.
14. Mesa-Lago, *Socialist Cuba*, 119.
15. *La Prensa*, July 10, 1984.
16. Brundenius, *Revolutionary Cuba*, 129.
17. Ibid.; Mesa-Lago, *Socialist Cuba*, 119.
18. Speech by Fidel Castro on November 19, 1974; reproduced in *Cuba Review* 14, no. 4 (December 1974).
19. Gil Green, *Revolution Cuban Style*, 80; *La Prensa*, August 4, 1984.

20. Brundenius, *Revolutionary Cuba*, 129.
21. *La Prensa*, July 27, 1984.
22. Jean Stubbs, *Tobacco on the Periphery*.
23. Green, *Revolution Cuban Style*, 101–2.
24. Dominguez, *Cuba*, 271.
25. *Cuba Review* 14, no. 4 (December).
26. The Family Code represented the publication of a law passed February 14, 1975, which supposedly made women wage-earners equal to men and attempted to eliminate discrimination against both women and children.
`27. Dominguez, 501.
28. Ibid., 32–33.
29. Green, *Revolution Cuban Style*, 119.
30. *La Prensa*, July 14, 1984.
31. *Bohemia*, 1977.
32. *La Prensa*, August 4, 1984.
33. Dominguez, *Cuba*, 55, 57.
34. Ibid., 136, 137; Brundenius, *Revolutionary Cuba* 59, 66; Mesa-Lago, *Socialist Cuba*, 118.
35. Brundenius, *Revolutionary Cuba*, 73, 134, 136.

7

Health Care and Medicine in Cuba

J. C. Rosenberg

This chapter results from personal encounters with physicians and medical educators in Cuba, along with visits to hospitals and clinics in the Havana area during the summer of 1984. It is not meant to be a full evaluation, but one physician's experience. The current status of health care can be best understood from the perspective of the pre-Castro period.

In 1959, when the government led by Castro came to power, the disruption that took place in all phases of Cuban life was particularly evident in the availability of and accessibility to medical care. A problem that rapidly developed was a shortage of physicians. In 1959 Cuba had a physician population of 6000 to 6500 doctors; at least 3000 physicians were located in Havana. Within three years of the change in governments, close to half of all the physicians in Cuba joined the half-million people who fled the country.[1] Many of them came to the United States, and some went to South America. This placed a tremendous burden on the physicians who remained, since they had to provide care for the 6 million people on the island. Forty percent of the population lived in rural areas where the availability of health care had always been sparse. In a study based on a 1956 survey of agricultural workers, some 40 percent of Cuba's population, the Catholic University Association stated:

> The inquiry had three principal aims: to make, for the first time in Cuba, a detailed, accurate, statistical study of the living conditions of agricultural workers, which may serve as a firm base for analyzing economic and social problems and finding solutions to them; to give our members in the cities an opportunity to become aware of the reality of our countryside and learn its difficulties. And, last but not least, to be able to affirm, with certain knowledge and proof ready at hand, that the Cuban peasants find them-

selves in the no man's land between abandonment and helplessness, thanks
to national egoism, and that our nation cannot aspire to true progress
as long as it does not give proper attention to our countryside. The city
of Havana is enjoying an epoch of extraordinary prosperity, while the
countryside, and especially the agricultural workers, must live under almost
unbelievable conditions of stagnation, misery, and hopelessness.[2]

The burden that fell on the physicians who remained was a severe
one. In addition to the responsibility of caring for the sick of Cuba,
they were under pressure to make good on a promise Castro had made
to the Cuban people when he led the fight against the Batista regime;
namely, that his government would see to it that Cubans would be provided with better medical care. This was a major component of his program and propaganda.

The exodus of physicians from 1959 to 1961 left behind a coterie
of doctors who were very dedicated to promoting the welfare of the
Cuban nation and the Cuban people. Especially important were a group
of physicians who had worked in the field of tropical medicine and
parasitology.[3] The idealism of these doctors and their commitment to
the socialist form of government expressed itself in the health care
system they developed. Their dedication to Cuba and the new political
philosophy accounted for the fact that the health care system they instituted is physician-dominated, places physicians in a very high status
in the social order of Cuba and, most important, accounts for the successes the Cuban health care system has achieved. First we will examine
the delivery of health care in Cuba.

Community-Oriented Primary Care

Primary care can be most simply thought of as routine, nonemergent,
uncomplicated health care. The Cubans selected an Eastern European
model for the delivery system of this kind of health care, in particular
borrowing heavily from the one in place in Czechoslovakia.[5] It is similar to the system in other countries in Europe. The Cubans maintain
links with their Eastern European colleagues through a continuing interchange of ideas and information.[6] The portal of entry is the polyclinic, the principle facility for ambulatory care and the health care
center for the community, first introduced in 1965. If a Cuban has a
medical problem he will likely go to the outpatient facility known as
a *policlinico*, where the primary level of care is given.

Four-hundred polyclinics are scattered throughout the country, and
they are to become double this number by the year 2000. All are headed
by a physician-director and deliver a fairly standard core of prescribed
services. The urban polyclinics are designed to serve anywhere from
20,000 to 30,000 people, but in remote rural areas as few as 7500 people may be served.[7]

The Cuban political philosophy is reflected in the health care system they developed. This is represented by an effort on the part of the Cuban Ministry of Public Health to develop what we would call "a community-oriented primary care system." The prevention and treatment of illness in a prescribed area with a given population is their goal. They not only want to satisfy the people's health needs; they want the patients to participate in decisions that involve their care.[8]

Community-oriented primary care has been practiced and implemented in such diverse places as the southwestern United States (among Native American Indian communities), in Israel, and in the Dominican Republic. Unlike most health care systems that provide for episodic care of patients when they present themselves with complaints, community-oriented primary care attempts to integrate health care into community life by taking all aspects of an individual's activities into account when treating him. It also entails becoming involved in the community's health needs and following through to see that they are met.

Tertiary care, which is hospital-oriented, high-technology care, has consumed most of the efforts and energy of medical scientists throughout the world. Public health services have also received a great deal of attention. On the other hand, very little has been devoted to primary care based in neighborhoods of cities, rural villages, or other local communities. This community-oriented primary care attempts to incorporate elements of public health and medical administration. It considers the community as a whole as well as the individual patient. Comprehensive medical care is one of its goals.

When a patient comes to a polyclinic in Cuba, he or she is not seen by whatever doctor happens to be on duty, but is treated by his or her own physician. But unlike the health care system in the United States, the patient cannot select his physician. Each doctor is responsible for a given number of families in the community. (Cuba's eventual goal is to have one family doctor for 120 families.)

Office hours start at 9:00 A.M., and the clinics stay open until late afternoon. Appointments are not required, and patients have to wait before being seen. The delay can be considerable, especially during the busy morning hours. After lunch most doctors and nurses are in the field, making house calls, visiting patients at risk in their homes and workplace on a non-demand basis, and surveying local health conditions.

The polyclinic I visited in Havana was a three-story structure in a working-class neighborhood, the Policlinico de la Plaza de la Revolucion. Its director, Dr. Cosme Ordonez Carceller, was also a Professor of Epidemiology and obviously proud of his showcase clinic. Tall, imposing, and enthusiastic, he spoke eloquently and knowledgeably, in excellent English, of the medical care situation in Cuba. The Plaza Polyclinic was a pioneer as a teaching facility, designed to serve as a model for community health care.[9] It was one of 32 such training centers for ambulatory care in Cuba, 20 of which are located in Havana. The administrative team consists of heads of the sections of Internal Medicine, Pediatrics, Obstetrics and Gynecology, Nursing, Psychology-Social Work, Education, Statistics and Administration. All section heads answer to Dr. Ordonez. The physicians who are section heads are assigned to the clinic full time, and since this is a teaching facility, they are professors in their respective fields. Dr. Ordonez also maintains a research program in public health. Shortly before I was in Havana he and a colleague published an analysis of risk factors in coronary disease, assessing the relationship of hypertension to smoking, regular exercise, and diet.[10]

To deliver health care, the clinic has broken down the population to be served into groups of approximately 5000 people. A pediatrician, obstetrician, internist, and a nurse are assigned to each group. Every three months these health teams analyze the state of health of the community and make recommendations on how to improve it. Dr. Ordonez admitted that they still have problems with this system. Apparently there is little enthusiasm for the field work. Another type of team approach which they use combines the expertise of a physician, a health worker, a nurse, a psychologist, and a social worker.

Prevention has come to assume an equal emphasis with cure in the polyclinics. All adults receive vaccinations against tetanus and typhoid, and persons over 45 are checked every two years for high blood pressure. Particular care is given to pregnant women and to children. In addition to extra rations of milk, pregnant women receive a series of thirteen checkups and children under a year are examined monthly. Women are encouraged to obtain cervical smears every two years.[11]

Within the community, each block has a health care worker who integrates the programs of the polyclinic with the citizenry. Occasionally these efforts are aided by the Committees for the Defense of the Revolution (CDRS), manned by individuals in the community with a strong political and civic commitment to supporting and promoting the goals of the government and advancing the welfare of the Cuban people.[12] In addition, the Federation of Cuban Women, to which over 75 percent of adult women belong, cooperates with the Ministry of Public Health, referred to as MINSAP, in programs for childcare, blood donations, vaccinations, and the drive against endemic diseases.[13]

Secondary and Tertiary Care in Cuba

Tertiary care is also a necessary component of all health care systems. but this aspect of medical care in Cuba has not experienced the advances that have been achieved in the areas of primary care and public

Table 1

Medical Institutions   1984

General Urban Hospitals	97
Rural Hospitals	56
Maternity Hospitals	20
Maternity and Pediatric Hospitals	25
Pediatric Hospitals	27
Specialty Hospitals	43
Other Hospitals	2
Polyclinics	403
Rural Medical Stations	218
Other Medical Stations	82
Dental Clinics	148
Hygiene and Epidemiology Laboratories	22
Hygiene and Epidemiology Centers	171
Maternal Homes	103
Blood Banks	23
Spas	3

health.[14] In 1959 there were fifty-eight hospitals in Cuba, and 60 percent of all the hospital beds were in Havana. Since then the number of hospitals has increased to 256. The number of hospital beds has almost doubled, from 28,563 in 1959, to 51,872 in 1984. Most of this increase has taken place outside Havana, in rural areas and in other cities and towns. For example, in 1959, the first year of the Castro government, fifty hospitals of 30 beds each were built in rural areas, principally in the provinces of Oriente, Las Villas, and Pinar del Rio.[15]

Hospitals vary in the degree of care they supply. Most are general hospitals that can deliver routine or so-called secondary care. These general hospitals are the regional and municipal hospitals. Cuba is divided into fourteen provinces, and in the provincial hospitals tertiary care is given, along with other hospitals that specialize in areas such as orthopedics, ophthalmology, psychiatry, pediatrics, and obstetrics. Almost all children are born in maternity hospitals and cared for in hospitals devoted solely to them. In 1966, ten institutes were established to promote the development of advanced care, research, and training in such areas as cardiac disease, endocrinology, nephrology, and oncology. These are multispecialty institutes that confine themselves to their particular field.

The doctors who staff the hospitals and institutes are not the same as those who staff the polyclinics. If a patient requires hospital care, he or she is referred to the appropriate facility by the doctors in the polyclinic. In this respect the Cuban system is similar to the British National Health Service. Physicians in the hospital practice only in the hospital, but may occasionally consult at a polyclinic. Physicians practicing in the polyclincs do not care for hospitalized patients.

Hospitals are equipped with instruments of Japanese or European make. Very little American-made equipment is in evidence because of the twenty-five year U.S. embargo on trade with Cuba. At least 80 percent of all drugs is manufactured in Cuba, with the rest coming from the U.S.S.R., Eastern Europe, Sweden, Mexico, or Spain. Great efforts are made to conserve drugs in short supply. One expensive anticancer agent, methotrexate, is recovered from the urine of patients receiving the medication and purified for reuse. The hospitals have emergency rooms and outpatient clinics that are frequently busy and crowded. This is partly because of the Cubans' propensity to show up hours before their scheduled appointments, and also because of their belief that the "real doctors" are to be found in the hospitals.

The Instituto Nacional de Oncologia and Radiobiologia is housed in a hospital and directed by Professor Zoilo Marinello, a dynamic man who has led the advance for better care of Cuban patients with malignant disease since becoming director of the Institute in 1961. The hospital is an old one, located near the center of Havana in a pleasant residential area. Like many buildings in tropical and subtropical parts of the world, it is an open, rambling structure only five or six stories high. The rooms contain beds for seven to ten patients, and there is an occasional private room for the "VIP." A family member may stay with a patient 24 hours a day, a practice introduced in 1978. It is encouraged to the extent that these visitors are even given free meals while they stay with the patients. This practice started in 1969 when parents were encouraged to stay with their hospitalized children, and given room and board while they were there.

The intensive care unit has stricter sterile technique precautions than would be required in the United States. As is generally true of the technological level in this and other hospitals, the instrumentation in the intensive care unit is less advanced than in the United States. Radiation therapy is given by cobalt units, since the $1 million available for radiation therapy can purchase four cobalt units but only one linear accelerator, the normal equipment in the United States.

The Clinico Quirurgico Joaquin Albarran is one of fourteen teaching facilities attached to Havana's medical school. The hospital has a staff of 160 physicians, 160 nurses, 200 technicians, 50 administrators, and more than 600 additional personnel. It serves a community of 86,000 people and six polyclinics. It is a general hospital but does not accept pediatric, obstretric, nor psychiatric patients.

The hospital also housed the Instituto de Nephrologia on its fifth floor. Directed by Professor Abelardo Busch Lopez, the Institute began a hemodialysis program for kidney patients in 1963. Dr. Busch instituted the program after spending four months in Czechoslovakia to obtain experience in this area. This was followed in 1968 by a chronic hemodialysis and kidney transplant program; the first kidney transplant was performed on February 24, 1970. Professor Busch was proud to tell me that the patient was still doing well. In 1973, a $1 million loan from Sweden enabled them to replace the old American-made units (hard to maintain because of the embargo) with new ones from Sweden. As of the beginning of 1984, they had performed a total of 637 transplants and have established three other dialysis and transplant centers in other parts of Cuba.

The hospital that Cubans are most proud of is the Hospital Clinico-Quirurgico Hermanos Ameijeiras, which was opened in 1982. The 25-story, 950-bed structure is named for three brothers who lived in the area the hospital serves and died in the struggle against the Batista government. It is a beautiful, impressive facility containing the most up-to-date medical technology, and unlike any other in Cuba. The building was originally built for the Havana Stock Exchange shortly before the revolution and was converted by the new government. It is well equipped with x-ray equipment, CAT scanners, and modern microscopes in the laboratories.

The Organization of Medical Care, Education, and Research

The Ministerio de Salud Publica (Ministry of Public Health), MINSAP, controls and coordinates service, teaching and research in medicine.

Table 2

Research Capacity   1983

Type of Institutions	Number of centers	Research projects	Research personnel
Research Institutes	12	453	626
Institutes of Higher Education in Medical Sciences	46	344	831
Medical and Pharmaceutical Industry	3	47	82
Provincial Centers	151	539	1,153
Total	212	1,383	2,692

All the hospitals and polyclinics are under its control, as are the twenty-six medical schools as of 1984, eight of which are in Havana. It not only employs all the island's doctors and other health care workers, it also runs the nursing homes, pharmacies, pharmaceutical industries, and anything remotely connected with health. In 1959 there were only three medical schools in Cuba, all of them connected to universities. In 1966 they were placed under MINSAP, and as a result there is little connection between Cuban universities and the training of doctors. Academic medical people have remained concerned that the training is too pragmatic, but the magnitude of these concerns has been mitigated by the overall success of Cuba's health program.[16]

Students with high grades and the "right moral character" are admitted to medical school at eighteen years of age. Half are women; some are from other Latin American countries and Africa, and some are Palestinian Arabs. There is no tuition, but all medical students are required to perform rural service and practice community medicine after they graduate. Training in one of the specialities such as surgery, can take place only after completion of compulsory service.

Those who choose a career in research need not serve in this capacity, but can go directly into their investigative work. Cuban medical research supports ten professional journals, including ones in surgery, hygiene and epidemiology, pharmacology, pediatrics, and tropical medicine. Research is concentrated on immunology, environmental diseases, prenatal growth and development, genetics, nutrition, heart disease, and cancer.[17]

The medical schools have turned out large numbers of physicians to man the hospitals and polyclinics. Before 1959 an average of 300 doctors graduated each year; this figure was tripled within ten years.[18]

More than 20,000 students were enrolled in medical school in 1984. By 1986 Cuba had about 23,000 physicians, and was graduating nearly 3000 a year.[19] Two thousand were in dental school and 7000 were enrolled in nursing programs. Whereas there had been one doctor for 1000 people in 1959, there is now one for every 500 Cubans, or 20,000 physicians for a population of 10 million. This is the same physician-to-population ratio as in the United States. Cuba hopes to have 70,000 doctors by A.D. 2000.

Training of nurses and other health care personnel has also been accelerated. In 1959 around one hundred nurses graduated annually. By 1979 the number of nurses in Cuba had reached 42,000. The goal set by MINSAP is one doctor for every 500 to 525 inhabitants, one dentist for every 2050 to 2200 persons, and 3.75 nurses for each doctor, ratios equivalent to the most advanced nations.[20]

Medical care has also become an exportable commodity. Cuban physi-

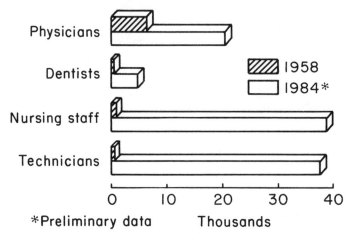

PHYSICIAN, DENTIST, NURSING STAFF AND TECHNICIANS 1958 AND 1984

Figure 7.1

cians in sixteen countries and many Third World nations look to Cuba for guidance in medical care.[21] Special cases are sometimes brought to Cuba for treatment, from Central America and from Africa.

The financial commitment that has been made to medical care has been more than in any other Third World country and is even proportionately greater than the United States dedicates to health care. The Cuban people themselves pay little for the services they receive. They must pay for drugs (other than anti-tuberculous and anti-cancer drugs), but all else is without charge. But like everything else in life, nothing is free: the cost of the health care system as a percent of the GNP of Cuba is very high, higher than in the United States. It has been estimated that the bill for all these services comes to more than 15 percent of Cuba's GNP, in contrast to the 10 percent of the GNP in the United States and the 8 percent in Canada.

Advances in Health Care

The result of all this effort and expense has been improved health care. Life expectancy has increased from 65.1 years in 1960 to 73.5 in 1984. The infant mortality rate, which was 60 per 1000 births, is now 16.3 per 1000 (the U.S. rate stood at 13.0 in 1985). The pattern of disease causing mortality and morbidity has changed. Infectious problems such as polio, diphtheria, tuberculosis, tetanus, and gastroenteritis have been drastically reduced. Chronic degenerative diseases are the most prominent problems, as they are in developed countries. Heart diseases, cancer, and strokes are the current major health problems. Efforts have begun to discourage the most pernicious health problem in Cuba, smoking. Sixty-two percent of the adult population smoke cigarettes, more than twice as many as in the United States.[22]

Whatever one's political philosophy, one cannot deny that the current Cuban government has used its power to make impressive advances in health care.[23] They have implemented a community-oriented primary care system and public health measures that have elevated the health of their people to the level of developed countries. Tertiary care has not improved to the same degree as primary care and public health, but this has had little impact on the overall status of health care in Cuba.[24]

POLYOMYELITIS AND DIPHTHERIA CASES
1959-1984

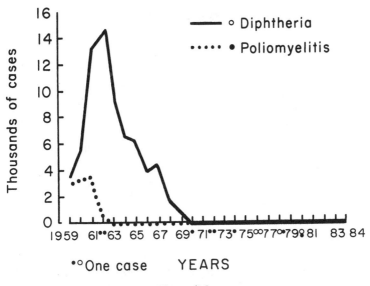

Figure 7.2

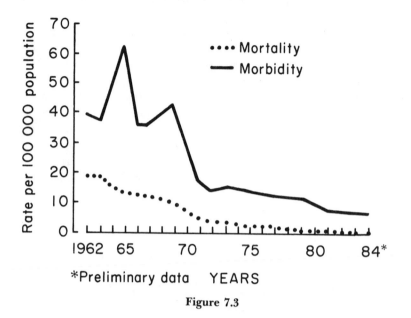

TUBERCULOSIS MORBIDITY AND MORTALITY
1962-1984

*Preliminary data   YEARS

Figure 7.3

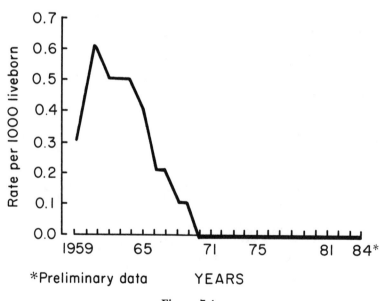

NEWBORN TETANUS MORTALITY
1959-1984

*Preliminary data   YEARS

Figure 7.4

126

MORTALITY FROM INFECTIOUS AND PARASITIC DISEASES AND ACUTE DIARRHEAL DISEASES 1962–1984

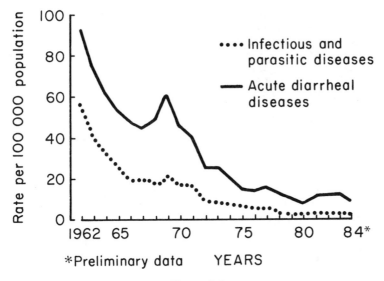

Figure 7.5

MAIN CAUSES OF DEATH 1984*

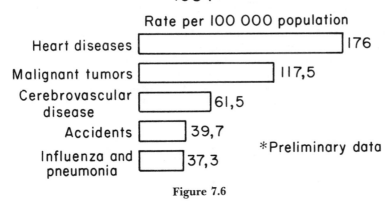

Figure 7.6

Notes

1. Philip M. Boffey, "Health Care as a Human Right: A Cuban Perspective," *Science* 200 (June 16, 1978): 1247.

2. Melchor W. Gaston, Oscar A Echeverria, and Rene de la Huerta, *Por que Reforma Agraria* (Havana: Agrupacion Catolica Universitaria, 1957), 6, as quoted

in translation in Ricardo Leyva, "Health and Revolution in Cuba," in Rolando E. Bonachea and Nelson P. Valdes, *Cuba in Revolution* (Garden City, N.Y.: Double-day, 1972), 457–58.

3. Ross Danielson, *Cuban Medicine*, 132.

4. See the review of the Cuban public health system published as a party of the First Congress of the Cuban Communist Party: *Cuba: la salud en la revolucion* (Havana: Editorial Orbe, 1975).

5. Danielson, *Cuban Medicine*, 144, 163–65, 179–80.

6. See, for example, Jiri Zahradka, "Organizacion y funciones de los servicos de salud publica territoriales en Checoslovaquia," *Revista cubana de administracion de salud* 10, no. 1 (February-March 1984): 81–83.

7. Boffey, "Health Care," 1250.

8. E. Connor and F. Muller, eds., "Community Oriented Primary Care," *Conference Proceedings, Institute of Medicine, Division of Health Care Services* (Washington: National Academy Press, 1982).

9. Danielson, *Cuban Medicine*, 197–98.

10. Cosme Ordonez Carceller and Pedro Pons Bravet, "Prevalencia de factores de riesgo coronario en area de salud del policlinico comunitario docente 'Plaza de la Revolucion,' " *Revista cubana de administracion de salud* 10, no. 1 (Feb.-March 1984): 15–21.

11. Paul Harrison, "Cuba's Health Care Revolution," 6–7.

12. Boffey, "Health Care," 1246.

13. Adolfo Valdiva Dominguez, "Stimulating Community Involvement Through Mass Organizations in Cuba: The Women's Role," *International Journal of Health Education* 20, no. 1 (1977): 57–60.

14. R.N. Ubell, "High Tech Medicine in the Caribbean: 25 Years of Cuban Health Care," 1468–72.

15. Cuba: Ministerio de Salud Publica, *Fundementacion para un nuevo enfoque de la medicina en la comunidad* (Universidad Autonomia de Santo Domingo, 1977), 9–10.

16. For the organization of MINSAP, see Armando Aguirre Jaime et al., "Informe preliminar sobre la elaboracion de propuesta para los dos primeros niveles del arbol de objetivos del Sistema Nacional de Salud," *Revista cubana de administracion de salud* 10, no. 1 (Feb.-March 1984): 260. Danielson, *Cuban Medicine*, 136–38, describes the battle within the university.

17. Lynn Margulis and Thomas H. Kunz, "Glimpses of Biological Research and Education in Cuba," 635.

18. Leyva, "Health and Revolution," 14.

19. *Granma*, June 22, 1986, 2.

20. Norberto Fuentes, "Una vocacion priorizada," *Cuba Internacional* 11, no. 116 (July 1979): 24–27; *Socioeconomic Guidelines for the 1981–1985 Period* (Havana: Political Publishers, 1981), 125.

21. Paul H. Grundy and Peter P. Budetti, "The Distribution and Supply of Cuban Medical Personnel in Third World Countries," 717–19.

22. Tad Szulc, *Fidel: A Critical Portrait*, 84, relates Castro's decision to set an example by giving up his cigars.

23. See Danielson, *Cuban Medicine*, 229–33, for a statistical appendix on health care. Also see Sergio Diaz-Briquets, *The Health Revolution in Cuba*.

24. Larry R. Oberg, *Human Services in Postrevolutionary Cuba* (Westport, Conn.: Greenwood Press, 1984), 275–99, has a bibliography on public health and medicine.

8

Cuban Art and Culture

David Craven

Since the early 1960s, Cuban culture has assumed a unique position internationally. At once distinctively Caribbean yet also exemplary of developments worldwide, Cuban art has diverged from Eastern bloc traditions, as well as those of the West, to arrive at a seminal position for Third World cultural advances. Indications of this later achievement surfaced during the early 1960s when Che Guevara criticized both the Stalinist doctrine of "socialist realism" *and* the Western fetish for isolated "personal expression."[1] Similarly, in this same period Fidel Castro opposed the institution of any official style that would set narrow formal limits to the conception of art. While Khrushchev, in the early 1960s, condemned all modern art as counterrevolutionary, Fidel significantly disagreed, with the observation: "Our enemies are capitalists and imperialists, not abstract art."[2] As a corollary to this position, Fidel enunciated the basic axiom of Cuban cultural developments since 1959: "Within the Revolution, everything. Against the Revolution, nothing."[3]

From the beginning, the cultural progress of the Cuban revolution has been characterized by an unprecedented breadth in several respects. Perhaps the most profound manifestation of this advance has been a sustained commitment to what the Cubans call "cultural democracy," an expansive process whereby the populace has assumed a far more participatory role in the cultural life of the country than normally prevails elsewhere in the world. As a result, the Cuban revolution has not only greatly expanded the audience for the arts, it has also substantially increased the number of those engaged in the arts. In addition, this newly enlarged public sphere and aesthetic context have led to an artistic vocabulary of remarkable formal, as well as conceptual, scope. Components range from pre-colonial African traditions and U.S. pop culture to pre-Columbian forms and European high culture. At its most profound, the art production of Cuba has gone beyond mere eclecticism to a new synthesis, both internationalist in general orientation yet specifically expressive of major issues confronting the Third World. This impressive accomplishment, along with an extension of cultural democracy, explains why "Cuba has been at the center of cultural activity in the Hispanic world for the past 20 years."[4] Furthermore, these factors also make clear why Cuban art and culture will in all probability continue to occupy a prominent position among countries around the world, which are now confronting the phenomenon of cultural underdevelopment interrelated with economic dependency.[5]

To address the important cultural dynamic of Cuba since the revolution, several things are needed. (a) We must first discuss the concrete cultural policies instituted after 1958, as well as the theoretical basis for them. Such a discussion will entail a consideration of cultural democracy and the transformed public sphere it presupposes, in order to determine whether the arts have indeed become much more accessible to the Cuban populace as part of an emphatic decentralization of political power since the revolution, particularly since the mid-1970s. Concomitant with this consideration will be an assessment of the Cuban concept of "popular culture"—a concept to be sharply distinguished from populism and mass culture. (b) We will also examine a few of the many notable artistic achievements engendered by this new cultural matrix: Nueva Trova music, the National Ballet under Alicia Alonso, the New Theater of Escambray and Cabildo Teatral, the criticism of Roberto Fernández Retamar and Roberto Segre, the highly regarded graphic design of posters for the Film Institute, the paintings of René Portocarrero and Raul Martínez, and, of course, the celebrated films of directors like Tomás Gutierrez Alea, Pastor Vega, Santiago Alvarez, Marisol Trujillo, and several others. (c) Finally, having discussed the cultural successes since 1959, we will consider significant problems within the realm of art and culture that have yet to be resolved.

Cultural Policies Since 1959

Cuban Minister of Culture Armando Hart Dávalos stated: "What we hope to achieve in the future . . . is for art to penetrate all spheres of life."[6] Whether or not this goal will be attained is, of course, yet to be seen, but other achievements related to it are no longer in doubt. Prominent among these accomplishments is the immense progress already achieved toward incorporating diverse cultural activities into the everyday experience of the Cuban public. During the first decade of the revolution, the centralization of political power and the rationalization of the economy were accomplished by the institution of numerous cultural agencies on the national level. One of the first cultural acts of the revolutionary government, in March 1959, was the founding of the National Film Institute (ICAIC). This followed the consensus at the

1st National Congress on Education and Culture in Cuba that cinema is "the art *par excellence* in our century."[7]

Several other state institutions of considerable importance were also established in 1959: the National Ballet, the National Folkloric Ensemble, the National Chorus, and Casa de las Americas, the International Center for Latin American Art and Literature, whose journal and prestigious literary awards occupy a fundamental role in the intellectual life of the Spanish-speaking world. Indeed, Casa de las Americas, along with Cuban Cinema and the National Ballet, has played a major part in fostering a "pan-Hispanic identity" for artists throughout Latin America.[8] The early 1960s were hardly less noteworthy for the foundation of new agencies. First came the creation of the National Symphony Orchestra and five provincial concert orchestras, then Cinemateca de Cuba, which today contains the largest collection of Latin American films in the world. Also occurring in 1960 was the establishment of the Consejo Nacional de Cuba (National Council of Culture), which was to be replaced in 1976, during the decentralization process, by the present Ministry of Culture, a more wide-ranging and flexible agency responsible for coordinating events among the various provincial centers of culture.

It was through its National Literacy Crusade in 1961, however, that Cuba's cultural transformation was advanced most substantially. Considered by UNESCO and other international educational organizations to be one of the most significant events in the modern history of education, this *alfabetización* elevated Cuba's rate of literacy from 72 percent to 98 percent, the highest in Latin America and one of the highest in the world.[9] A consequence of the advance was an end of what Paolo Freire, the Brazilian educator, has labeled the "culture of silence"— that state of cultural disempowerment linked to economic impoverishment and political disenfranchisement that afflicts the majority of people in the Third World.[10] A revealing monument to the cultural rejuvenation made possible by the literacy campaign is the case of José Yañes. Now one of the leading poets in Cuba, Yañes was an illiterate worker in a sausage factory before the literacy crusade.

Along with this quantitative expansion in readership has come a qualitative extension in terms of what is read. The Cuban public is now much more sophisticated, as evidenced by the fact that the most popular authors are among the finest writers in recent Latin American literature: Gabriel García Márquez, Julio Cortázar, Ernesto Cardenal, and, of course, Jose Martí, Nicolás Guillén, and Alejo Carpentier. Among non-Hispanic authors, Proust, Kafka, Sartre, Robbe-Grillet, Genet, Faulkner, and especially Hemingway (who was always a strong supporter of the Cuban revolution as well as a friend of Fidel) are widely known and read.[11] In a book about the time he spent in Cuba during the 1960s, Ernesto Cardenal describes his pleasurable surprise at the

rapidity with which entire editions of literary works sell out in this country. He witnessed, for example, a 10,000 edition of his own poetry go
out of stock in a week, a 50,000 edition of writings by Mario Benedetti
of Uruguay sell out in a comparable period, and a 90,000-copy edition
of *Cien años de Soledad* (*100 Years of Solitude*) by García Márquez disap-
pear in a few weeks.[12] In fact, several million copies of this book have
now been sold in Cuba, which has a total population of only around
10 million. Gabriel García Márquez has personally experienced the
esteem his work enjoys there. On one occasion several years ago, the
Colombian writer visited Cuba to observe changes in some of the most
rural areas of the country. When García Márquez was introduced to
campesinos on a farm cooperative, however, they quickly asked if he really
were the author of *100 Years of Solitude*, a book they had all read and
deeply admired. Instead of asking questions about the farm cooperative,
García Márquez ended up answering questions about his own novel.

The mid-1960s saw a continuation of these early developments, with
1962 being the year that several more institutions were set up: the National Recording Institute for Music, the National School of the Arts
(Cubanacán), the National Institute for Radio and Television, and the
National Commission on Museums and Monuments, whose task is the
conservation, restoration, and classification of the country's architecture. Since the early 1970s, a number of more specialized national
centers, designed to advance scholarship in various art forms, have been
founded: the Alejo Carpentier Center for Cultural Promotion, the Juan
Marinello Cultural Center, Casa del Caribe (for the advanced study of
Caribbean art), the Center for Musical Studies, the Wilfredo Lam Center
for Plastic Arts, and the Center for Jose Martí Studies. In addition, and
perhaps more conspicuous, the Cuban government has sponsored a
lengthy list of both international and national art festivals. Among these,
the International Festival of Ballet (begun in 1961) is one of the oldest
and most successful, while the International Film Festival and recently
established Latin American Biennial in the Visual Arts (begun in 1984)
are among the newest and most promising. The list of national festivals
is a longer one, with celebrations being devoted to the rumba, the son
(a type of peasant music), salsa, and numerous other popular art forms.

Even a quick survey of the concrete results generated by these institutional changes is impressive. In 1958, for example, there were only 6 museums and not even 100 libraries in the entire country. Today,
there are over 230 museums and nearly 2,000 libraries. While before
the revolution, very few people had ever visited a museum, today the
museum attendance averages over one million a year (or 10 percent
on the population).[13] In 1958, almost a third of the Cubans were illiterate; today, *all* are literate and one of every three is a student in
some capacity. Prior to 1959, there were three university centers; now
there are forty, with a college population twelve times larger than before

the revolution. Of this number, 46 percent are women, one of the highest rates in the world.[14] In 1959, Cuba published less than a million books a year; today, it publishes over 50 million books a year, all of which are sold below production costs, with school textbooks being free to students (incidentally, the first book published in an extremely large edition was *Don Quixote*, which is probably still one of the most widely read books in Cuba). In 1962, the National Council on Culture sponsored events attended by 4 million spectators, or half the population. During 1975, the Ministry of Culture sponsored events in the arts attended by 67 million spectators, or almost seven times the national population.

In 1958 there was no national film industry, although Cuba had one of the largest per capita audiences in the world, at 1.5 million cinema goers per week from a population of less than 7 million at the time.[16] Consequently, grade B movies from Hollywood constituted more than 50 percent of the films shown, a situation that is still endemic to many Latin American countries. Now Cuba has a highly esteemed film institute that regularly wins awards in international competition, which produces an annual average of 40 documentaries, 4 to 6 feature films, 5 to 10 animated films, and 52 weeklies. Nonetheless, Cuban films still make up only 5 percent of the 140 or so shown per year in over 510 theaters, with the vast majority of films coming from Europe and other Third World countries. According to the terms of the American economic embargo, North American cinema companies are prohibited by U.S. laws from sending films there on a regular basis.[17]

Extending, as well as complementing, these other gains has been a structural shift accompanying the transition to *poder local* (local power) that began in the mid-1970s. Foremost in this development has been the establishment of a national network of Casas de Cultura (houses of culture). As noted by the Ministry of Culture in a UNESCO publication, the object of the Casas de Cultura "is to bring people into direct contact with art, to disseminate culture, to raise the educational level of the population, and to provide it with opportunities for leisure and recreation."[18] Now around 200 nationally, Casas exist in each of the 169 municipalities that function as the basic political units within the country. Administered by the municipalities in conjunction with the Ministry of Culture, these Casas include a library, a museum, an amphitheater, an auditorium, conference rooms, music halls, and art studios. Here young people can study dance, music, and painting free; local artists and artisans can display their work; touring exhibitions are shown; and musical or theater performances by both visiting professionals and local amateurs take place.[19] As statistics demonstrate, a direct consequence of these Casas de Cultura has been a reinforcement of the immense increase in amateur groups involved in music, theater, dance, and the plastic arts. In 1964 there were 1,000 such groups. By 1975, when the Casas were first set up, that number had risen to 18,000 groups, with the number of children participating in the arts exceeding 600,000.

Cultural Democracy and Dialogical Art

All these accomplishments notwithstanding, questions still remain about the nature of this new public and just how much it has made the transition from passive consumption to critical engagement. Such questions are all the more pressing because of the situation that currently prevails in Western Europe and the United States. As Pierre Bourdieu has demonstrated, cultural consumption in France and indeed the West as a whole continually generates ideological legitimacy for social differences, differences that sustain what he terms the "aristocracy of culture."[21] Bourdieu's survey has further delineated the direct connection between one's educational level, class standing, and nature of interest in the arts. In France and Holland, for example, less than 1 percent of those with only a primary education visit a museum, while more than 15 percent of those with at least a secondary eduction frequent museums.[22] Even more revealing is the fact that 66 percent of all blue collar workers in these countries associate a museum with a church whose religion remains mysterious, hence off limits, while most of the managerial sector (54 percent) tends to view the museum as analogous to a library, a lecture hall, or some other site for learning.[23] In other words, there is a further correlation between one's degree of workplace self-management and one's sense of having access to the arts. Thus Bourdieu's survey shows how only the dominant political grups in the West—the most educated and economically ascendant sectors of the middle class (bourgeoisie)—feel entitled to "the right to speak" on all substantive issues, whether political, economic or cultural.[24]

How then has Cuba, formerly a Western colony deeply characterized by the cultural asymmetry associated with the West, been transformed to enlarge the number of those who feel they have "the right to speak" about the arts? It is one thing to eradicate the "culture of silence" and quite another to foster a vigorous public discourse by the majority. In light of Bourdieu's findings concerning the connection between class power and cultural empowerment, it is clear that any look at the formal devices for opening up public participation in the arts must also include a discussion of how this cultural development is, or is not, grounded in a comparable progression in the sphere of political economy. In short, has cultural democracy in Cuba been advanced, as Bourdieu implies it would be, by a marked democratization of the workplace, as well as by a decentralization of political power on the part of the silenced majority in pre-revolutionary society? Only if the latter two preconditions have been met would it seem plausible to speak of any expanded public sphere for the arts predicated on a principaled and rational exchange open to all sectors of society.

The answer to the first part of the above query is one that most visitors who have attended cultural events in Cuba can provide. Concrete avenues for expanding public discourse about the arts are the ever-present, generally lively, often-lengthly dialogues that accompany most cultural activities and are considered essential to cultural democracy. These dialogues, which occur along with most cultural events, involve informal discussions unquestionably attended by people from all sectors of society, particularly factory workers, and are led by recognized writers, filmmakers, musicians, or visual artists. Such well-attended public dialogues accompanied, for example, the various showings of *La Habanera* (1984), a controversial new film by Pastor Vega. After one projection of the film, at the Foundation for Cultural Heritage in Havana, there was an especially vigorous debate about the merits of the film, with Pastor Vega himself moderating the discussion. Set in the psychiatric ward of a major Cuban Hospital, the film explores the gender relationships within this stratum of society. Above all, it focuses on the contradictions of the woman who heads her unit, yet is unable to apply the insights from her profession to her own private life.[25]

The open discussion after the film intensely engaged a very heterogeneous audience representing various sectors of Cuban society—from assembly line workers to members of the intelligentsia. Questions were raised about the plausibility of the ending, about the use of photography, about the style of the film and, above all, about the lifestyle of the main protagonists. One young worker stated that everyone in his factory had seen *La Habanera* and that most of them had difficulty relating to the film because of the material benefits, specifically consumer products, enjoyed by the medical profession.[26] (Although factory workers and physicians enjoy the same access to education, health care, and food, doctors do in fact receive larger salaries, hence, access to more consumer goods.) It is significant that the basis of controversy surrounding *La Habanera*—the continued existence of a material inequality that contradicts the even more egalitarian society still being aspired to through the revolutionary process—has itself been the major theme of a profound, and also widely discussed, new film. In *Hasta Cierto Punto* (Up to a Certain Point), Tomás Gutierrez Alea engages in a self-critical focus on how a Cuban filmmaker intent on shooting a film about the residual *machismo* among workers, with whom he has several dialogues in the film, is forced to confront his own otherwise unacknowledged sentiments in favor of gender inequality. His own *machismo*, the *machismo* of an intellectual, manifests itself in a more oblique way, owing to his higher educational level and different lifestyle.

Figure 8.1 Alfredo Rostgaard, "Death of a bureaucrat," 1967 (poster).
Photo by Dawn Van Hall.

Figure 8.2 Raul Martínez, "Lucia," 1968 (poster).
Photo by Dawn Van Hall

Figure 8.3   René Portocarrero, "I am Cuba," 1964 (poster). *Photo by Dawn Van Hall.*

Figure 8.4   Manuel Mendive, untitled painting, 1981. *Photo by Dawn Van Hall.*

Through public dialogues about films like *La Habanera* and *Hasta Cierto Punto*, one realizes that Cuban people from all sectors are neither reluctant to speak out nor afraid to criticize what they have seen. This is especially true of dialogues about the film medium in a country where almost all people consider themselves film critics. As a North American correspondent recently observed in the *International Herald Tribune*, a visitor definitely leaves these debates with the sense that "culture is everybody's business" because these dialogues convey a "feeling that the opinion of the simple man in the street counts. Just as every sector of the population participates in music, or could be seen at the Biennial art exhibition, so people from all strata of society attended the film debate [about *La Habanera*]."[27]

In fact, these dialogues have themselves inspired poetry and become ancillary themes in cinema. A masterful use of this motif occurs in Tomás Gutierrez Alea's *Memories of Underdevelopment* (1968), one of the finest films ever produced in Latin America. During a brief part of this densely kaleidoscopic work, there is a public debate about the problem of underdevelopment, its historical origin, and so on, which prompts a North American in the audience to remark caustically: "Can't you people do anything more revolutionary than talk to each other?" His dismissive statement in turn strikes a sympathetic response in the mind of the main protagonist—a handsome, wealthy, and well-educated man still holding firm to old privileges and inequities in the midst of these strange new social phenomena. This protagonist, an ironic embodiment of Hollywood "perfection," leaves the open dialogue with the clear assumption that this new public discourse is simply an unpleasant symptom of underdevelopment per se. As such, Gutierrez Alea incisively focuses on the pervasiveness of these new public dialogues yet through the eyes of one unsympathetic to them, thus necessitating the critical intervention of the film audience to resolve this debate within the film and in turn to decide the fate of these dialogues outside the film.[28]

A poem by Nelson Herrera Ysla, "Colloquialism" (1979), celebrates these everyday dialogues as a seminal force for the art form he practices.

> Forgive me, defender of images and symbols.
> I forgive you, too.
> Forgive me, hermetic poets for whom I have boundless
>   admiration, but we have so many things left to say in a way
>   that everyone understands as clearly as possible, the
>   immense majority about to discover the miracle of language
> Forgive me, but I keep thinking that Fidel has taught us
>   dialogue and that this, dear poets, has been a decisive
>   literary influence.
> Thank you.[29]

These dialogical tendencies in the construction of artistic meaning are reminiscent of Paolo Freire's contention that henceforth advanced culture must be arrived at through a dynamic interchange involving the majority versus the hegemonic concept shared both by conservatives and certain sectors of the *avant-garde* of high culture as a closed set of exclusive values simply transmitted to the majority. Film directors in Cuba have engaged this dialogical process of cultural democracy by means of directorial self-criticism and a critique of the medium, thus calling attention both to the open-ended nature of cinematic statements and to the consummative critical role of the public. In this way, the best Cuban films (several of which have already been noted) initiate a critical dialogue, rather than presenting an artistic monologue. As Alfredo Guevara, Director of the National Film Institute, said, a major aim has been "to demystify cinema for the entire population; to work, in a way, against our own power . . . to dismantle all the mechanisms of cinematic hypnosis."[30] This process, which Guevara and others call "cultural decolonization," features an advanced use of medium self-consciousness to call attention to the social limits and ideological dimensions of the medium often assumed to be conceptually transparent and only technically problematic. Various formal strategies with extra-formal consequences for the viewer's participation in a critical dialogue are used in the most significant Cuban films. These devices have both derived from the substantially extended innovations by Godard, Pasolini, and Italian Neo-Realism, the great Russian filmmakers (Dziga Vertov, Sergei Eisenstein) and Brazilian Cinema Novo. Among these formal strategies for triggering interpretive involvement by the audience the following are: a Brechtian use of temporal dislocation to undermine linear narrativity, a focus on the actual mechanics of film-making (hence, also, on art production as a form of labor), a montage shifting between documentary footage and fictional passages, and a parodistic use of Hollywood genres like westerns or war films.[31] Among Cuban films, those of Tomás Gutierrez Alea, Julio García Espinosa, Sergio Giral, and Marisol Trujillo (one of the most impressive new directors) seem to feature these critical techniques most often, while the works of Pastor Vega and Humberto Solas, for example, appear to incorporate them the least. Furthermore, aside from creating films to accommodate the new public participation, Cuban cinema is exemplary in another respect. As Alice Walker, the black North American novelist, has approvingly observed of Cuban films: they "are excellent examples of how a richly multiracial, multicultural society can be reflected unselfconsciously in popular art."[32]

Cuban literature, as well as song-lyric writing, features formal elements and conceptual engagement analogous to that in films. While Cuba's greatest contemporary writers, Nicolás Guillén (b. 1902) and

Alejo Carpentier (1904–1980) grew to artistic maturity prior to the revolution, they nonetheless did so by means of indigenous Afro-Cuban idioms and European traditions, which have gained widespread influence only since the popular transformation of culture since 1959. It is, above all, fitting that the poet laureate of the revolution, as well as the current president of the Union of Cuban Writers and Artists (UNEAC), is Nicolás Guillén, a black man, who has long written poetry synthesizing various popular art forms with high culture to great public acclaim. If the revolution has yet to conceive another Guillén or Carpentier, it has nevertheless created a new and dynamic interchange between recognized writers and the Cuban populace. At present, the most notable Cuban novelists, as well as poets, such as Miguel Barnet (*Canción de Rachel*) or Reynaldo González (*La fiesta de los tiburones*), are advancing the synthesis achieved in Guillén and Carpentier by means of a collage approach that both questions the role of the author and presents the activity of reading as a sociopolitical act, as well as an aesthetic one.[33] An excellent example of some of these traits engaging the public to a greater degree can be found in the song-lyrics of Silvio Rodriquez. One of the major figures in *Nueva Trova* (New Troubador) folk music—along with Sara Golzalez and Pablo Milanés—Silvio Rodriquez uses an acute sense of authorial self-criticism along with deft *double entendres* on historical events in his popular song "Playa Girón." This title is replete with multiple meanings, since it is the Spanish phrase for what is referred to in English as the "Bay of Pigs" and is also the name of a fishing vessel upon which Rodriquez once worked:

> *Compañeros* poets:
> taking into account the lasts events in poetry
> I'd like to ask—it is urgent—
> what kind of adjectives should be used to make
> the poem of a boat without its getting sentimental,
> apart from the vanguard or obvious propoganda
> if I should use words
> like the Cuban Fishing Flotilla and *Playa Girón*.
>
> *Compañeros* musicians:
> taking into account those polytonal and audacious songs
> I'd like to ask—it is urgent—
> what kind of harmony should be used to make
> the song of this boat with men no longer children
> men and only men on deck
> men black and red and blue
> the men who man the *Playa Girón*.
>
> *Compañeros* historians:
> taking into account how implacable truth must be
> I'd like to ask—it is so urgent—

what I should say, what limits I must respect
if someone steals food and afterward sacrifices his life
    what must we do
how far must we practice the truths:
How far do we know.
Let them write—then—the story, their story
the men of the *Playa Girón*.[34]

New directions in Cuban theater have arisen since the mid-1960s, with the express aim of engaging portions of the public otherwise unattracted to the classical European drama presented in the major urban centers. Two professional groups, one originating in Santiago and the other in Havana, decided to reclaim much older forms of street theater, called simply *relaciones*, that were based on indigenous Afro-Cuban music, dance, and masks. In 1971, the Santiago group became known as Cabildo Teatral, a title adopted from a colonial word meaning both an assembly of civic leaders and the general grouping of black citizens. The new *relaciones*, which draw on stock characters from the Golden Age of Spanish drama, Afro-Cuban myths including traditional music and dance, along with social values from the Cuban present, were first staged in the main plazas of the low-income, black neighborhoods of Santiago. When performing in other demographic areas, such as agrarian ones, Cabildo Teatral performs street theater drawing on folk music and dance like the *décima*, the *guajira*, the *son*, and other forms of *campesino* popular culture.

The second tendency of New Theater in Cuba is represented by the Grupo Teatro Escambray, which began in 1969 when professionals from Havana took *relaciones* to some of the most underdeveloped parts of the island. A number of their works deal with rural folklore and historical events peculiar to the area. Now numbering at least twenty, these groups, such as Cabildo Teatral and Teatro Escambray, work in consultation with local mass organizations like worker councils in factories. Their main objective, as well as major success, has been to involve their audiences, normally not audiences who attend the theater, in the structure of the production itself. In some, public discussions are used as a starting point for the *relaciones*, while in others the performance is designed to end with the audience turned into a public assembly. Folk music typical of the region may be used in the choreography, with performances often terminating in an early Cuban form for festivals, namely the *guateque* (dance line) formed by spectators and performers weaving around the city streets.[36]

The success of street theater both in appealing to and involving the working class has been noted by an actress of the Participating Theater Group, which often performs near the loading docks of Havana's maritime port: "No one here ever used to go to the theater. Now, hundreds of workers have been turned on to serious theater as a worth-while activity. Going to a play has become something they like to do in the evening. First, the dockworkers came out of curiosity to see their fellow workers acting. . . . Now, you'll find them at any performance in the city."[37]

But, what are the political and economic foundations for these remarkable gains in cultural democracy? This democratization of the arts hardly seems plausible without substantial changes not only in the national level of education, but also in terms of worker self-manage-ment, that is, in the democratization of the workplace. While from the beginning Cuba's political life has been characterized by a leadership of considerable accessibility and "a continuous informal dialogue that is found in few other countries of the world,"[38] there was a disturbing tendency in the early 1960s toward an excessive centralization of power along with a matching growth of bureaucratization. This latter develop-ment became an issue of national controversy when Tomás Gutierrez Alea, in his immensely popular film *The Death of a Bureaucrat* (1967), deftly satirized the debilitating consequences of this mushrooming bureaucracy. The former topic, that of the monopoly of decision-making by the managerial sector, became a much-debated issue when in 1970 both Jorge Risquet, the minister of labor, and Fidel Castro publicly at-tacked the lack of workplace democracy and the absence of worker self-management.[39]

After this period of national discussion in the late 1960s and early 1970s, the Cuban people embarked on a process of pronounced decen-tralization and one of marked debureaucratization. This dynamic, which is spelled out in the new Cuban Constitution of 1976, has led to a shift in political power from the national level to *poder local* (based on the popularly elected assemblies of the municipalities) and to a degree of *autogestion*, or workplace democracy, hardly matched anywhere else in the world. The election of worker representatives to the Management Council, along with quarterly meetings between the council and fac-tory delegates, ensure the ongoing managerial involvement of ordinary workers. By 1976, 80 percent of all workers felt they were able to make decisions of importance to their production assemblies. In 1980, the national economic plan was discussed in 91 percent of all Cuban fac-tories, with workers' suggestions being used to amend the plan in 59 percent of all enterprises.[40] Cuba's advanced level of worker self-management is even more impressive when one realizes that this coun-try still has a majority of its labor force in the sphere of production (54 percent), with the service sector being 20 per cent, the professionals and technicians being 18 percent, and the administrative sector (in-cluding party cadres) being only 8 percent.[41]

The elected trade union committees, labor councils, and other mass organizations are involved with making decisions not only regarding production levels and working conditions, but also about cultural activities both in the factory and in the community at large. In fact, there are few factories without dance troupes, music groups, or some other cultural brigade. One such factory-based dance troupe appears in Pastor Vega's very fine film *Portrait of Theresa* (1979).

The coterminus achievements of cultural democracy, workplace self-management, and decentralized political power also follow from the dynamic intersection of certain developments in Cuban history. Two experiences before 1959 were common to the majority in Cuba: a deferred national revolution, which occurred when in 1898 U.S. capital replaced Spanish colonialism as the dominant economic determinant on the island, and a deferred social revolution, which happened in 1934 when Cuba workers rose up to establish the first soviets in the Western Hemisphere, only to have them suppressed in a military coup backed by the United States. The Cuban revolution become the overdetermined historical juncture at which these postponed developments were first able to reemerge, converge, and finally be realized interdependently. Thus, the last Latin American country to overcome colonialism, Cuba ironically became the first Latin nation to resist Western imperialism.[42]

Further, the means whereby this advance was possible rested most considerably on a mobilized working class, both urban and agrarian. During the crucial 1959 deadlock within the revolutionary government — between President Urrutia (speaking for the middle class) and the guerrillas (75 percent of whom were rural wage laborers, *not* to be confused with landed peasants) — it was precisely this mass base that definitively resolved the dispute in favor of the latter. Not a recourse to arms by the guerrillas, but the massive general strike of June–July 1959 led by the Cuban Confederation of Labor (CTC) determined most deeply the trajectory of the Cuban revolution.[43] Hence, cultural democracy, far from being a simple vanguard accomplishment, has in fact been yet another expression of the Cuban populace's active participation in national affairs. The degree to which this majority participation has greatly expanded the cultural resources of Cuba helps us to understand what a critic for the *New York Times* could not, when, in 1979, he praised the exceptional quality of the Cuban National Ballet as being all out of proportion to the country's small size and beyond its limited resources.[44]

The Problem of Popular Culture

In concluding our discussion about the democratization of culture and the transformation of the public, some general observations are in order about the nature of art fostered by these new circumstances. As is now clear, concomitant with an altered view of art's relation to society has been a redefinition of art itself. To a greater degree than in most other countries, Cuba has advanced a fundamental insight by Caribbean writer Frantz Fanon in his book *The Wretched of the Earth* (1961). As Fanon noted, and as Cuban critics like Roberto Fernández Retamar or Roberto Segre have further shown, there are crucial differences between a progressive popular culture drawing on indigenous art and a regressive cultural populism based on Western mass culture.[45] Far from being the mere revival of static forms from the past, popular culture entails the collective effort of a people in the ongoing process of self-definition — a process of self-definition that both draws on the past and progresses beyond it by means of new ideas from the present.

While the populist images of Western mass culture (Coca-Cola billboards, Walt Disney comics, Las Vegas architecture, TV soap operas) are entirely engineered from above by multinational corporations to sell products, inculcate hierarchical values, and further ethnocentrism, the genuine popular culture of a Third World country is necessarily generated from below by the most exploited sectors and in marked opposition to the above-mentioned values of corporate capital.[46] Such a process of cultural self-realization leading to the construction of a popular culture is necessarily based on an appreciation of ethnicity that, mediated by international solidarity with others involved in a comparable national struggle for equality, precludes ethnocentrism, always an ideology of privilege. It is significant that one of the most salient characteristics of Cuban art, and a trait for which Cuban posters and paintings are especially well known, is an internationalist orientation that complements the immense amount of aid (medical, educational, engineering, and military) Cuba provides to more than thirty countries in the Third World.[47]

Cuban posters, which were influential in the 1960s on the New Left, are among the most famous artworks produced since 1959. Many of these posters are indicative of an acute internationalism, particularly those of Elena Serrano and Antonio Perez, who use the visual dynamics of European op art; by Raul Martínez, who draws on the bold graphic design of North American pop art; by Eduardo Muñoz Bachs, whose playful draughtsmanship bears an affinity to that of Paul Klee; by Alfredo Rostgaard, who uses a sensual line couple with simplified forms, reminiscent of Matisse and the Mediterranean tradition; and by Felix Beltrán, who uses the formal reduction of minimalism. All of these visual references are further expanded by the subtlety and singularity with which contemporary issues are addressed, both on a national and international level.[48]

Related tendencies exist in oil painting, some of which started before 1959. Wilfredo Lam, a younger member of the Surrealist group and one favorably regarded by André Breton, created a Picassoid style featuring the spatial plenum of Caribbean foliage with a variable palette.[48] A partisan of the Cuban revolution until his death in 1982, Lam was an important transitional figure from avant-garde radicalism to revolutionary art. From the 1930s, Lam consistently reaffirmed Afro-Cuban elements within a European framework, thus being a seminal figure in oil painting. Another major artist responsible for synthesizing various visual traditions from the Mediterranean, the Caribbean, the Mesoamerica was René Portocarrero who, until his death in 1985, was Cuba's most acclaimed artist. Portocarrero, who was given a large retrospective last year at the Museum of Contemporary Art in Spain, often used a dense all-over of Caribbean sensibility with a deft calligraphic line sometimes recalling Matisse, as well as the outlined contours of colonial vitrales in Cuba. In addition, his work uses a broad tropical palette and, sometimes, clear references to the ceremonial plumage of ancient Mayan art, as well as allusions to the revolutionary symbol *manigua redentora* ("redemptive bushland").[50]

The work of the Cuban poster artists, along with that of Lam and Portocarrero, is significant because of the way it expresses a synthesis of popular culture with international concerns. This art underscores Fanon's correlation of the difference between popular culture and populism with the distinction between national self-determination and nationalism. Indeed, Samir Amin has written—in light of the modern history of Western colonialism, as well as the contemporary underdevelopment of many countries by the West—that the aspiration to national self-determination is as important for ending the dependency of the Third World as the threat of nationalism in the West is essential for maintaining that dependency.[51] A corollary of the impetus toward national sovereignty when self-determination is pursued in a consistent and systematic way by one country is that the peoples of all other countries have an equal right to national self-determination as well—an idea patently at odds with the dictates of nationalism that permit such routine references to neighboring countries as "our backyard" or "our sphere of influence." The latter tendency of Western nationalism, especially in a more advanced form known as fascism, invariably appeals to a restoration of the "aristocratic" order "ordained" by nature.[52]

A danger facing any country struggling for cultural self-determination is to simply reject Western European culture in toto, in favor of an uncritical revival of indigenous art forms. Among those who warned against an undialectical displacement of the gains of hegemonic high culture with a simple reversion to subaltern popular tradition was Antonio Gramsci, who has been a major influence on the architectural criticism of Roberto Segre.[53] In noting that any subaltern culture will attest to the never entirely dominated aesthetic impulses of a subjugated people, as was the case with the musical culture produced by Afro-Cuban slaves within colonial society, Gramsci observed that such a subaltern culture would also be branded by the intellectual insularity of those denied access to other bodies of knowledge and cultural traditions. Furthermore, as is the case with *Santería* (or voodoo), which draws on ancient African religions and now enjoys some popularity in Cuba, such popular traditions can be characterized by hierarchical relations at odds with genuine social equality, by a recourse to irrationalism or mysticism at odds with the requisite rational discourse for majority rule, and by a closed set of repeated cultural rituals at odds with any historical process of social transformation and rigorous self-criticism in the cultural sphere.

Gramsci's reservations about an uncritical use of indigenous culture have often, if not always, been shared by the populace in Cuba. Consequently, the elevation of popular cultural traditions as a vocabulary for new art has been accompanied by the increased accessibility of European high culture, such as ballet, symphonic music, and Western visual art, as a common part of the public's artistic experience. One of the most remarkable successes of recent cultural developments has been the way ballet, with hardly any Cuban audience before 1959 and still one of the most elite cultural forms in the West, has become one of the most popular art forms in Cuba. At present, the demand for ballet classes around the country is such that the Casas de cultura and the Ministry of Culture cannot keep up with it. Not only has it produced a number of newly acclaimed ballet dancers in the tradition of Alicia Alonso, Cuba has also been influenced in its gender relationships by this success. In the early years after the revolution, there was much opposition to the training of boys as ballet dancers, since this art form was considered effeminate. Now the opposition has dissipated and Cuba has produced some famous male dancers, such as Jorge Esquivel. Furthermore, the National Ballet of Cuba has effectively incorporated popular dance forms into its own performances, thus synthesizing European and Afro-Cuban culture. Ernesto Cardenal had precisely such developments as these in mind when he wrote: "In Cuba, as contrasted with Russia, there has been no attempt to create a simple art that can be immediately understood by the people; rather there has been an education of the people to the point where they understand the complexity of art. I was told that this has been the official policy of the revolution."[54]

Further Barriers to Cultural Democracy

To say that much has been achieved is neither to claim that little is left to be done nor to deny that serious problems have yet to be re-solved. Indeed, when Cardenal asked a Cuban poet about the role of writers in the revolution, the poet responded, "For us that function must be criticism."[55] Further, Cardenal himself observed that in Cuba it is very easy to distinguish true revolutionaries by the way they discuss the revolution: true revolutionaries are critical in their discussions of it, false revolutionaries are not. Nonetheless, this observation is misleading if not accompanied by the recognition that there are still barriers to publishing such criticism. While critical remarks can and do appear in films or public dialogues, criticism in printed form is much less common because both daily newspapers are controlled by the Communist party.

The absence of independent daily publications of the labor unions, as well as other mass organizations not formally linked to the Communist party, attenuates the further expansion of public discourse and constricts essential avenues for constructive criticism. Thus, the situation of the press—which has been criticized as inadequate by Julio Cortázar and Mario Benedetti, both of whom were strong partisans of the revolution[56]—also contradicts the general tendency, since the 1970s, to decentralize power and to democratize decision-making. The only two daily newspapers in Cuba are official organs of an organization that constitutes a very small minority of factory workers and of the population in general. Even Fidel Castro has conceded that this situation is "unhealthy."[57] Yet, so far, the requisite measures to change these circumstances have not been forthcoming.

Contrary to Western ideology about what constitutes a "free press" (private ownership of it, coupled with minimal governmental, or public involvement), the democratization of the daily mass media in Cuba would hardly be achieved by any regression to a press privately owned, hence necessarily antidemocratic in structure. A public (decentralized) culture is inherently incompatible with a private (centralized) press. Indeed, the existence of such a private press in the United States, as well as in Western Europe, is a major means whereby the "aristocracy of culture" so profusely documented by Bourdieu is sustained. The reason for the utter exclusivity of the mainstream Western press—which generally functions as a corporation both logistically and ideologically, and is in turn largely owned by a consortium of the most powerful multinational corporations—has been well summarized by A.J. Liebling: freedom of the press belongs to those who own one.[58] Or in other words, since a prerequisite of "free speech" on an extended basis is the extensive accumulation of capital, "freedom of the press" in the West is not an affair of the majority, who are unable to buy a press in order to be heard on a national level. (Here one is reminded of Marx's acute observation that the first guarantee of a free press is that the press not be a business.) Thus, Cuba's pressing dilemma with regard to the press cannot be resolved by recourse to the Western model—a model utterly unaccountable to the majority in both managerial and editorial terms, as if multinational corporations alone have the right to discuss issues in a "public" arena.

Yet it does not follow, as the problem in Cuba shows, that to have public control over the mass media is synonymous with public access to the mass media. Insofar as a small minority speaks for, rather than with, the majority, there is an unacceptable passivity intrinsic to the majority role, even when the majority is in complete agreement with the minority. Thus, a necessary though not sufficient precondition for democratizing the press is the further decentralization of power, so that the state does not speak for the public, but instead implements consensual decisions arrived at in the broadest possible public debate.

Nonetheless, this process of augmenting the public domain will not automatically translate into a greater public access to running the press, even though such a change would enhance the dynamic toward *poder local* and *autogestion*. In fact, the 1976 Constitution of Cuba, which guarantees "freedom of speech" to all citizens (Article 52), attests to the still somewhat uncertain political relationship between the party and the populace as whole—an uncertainty that explains in part the unresolved predicament of the press with regard to cultural democracy. Article Four of the Constitution gives ultimate political power to the municipal governments, which directly represent the majority, while Article Five grants final decision-making power to the party, which as an internal organization of select members is accountable only indirectly to the majority of people in Cuba. So far, the daily mass press has tended to function with regard to Article Five rather than with respect to Article Four, even though these two articles are obviously assumed to be mutually determining.[59]

As a last note, it should be pointed out—primarily because of a misguided notion religiously repeated in the Western press—that the still uneven and sometimes ambiguous relationship between the party and organs of *poder local* has not resulted in an unremitting stream of dictatorial decisions in the press. Vigorous debates over the nature of art, as well as the quality of particular artworks, have occurred in print in the major journals of arts and letters (but not as often, unfortunately, in the daily press).[60] Casa de las Americas has recently published strong criticisms by Julio Cortázar of the Cuban government in its handling of the notorious 1971 Padilla case.[61] Probably the worst mistake made so far in the cultural realm with Cuba, this error involved the detention and interrogation of author Heberto Padilla for four weeks, because the black tone of his writings was perceived as "counterrevolutionary" in certain governmental circles (although Padilla was honored in other groups). After Cortázar and other Latin American, as well as European, intellectuals sharply disagreed with these actions, the Cuban government backed off sheepishly, with Fidel Castro himself personally intervening to secure Padilla another job. Cubans have now come to view the Padilla case as in contradiction with the other cultural advances being made. The commendable publication in Cuba of Cortázar's criticisms is a further public concession that the Padilla case was a grave mistake that should not be repeated.

While the treatment of Padilla in Cuba was disturbing, the continued iteration of this treatment in the Western press is deplorable. Far from seeing this as an unusual case—which, of course, accounts for its notoriety—the mainstream media in the United States and Western Europe have presumed it to be the normal state of cultural affairs in Cuba. Even the clearly documented facts of the case have been misrepresented, with a recent article in the *New York Times* referring to Padilla's imprisonment as being ten years in duration! Furthermore, a lack of rigor in examining this case coupled with a dearth of serious scholarship in general has led publications like the *Village Voice*, a liberal weekly, to impute Padilla-style treatment to other Cuban artists as well. In fact, in August 1984, a Cuban exile named Nestor Almendros claimed in the *Village Voice* that Gutierrez Alea's aforementioned film *Hasta Cierto Punto* had been banned in Cuba and the film director placed in a precarious position. But one week before reading this article, I personally watched *Hasta Cierto Punto,* while visiting in Havana, spoke to people at the Film Institute about it (most of whom praised it), and discussed the film with several ordinary Cubans (who had a variety of reactions to it). Only half a year later did the *Village Voice* bother to ascertain whether or not all these easy accusations against the Cuban government were correct (no small matter itself since the Reagan administration has revoked "freedom to travel" to Cuba for almost all U.S. citizens who are not academicians). When, however, the *Voice* did finally run an interview with Tomas Gutierrez Alea, the Cuban filmmaker disproved what they had earlier maintained.[62]

Here as elsewhere, the mainstream Western press can maintain that a "free press' exists in the United States, and is completely absent in Cuba only by a monumental case of historical amnesia. Yet when we weigh the Cuban improprieties with Padilla against the U.S. expulsion of Charlie Chaplin and Angel Rama purely for political reasons, along with the denial of U.S. travel visas to Pablo Picasso, García Márquez, Julio Cortázar, and Graham Greene, to name only a well-known few, it is quite clear that the above formulation of "free speech" in the United States versus "nonfree speech" in Cuba is simple-minded at best.[63] Nor did the *Village Voice,* when it creatively imagined the mistreatment of Gutierrez Alea in Cuba, care to mention the U.S. censorship of

Gutierrez Alea here. In 1973, for example, after Gutierrez Alea was given a special award by the U.S. National Society of Film Critics and was to be honored at a banquet, the Cuban filmmaker was not allowed into North America by the U.S. State Department. Further, and more shocking, when the First New York Festival of Cuban Cinema was opened in 1973, the federal government closed it down, confiscated all the films, and drove the cosponsor of the festival, American Documentary Films, into bankruptcy.[64] All this makes clear that the current presence in Miami of Heberto Padilla has less to do with any sincere commitment to "free speech" on the part of the United States than it does to the *type* of ideological speech Padilla has now come to symbolize.

It is ironic that the mainstream Western media, particularly those in the United States, will be unable to criticize Cuban culture legitimately until they gravitate away from the uncritical and utterly reflexive dismissal of Cuban culture. Here as elsewhere, a scholarly grasp of the pertinent data remains a *sine qua non* for focusing on the failings — failings which can only be assessed fairly in the context of concomitant successes. The problem is not that the U.S. media and many in academia criticize Cuba, but rather that they do so for reasons hopelessly misinformed and transparently self-serving. Yet, only criticism that is based on extensive knowledge, as well as being devoid of hypocrisy, is worthwhile in assessing the cultural development of revolutionary Cuba. When such constructive criticism of Cuba is finally accomplished on a regular basis in the United States, a considerable service will have been done not only the Cuban People, but also the North American public. Then, and only then, will cultural democracy be advanced in both countries at the same time.

Notes

1. Ernesto Che Guevara, "El Socialismo y el hombre en Cuba," in *Escritos y Discursos*, vol. 8 (Havana: Editora Política, 1977), 264–67.

2. Eva Cockcroft, "Cuban Poster Art," in *Cuban Poster Art: 1961–1982* (New York: Westbeth Gallery, 1983), 3–4. For a further look at Khrushchev's opposition to modernity in the visual arts, see John Berger, *Art and Revolution: Neizvestny and the Role of Art in the USSR* (London: Penguin, 1969).

3. Fidel Castro, *Palabras a los intelectuales* (Havana: Editora Política, 1961), 15.

4. Roberto González Echevarría, "Criticism and Literature in Revolutionary Cuba," in Halebsky and Kirk, eds., *Cuba*, 155.

5. See, for example, Fidel Castro, *La crisis social y económica del mundo* (Havana: Publicaciones del Consejo de Estado, 1983).

6. Armando Hart Dávalos, *Cambiar las reglas del juego* (Havana: Editorial Letras Cubanas, 1983), 12–13.

7. Cited in Julianne Burton, "Film and Revolution in Cuba," in Halebsky and Kirk, eds., *Cuba*, 135.

8. González Echevarría, "Criticism and Literature," 155. José Martí was an early advocate of this identity. See José Martí, "Our America," in Philip S. Foner, ed., *Our America*, trans. Elinor Randall (New York: Monthly Review Press, 1977).

9. Confirmation of this literacy level can be found in such sources as the Quality of Life Index of the Overseas Development Council. Also see Samuel Bowles, "Cuban Education and Revolutionary Ideology," *Harvard Educational Review* 41, no. 4 (November 1971): 472–500.

10. Paolo Freire, *Pedagogy of the Oppressed* (New York: Continuum, 1972).

11. Lee Lockwood, "The Arts," in *Castro's Cuba, Cuba's Fidel* (New York: Random House, 1969). Also see Fidel Castro, "Recuerdos de Hemingway," in *De los recuerdos de Fidel Castro* (Havana: Editora Política, 1984), 81–87; and Angel Capellan, *Hemingway and the Hispanic World* (Ann Arbor: Univ. of Michigan Press, 1985), 14.

12. Ernesto Cardenal, *In Cuba*, 76.

13. Judith Weiss, "The Emergence of Popular Culture," in Halebsky and Kirk, eds., *Cuba*, 119–20.

14. Marvin Leiner, "Cuba's Schools: 25 Years Later," in Halebsky and Kirk, eds., *Cuba*, 31.

15. Weiss, "Popular Culture," 121.

16. Burton, "Film and Revolution," 136.

17. Ibid., 148. See also Susan Fanshel, "The Cuban Film Institute: An Interview with Jorge Fraya," in *A Decade of Cuban Documentary Film: 1972–1982* (New York: Young Filmmakers Foundation, 1982).

18. Jaime Saruski and Gerardo Mosquera, *The Cultural Policy of Cuba* (Paris: UNESCO, 1979), 25.

19. Weiss, "Popular Culture," 124–25. See also Mirta de Armas, "Cases de Cultura," *Revolución y Cultura* 61 (1977): 27ff.

20. Saruski and Mosquera, *Cultural Policy*, 25.

21. Pierre Bourdieu, *Distinction: A Social Critique of the Judgement of Taste*, trans. Richard Nice (Cambridge: Harvard University Press, 1984), 7.

22. Pierre Bourdieu and Alain Darbel, *L'Armour de L'Art* (Paris: Editions de Minuit, 1969), App. 5, table 4.

23. Ibid., App. 4, table 8.

24. Bourdieu, *Distinction*, 411.

25. Jeanne Brody, "Cuban Culture Dances to a Popular Beat," *International Herald Tribune*, November 23, 1984, 9–10

26. Ibid.

27. Ibid.

28. For an excellent discussion of this aspect of the film by Gutiérrez Alea himself, see "An Interview with Tomás Gutiérrez Alea," in *The Cineaste Interviews*, ed. Dan Georgakas and Lenny Rubenstein (Chicago: Lake View Press, 1983), 156–160.

29. Nelson Herrera Ysla, "Coloquialismo," in *Canto Libre*, vol. 3, no. 7 (1979). Cited in Lucy Lippard, *Get the Message?* (New York: E.P. Dutton, 1984), 118. See also idem, "Beyond Pleasure," in *Get the Message*, 230–34, which discusses her reaction to Cuban Art.

30. Quoted in Majorie Rosen, "The Great Cuban Film Fiasco," *Saturday Review*, June 17, 1972, 53. See also Tomás Gutiérrez Alea, *Dialéctica del espectador* (Havana: Ediciones ICAIC, 1982).

31. Burton, "Film and Revolution," 140.

32. Alice Walker, "Secrets of the New Cuba," *Ms.* 6, no. 3 (September 1977): 99. Concerning the issue of black filmmakers, see Julianne Burton and Gary

Crowdus, "Cuban Cinema and the Afro-Cuban Heritage: An Interview with Sergio Giral," *The Black Scholar* 10, nos. 8–10 (Summer 1977).

33. González Echevarría, "Criticism and Literature," 170.

34. Cardenal, *In Cuba*, 75. See also Leonardo Acosta, "La Nueva Trova," *Revolución y Cultura* 63 (1977): 80–83.

35. Weiss, "Popular Culture," 127–80. See also Carlos Padrón, "Conjunto Dramático de Oriente," *Revolución y Cultura* 64 (1977): 64–72.

36. Ibid. See also Graziella Pogolotti, *Teatro Escambaray* (Havana: Instituto Cubano del Libro), 1978; and Laurette Sejourne, *Teatro Escambray: Una experiencia* (Havana: Instituto Cubano del Libro, 1978).

37. Quoted in Margaret Randall, "To Create Themselves: Women in Art," *Women in Cuba* (Brooklyn, N.Y.: Smyrna Press, 1981), 111.

38. James Petras and Morris Morley, "The Cuban Revolution," in Halebsky and Kirk, eds., *Cuba*, 431.

39. Andrew Zimbalist, "Cuban Economic Planning," 217–18.

40. *JUCEPLAN, Sequenda Plenaria Nacional de Chequeo de la Implantacion del SOPE* (Havana: Publicaciones del Consejo de Estado), 27. See also Marta Harnecker, *Cuba: Dictatorship or Democracy?*; and Andrew Zimbalist, "Worker Participation in Cuba," *Challenge: The Magazine of Economic Affairs* (November–December 1975).

41. Joaquín Benavides Rodriquez, "La ley de la distribución con arreglo al trabajo," *Cuba Socialista* (March 1982): 70–73; and Marifeli Perez-Stable, "Class, Organization, and *Consciencia*: The Cuban Working Class After 1970," 291–306.

42. James Petras, "The Cuban Revolution in Historical Perspective," *Politics and Social Structure in Latin America* (New York: Monthly Review Press, 1970), 108.

43. Ibid., 110.

44. Michael Robertson, "A Cuban Ballet Star Who Cuts Sugar Cane," *New York Times*, July 15, 1979, D, 18ff.

45. Frantz Fanon, *The Wretched of the Earth*, trans. C. Farrington (New York: Grove Press, 1968), 232. See also Roberto Fernandez Retamar, *Caliban* (Mexico City, 1972).

46. See, for example, Ariel Dorfman and Armand Mattelart, *Para Leer al Pato Donald* (Valparaiso: Ediciones Universitarias, 1971); and Ariel Dorfman, *The Empire's Old Clothes* (New York: Random House, 1983).

47. Susan Eckstein, "Cuban Internationalism," 372–90.

48. For further discussion, see David Kunzle, "Uses of the Portrait: The Che Poster," *Art in America* 63, no. 5 (October 1975); and idem, "Public Graphics in Cuba," *Latin American Perspectives* 7 (1975). See also Cockcroft, "Cuban Poster Art."

49. André Breton, "Wilfredo Lam," in *Surrealism and Painting* (New York: Harper & Row, 1975). See also Antonio Nuñez Jimenez, *Wilfredo Lam* (Havana: Editorial Letras Cubanas, 1982).

50. *René Portocarrero: Colecciones del Museo Nacional de Bellas Artes, La Habana* (Museo Espanol de Arte Contemporaneo de Madrid, December 1984–January 1985).

51. Samir Amin, "Crisis, Nationalism, and Socialism," in *Dynamics of Global Crisis* (New York; Monthly Review Press, 1982), 167–232.

52. For a concise critique of fascist ideology, see Herbert Marcuse, *Reason and Revolution* (Boston: Beacon Press, 1954), 402–19.

53. For a discussion of Gramsci on popular culture, see Alberto Maria Cirese, "Gramsci's Observations on Folklore," in *Approaches to Gramsci*, ed. Ann Sasson (London: Reader's and Writer's Cooperative, 1982), 212–47. For a look at Roberto Segre's treatment of these themes, see, for example, Roberto Segre, *Diez años*

de arquitectura en Cuba (Havana: Editorial Letras Cubanas, 1970); idem, *Las estructuras ambientales en America Latina* (Havana: Editorial Letras Cubanas, 1978); and idem, "En busca de una arquitectura con vocación estetica," *Casa de las Americas* 149 (March–April 1984): 59–67.

54. Cardenal, *In Cuba*, 189.

55. Ibid., 239.

56. Ibid., 153.

57. Lockwood, "The Arts," 114.

58. See Michael Patenti, *Inventing Reality: The Politics of the Mass Media* (New York: E.P. Dutton, 1986); and Edward Herman, *The Real Terror Network* (Boston: South End Press, 1982).

59. *Constitution of the Republic of Cuba* (New York: Center for Cuban Studies, 1983), 3–4.

60. For a look at these polemics, see González Echevarría, "Criticism and Culture," 163–67.

61. *Casa de las Americas, Número monografico Sobre Julio Cortázar*, 145–46, (Havana, 1984). See the review of this monograph by Mariano Aquirre, "Tres Caminos hacia Cortázar," *El País* (Madrid), June 9, 1985, *Libros* 2.

62. Enrique Fernández, "Razzing the Bureaucracy," *Village Voice*, March 25, 1985, 45ff.

63. See, for example, "USA(2): Undesirable Aliens," *Index on Censorship* 9, no. 5 (October 1980): 8–11.

64. Burton, "Film and Revolution," 134–35.

9

Cuban Foreign Policy in the 1980s: Retreat from Revolutionary Perspectives or Maturation?

Gary Prevost

The U.S. assessment of Cuban foreign policy has been highly politicized ever since the 1959 revolution. For close to twenty-five years various U.S. administrations have fostered stereotypic views of Cuba and her role in the world in order to justify a policy of continued embargo and attempts to isolate Cuba from other Western Hemisphere nations. The result of these efforts, which have been bolstered by long periods of restricted travel to Cuba by U.S. citizens, is that the subtleties and changes in Cuban foreign policy have been lost on key foreign policy makers in Washington. To assess the changes that have occurred over time and to analyze objectively where Cuba stands in the world today, it is necessary to go beyond the stereotypes of Cuba. One specific question: Do Cuba's current policies reflect a definite retreat from revolutionary perspectives or only the natural maturation process of a revolution that has been institutionalized?

What stereotypes dominate the U.S. view of Cuba and her role in the world? The stereotypes can be described as follows: (a) Cuba is a puppet of the Soviet Union with a hopelessly bankrupt economy. (b) Castro is a fiery revolutionary out to spread Communism to Latin America and to Africa under the direction of the Soviets. (c) As a result, Cuba is an isolated nation with few friends, particularly in the Western Hemisphere. These stereotypes are reflected in the long-standing U.S. policy to isolate Cuba through an economic embargo, to not negotiate with her on serious questions, and to work for the ultimate demise of the communist regime.

154

Cuban reality is far more complex, and the continuation of these stereotypes by policymakers in Washington does harm to both Cuba and the United States. Cuba's role in the world in general and in the Western Hemisphere in particular has undergone important changes in the last decade. These changes. while not transforming Cuba's basic dependent relationship with the Soviet Union, have further underscored Cuba's important and relatively independent role in world and hemispheric affairs. Whether it is appreciated or not, Cuba's long isolation from the governments of the rest of Latin America has begun to break. To understand where Cuba stands today, it is necessary to review the principles behind Cuban foreign policy and to review the practice of that policy since the 1959 revolution.

Cuba's relations with the world are a reflection of the current political leadership of the Cuban Communist Party and one hundred years of Cuba's search for national independence and sovereignty. As stated by the Cubans themselves, Cuba's foreign policy is rooted in normal relations between nation-states based on mutual respect, recognition of national sovereignty, and nonintervention. These basic principles are generally carried out by Cuba but within nuances flowing from her commitment to revolutionary internationalism. Revolutionary internationalism is defined by Cuba's commitment to provide resources and personnel to assist revolutionary movements and governments throughout the world, particularly in Africa and Latin America. This internationalism is crucial, because Cuba's commitment to it in spite of hardships and setbacks makes the Cuban nation stand out far out of proportion to her tiny size. Jorge Dominquez's claim that Cuba has been committed to revolutionary internationalism longer than any other government in a similar position with more commitment of resources relative to its size is borne out by a close look at Cuba's actions, particularly in Africa and Latin America.[1]

Cuban Goals

Cuba's primary foreign policy goals are the survival of the revolutionary government and the generation of economic resources to carry out the social and political programs of the leadership. Closely allied to these goals is Cuba's search for influence with other governments and with progressive political movements in the world, particularly those of a revolutionary nature. It must be understood that the Soviet Union plays an important role with regard to virtually all these goals, particularly survival and generation of economic resources. On the one hand it is not an overstatement to say that Cuba's very survival depends on the USSR; on the other hand, Cuba's differences with the USSR have often been profound, and the Cubans often go well beyond the intentions of the Soviet leadership in pursuing their revolutionary internationalism. While Cuba's principles may have remained the same since 1959, many important policy shifts have occurred.

The first ten years of the Cuban revolution (1959 to 1968) were its most idealistic and radical phase. During that era Castro advocated an uncompromising stance toward the Latin American elites and the United States. The basic outline of Catro's position from the Second Declaration of Havana saw revolution as inevitable in Latin America due to class oppression, economic exploitation, and oligarchical domination by pro-U.S. repressive regimes. Havana sympathized with such prospects and saw it as "the duty of every revolutionary to make the revolution."[2] As a strategy Castro called for armed revolution on a continental scale. The Cubans gave direct material support to revolutionary movements in Nicaragua, Guatemala, Venezuela and Colombia. Che Guevara, a leader of Cuba's own revolution, went to fight in Bolivia, where he was killed in 1967. Two conferences during this era epitomized the commitment of the Cuban leadership to the strategy of revolutionary guerrilla warfare. In 1966 Castro convened the Conference of Solidarity of the Peoples of Asia, Africa, and Latin America where, in his keynote speech, the Cuban leader attacked U.S. imperialism, Latin American elite governments, and also all political movements who opposed the necessity of armed struggle, including Communist parties. The strategy of guerrilla warfare was confirmed at the Latin America Solidarity Conference the following year in Havana.[3] While this strategy struck a responsive chord among revolutionaries throughout the Americas, the policy did isolate Cuba within the hemisphere. Her support for armed guerilla movements made normal relations with most governments in Latin America impossible and even served to bring Castro in conflict with significant leftist forces in the region. Castro directly attacked the reform-oriented approaches of the region's communist parties as a betrayal of revolutionary principles. Most communist parties in the hemisphere had renounced armed struggle as a viable strategy for power and were pursuing reforms within existing Latin American political structures.

Beginning in 1968 Cuban foreign policy underwent a shift from the emphasis on continent-wide guerrilla warfare and a sole focus on armed struggle to a broader strategy that included diplomatic approaches to the established governments of Latin America. The reasons for the shift could be found in the death of Che Guevara in Bolivia, the general lack of success of other armed struggles, and pressure from the Soviet Union. While the Soviet Union was always uneasy about Castro's attacks on the reform-oriented Communist parties in Latin America, the pressure did not become severe until Castro was brought into line following the Soviet invasion of Czechoslovakia. While Castro's first instincts may have been to criticize Soviet behavior in that invasion, it quickly became clear that deviations from Moscow's line would have severe economic repercussions for Cuba. Soon after, the election of Richard Nixon brought the prospect of détente and with it a strong desire by the Soviet Union to downplay revolutionary rhetoric in the Third World. Castro largely complied with the Soviet pressure and began to stress diplomatic initiatives in Latin America, which eventually bore fruit in several instances.

Diplomatic relations were reestablished during this period with Argentina, Peru, and Chile, three countries that underwent shifts to the left and who saw the reestablishment of relations with Cuba as a part of a foreign policy shift away from total domination by the United States. Later political changes, particularly the military coup in Chile and Argentina, damaged these relations, although relations with Argentina were never suspended. By the mid-1970s Cuba had shifted her own policy toward more normalized relations with the other countries of the Americas, but the general political circumstances, particularly the domination of Latin America by military regimes, made a significant breakdown of isolation difficult. It was in that context that Cuba began to project herself more aggressively within the Non-Aligned Movement and within Africa. While these overtures were carried out within the same wider strategy of gaining broader international influence, they each developed within specific political circumstances. The Cuban involvement in Africa will be explored first and in much greater detail.

Cuba and Africa

Cuba's policies in Africa in the 1970s signaled the beginning of a new era of Cuban foreign policy that was to be marked by an expansion of Cuban power and influence. Cuba's commitments to Angola and Ethiopia were not its first foray into the African political scene. Cuba had aided Algeria in 1963 and Zanzibar in 1964, but the actions of the 1970s were qualitatively different. By the end of 1977 Cuba had 35,000 troops on the continent, aiding the governments of Antonio Agostinho Neto in Angola and Lt. Col. Mengistu Haile Mariam in Ethiopia, in addition to personnel in numerous fields ranging from medicine to education.

The different circumstances in Ethiopia and Angola militated different Cuban involvement in the two countries. The context of the Cuban involvement in Angola was the military revolt in Portugal in April 1974 that ended that country's long dictatorship and intensified the struggle for Angolan independence. While the ultimately triumphant Popular Movement for the Liberation (MPLA) was only one of three liberation groups fighting against Portuguese control, Cuba's connections with the MPLA were by far the strongest, going back to the mid-1960s when MPLA officers studied guerrilla tactics in Havana. Yet the most important factors in the ultimate full-scale Cuban aid to the MPLA were directly related to the actions undertaken by other foreign actors to support the other two liberation groups, the National Front for the Liberation of Angola (FNLA) and the National Union for the Total Independence of Angola (UNITA). By mid-1975 the United States was sending significant aid to these groups to deny victory to the MPLA.[4] In that context Cuba established a military advisor mission in the country and committed itself fully to the banner of the MPLA, which was seeking a negotiated settlement with both Portugal and the other liberation groups. The invasion of Angola in November 1975 by South Africa was a turning point for both Cuba and the MPLA. Cuba responded to the South African invasion by dispatching more than 10,000 troops to the country who, by most accounts, were the decisive factor in turning back the South African incursion. The FNLA and UNITA cooperated with the South African forces and, in the eyes of Cuba and the MPLA, ceased to be legitimate liberation groups. Under this new situation the MPLA came to view these organizations as counterrevolutionaries with whom no dialogue was possible. By early 1976 the MPLA, with Cuban support, had firmly established itself as the government of Angola despite continual guerrilla activities by UNITA and the FNLA. Ten years later Cuba's involvement in Angola continues strongly and is justified by Cuba on several grounds, of which the most important is the Angolans' lack of trained military personnel in the face of continued guerrilla operations and repeated incursions by South African troops from Namibia.

Cuba's involvement in Ethiopia came after her entrance into Angola. There is little doubt that the success of the Angola operation laid the groundwork for Cuba's presence in Ethiopia. The catalyst for Cuban military entry into Ethiopia was the attack on Ethiopia by forces of Somalia. In 1977 Somali forces backed by Saudi Arabia and the United States entered the Ethiopian Ogaden region, claiming to do so on behalf of the Western Somalia Liberation Front. Initially Cuba sent approximately fifty military advisers, but following a renewed attack on the Ogaden in July 1977 by 40,000 Somalian troops, Cuba responded with 13,000 troops, who became an integral part of Ethiopia's counterattack. In early 1978 the united armies forced Somalia to withdraw. The Cuban commitment to Ethiopia was similar in size to Angola, but had greater confidence and professionalism gained from the military victory in Angola. While most of the African nations sided with Ethiopia in this war and respected Cuba's important military contribution, Cuba's overall involvement in Ethiopia was much more controversial than in Angola. The complicating factor in Ethiopia is the Eritrean Popular Liberation Front, which has fought for the autonomy of the Eritrean region for many years. In the late 1960s Cuba trained the rebels who were fighting against the feudal monarchy of Haile Selassie I. In aiding the revolutionary government of Mengistu, Castro did not ignore the Eritrean question and sought to act as a mediator to achieve a political solution. But when it became clear that a negotiated settlement was not possible, Castro reaffirmed Cuba's support for the Ethiopian government, which he justified by the need to defend Ethiopia against outside aggression from Somalia.

More than ten years after Cuba's initiatives in Africa began, what is the balance sheet? The policy has largely been successful. Cuba's stature among Third World countries was clearly enhanced by rapid response to the South African invasion and South Africa's hasty withdrawal. Because opposition to the South African government extends throughout the Third World, cutting across political and ideological differences, the Angola action gave Cuba the opportunity to gain more positive recognition from outside the socialist world than ever before. Cuba's commitment of trained technical personnel to Angola also demonstrated to Third World countries that Cuba's assistance could go beyond a military presence and become a real contribution to social and economic development. These contributions were most clearly acknowledged in Africa, giving Cuba access to a continent of potentially strong allies. These ties have been extremely important in Cuba's role within the Non-Aligned Movement.

While Cuba's Africa operations have been generally successful, there have been costs. While Cuba's actions in Angola and Ethiopia have been widely respected in the Third World, Western nations, particularly the United States, have taken a distinctly different view. Rather than portraying Cuba's actions as positive, the United States has viewed them as an expansion of Soviet influence in Africa that threatens vital U.S. interests. There is definite evidence that Cuban support for Ethiopia and continued presence in Angola was a major factor in the decision by the Carter administration in 1978 to pull back in its normalization of relations with the Cuban government.[5] Other Western countries also reacted to Cuba's new policies in Africa. In June 1978 Canada canceled $64.4 million in assistance, and West Germany had previously banned aid to Cuba in protest of its intervention in Angola. The burden of Cuba's military presence in Africa is not a small one. According to U.S. government sources, Cuba has 20,000 troops in Angola, 15,000 in Ethiopia, and a total of 1000 military advisers throughout the Congo, Guinea-Bissau, Mozambique, and Namibia. While the Soviet Union finances Cuba's military actions in Africa, it is still a significant expenditure of manpower on technical advisers in Angola and hosts more than 10,000 African students in Cuban schools.[6]

The Non-Aligned Movement and the Americas

The general popularity of Cuba's Africa activities, particularly in

Angola, were the key to Cuba's rise to prominence in the Non-Aligned Movement (NAM). In 1979 at the ministerial conference of NAM in Belgrade, Castro received strong endorsement of his Africa policies and in the following year was elected to the presidency of the organization. The presidency of the NAM represented a new high of prestige for both Fidel Castro and revolutionary Cuba, yet Castro's term as president was not without its setbacks. The early 1981 meeting of the organization was moved from Cuba to New Delhi as the result of disagreement over Cuba's position on the Soviet invasion of Afghanistan. Cuba had sided with the Soviet Union in a General Assembly vote on the invasion, while an overwhelming majority of the NAM members voted against the Soviet position. There is no doubt that Cuba's support for the Soviet Union in this instance lessened her stature as a leader of the NAM. Cuba's setbacks in the NAM over Afghanistan were reversed during the crisis over the Falklands/Malvinas Islands. In fact, Cuba's role during this crisis was another important factor in breaking down Cuba's isolation, particularly within Latin America. Argentina's attack on the Falklands/Malvinas in support of a long-standing claim gave Cuba her first opportunity in two decades to stand with the rest of the Latin American nations. Overt U.S. support for the British gave Cuba the opportunity to rally Latin American countries on a nationalistic basis against the United States. The NAM became a forum for Cuban and general Latin American opposition to the United States and Britain. On May 5, 1982, Argentina, a long-standing member of NAM, traveled to the coordinating bureau meeting in Havana to brief the delegates on developments in the first month of the war, the first visit by representatives of the Argentine government to Cuba in more than twenty years. As the spokesperson for NAM, Cuba gained a higher profile than other countries in denouncing the U.S. and British actions. Cuba successfully invoked Latin American unity by stating, "The cause of the Malvinas is the cause of the Argentine people and therefore the cause of Latin America and the Caribbean."[7] The character of Cuba's remarks toward the United States were by no means new, but the agreement with these harsh statements by many Latin American allies of the United States was extremely significant. That significance was acknowledged in an unpublished 1982 Defense Department report analyzing damage to U.S. interests in the Falklands/Malvinas war. The report expressed fears over Cuban and Soviet gains and recommended renewed military cooperation with the key countries of South America.[8]

The Cuban initiatives on the South Atlantic crisis, despite Argentina's defeat, bore specific results. On June 3, 1982, Cuba signed a trade agreement with Argentina, and recently the latter agreed to lend Cuba $200 million a year to purchase Argentine products.[9] In carrying out the agreement, Argentina surpassed Mexico as Cuba's foremost Latin

American trading partner. The return of civilian rule in Buenos Aires has been an important factor in further cementing ties between the two countries in the last two years.

The process of normalization has not been limited to Argentina, and during April 1985 alone Cuba scored several important diplomatic triumphs. Ecuador's right-of-center president, Leon Febres Cordero, became the first South American chief of state since Salvador Allende to visit Cuba. The Ecuadoran visit is a particularly good example of a new Latin unity in the face of obvious ideological differences, although subsequent Cuban-Ecuadorian relations have cooled. On another front, the new Uruguayan president, Julio Maria Sanguinetti, canceled the ban on trade with Cuba within his first week in office. Diplomatic relations were reestablished later in the year, and a Cuban trade mission was established in Montevideo. While Colombia does not have formal diplomatic relations with Cuba, Castro and Colombian President Belisario Betancur frequently consulted on significant matters, particularly the conflict in Central America. It is known that the former Colombian president considered Cuban participation in the Contadora process essential to its ultimate success. Castro has apparently indicated his willingness to participate, but such involvement is opposed by the United States. Other promising developments for Cuba on the diplomatic front during the last two years included solidifying ties with Bolivia and normalization of relations with Peru and Brazil. The latter would be particularly important to Cuba for its significant trading opportunities.[10]

The unity sentiment among Latin American nations has also been spurred on by the Reagan administration's Central American policies, which are generally unpopular throughout Latin America. Its seeming commitment to a military solution in Central America, including the destruction of the Sandinistas, is seen in sharp contrast to Cuba's and Nicaragua's willingness to compromise within the framework of Contadora. The Contadora process, initiated in 1983 by Mexico, Venezuela, Panama, and Colombia, is an expression of long-standing, nationalistic sentiment in Latin America for non-interference in the internal affairs of other nations. Continued U.S. opposition to a political settlement in Central America has opened the way for Cuba to support the Contadora process and ally itself with the major countries of Latin America against U.S. policy.

The most recent issue spotlighting Cuba has been the statements of Fidel Castro on the international debt crisis and the responsive chord they have struck in Latin America. The irony for U.S. foreign policy is that many in Latin America are convinced the Reagan White House does not care about their awesome economic crisis, and that Fidel Castro does. When Castro declared in March 1985 (in an interview with

Mexican newspaper *Excelsior*) that the Latin American foreign debt, which now stands at $380 billion, simply cannot be paid and must be canceled, he created widespread comment throughout the region. His arguments that the debt must be settled through government-to-government political negotiations and that Latin American nations ought to unite to create a "debt cartel" has also found sympathetic ears.[11] Of course, it should be pointed out that Cuba's own $3 billion debt to Western banks has not been renounced. In fact, she has recently negotiated a new payback agreement. The climate of acceptance of Cuba is thus not as much a function of pro-socialist sympathies in the Western Hemisphere as a spreading sense that Latin America must look after its own fate.

Support for Nicaragua

Paralleling Cuba's rise to prominence in the NAM and the reestablishment of her diplomatic contacts in Latin America has been the development of a very special relationship with revolutionary Nicaragua. This relationship has had an important impact on Cuba, for the triumph of the Sandinistas in Nicaragua in 1979 meant that Cuba was no longer the only revolutionary country in the Western Hemisphere, and it rekindled hope that revolutionary change was again on the agenda in the region. Yet the relations with Nicaragua have created new burdens and new challenges for Cuba.

Cuba's relationship with the Nicaraguan revolutionaries is long-standing. The Sandinista National Liberation Front (FSLN) was founded in July 1961 under the combined leadership of Tomas Borge, Carlos Fõnseca, and Sylvio Mayorga. The FSLN'S founding had its roots in the long struggle against the Somoza family dynasty and the domination of the country by North American political and economic interests.[12] The Front took its name from Augusto Cesar Sandino, the legendary Nicaraguan guerrilla fighter who fought a seven-year war against the U.S. Marines and the Nicaraguan National Guard from 1927 until his assassination in 1934.[13] The founding of the FSLN in 1961 had its main roots in the wars of Sandino and the subsequent struggles against the dictatorship, particularly the assassination of the elder Somoza in 1956 by Rigoberto Lopez. In that sense the FSLN was, and is today, a strongly nationalistic movement. Another important component in the birth of the FSLN was the triumph of Fidel Castro's 26th of July Movement in Cuba two years earlier. Like the FSLN, the 26th of July Movement was primarily a nationalistic movement that fought to rid Cuba of a hated dictator, Batista, and to end domination of the country by North American political and economic interests. As the FSLN would draw its primary inspiration from a nationalistic figure,

Sandino, the Cuban revolutionaries saw themselves as the continuation of a national liberation struggle led against the Spanish in the 19th century by Jose Marti. Carlos Fonseca, in his writings on the founding of the FSLN, consistently stressed the linkage between the nationalist and internationalist aspects of their revolutionary movement. The Cuban revolution is continually cited as the most important international influence on the founding of the FSLN.[14]

For its part, the Cuban leadership saw the FSLN and its challenge to Somoza as a crucial element in its strategy of continental guerrilla warfare. Where exactly did the FSLN fit into this overall strategic unity? In comparison to the strength and capacity of other guerrilla movements in Latin America, the FSLN was relatively small and weak, with probably no more than 100 combatants during its early years. But despite its small size, the FSLN was important to the Cuban leadership because of its link with the Sandino legend and because of the nature of the Somoza regime. While Cuba sought normalized state-to-state relations with many Latin American countries, Nicaragua was never the target of such overtures. Castro recognized Somoza's role as an unwavering ally of U.S. policy and in particular recognized his role in the overthrow of the Guatemalan government in 1954 and the aborted raid at the Bay of Pigs in 1961. For those reasons Castro reserved a particular hatred for Somoza and saw the FSLN as the likely vehicle for achievement of his downfall.

After 1968 Castro's focus shifted away from revolutionary activity somewhat, but that shift did not dramatically affect the Cuban relationship with the FSLN, since the diplomatic initiatives did not include Somoza's Nicaragua. As the revolutionary struggle heightened in Nicaragua following the earthquake in 1972, Cuba played an important support role for the FSLN. Although arms aid was apparently halted and training of FSLN cadres was reduced, Cuba remained a refuge for Nicaraguan exiles and Sandinista leaders. When four Sandinistas, including Carlos Fonseca, were released in prisoner exchange in 1970, they were given refuge in Cuba. In 1974 when fourteen Sandinistas were freed in Nicaragua as the result of a successful raid, they sought asylum in Cuba before eventually filtering back into Nicaragua.

During the years 1968 to 1978, Cuban support for the FSLN remained firm, but it appears in hindsight that the Cubans did not believe that a revolutionary triumph by the Sandinistas was imminent. Even after domestic opposition to Somoza grew following the January 1978 assassination of moderate opposition leader Pedro Joaquin Chamorro, the Cubans did not greatly increase their level of material support to the Sandinistas. Judging from Cuban press accounts at the time, Cuban officials did not believe that a revolutionary situation existed in Nicaragua,[15] and as late as 1978 neither the Soviet Union nor Cuba

was expecting a dramatic change in Central America and the Caribbean. The events in Nicaragua, El Salvador, and Grenada in 1978–79
probably caused as much surprise in Havana and Moscow as in Washington.[16]

Once Cuba assessed the potential for revolution in Nicaragua in the
fall of 1978, the Cubans did become a positive factor in the ultimate
triumph of the FSLN, but their relative weight compared to other factors should not be overestimated. As the revolutionary struggle heightened following the September 1978 offensive of the FSLN, Cuba's main
influence was political rather than financial or military. Castro's main
contribution to the success of the FSLN was his role in the merging
of the three factions of the Sandinistas in early 1979. His negotiating
skill and political prestige brought the feuding factions together and
paved the way for the "final offensive" that began in May 1979. Without
Castro's crucial mediation the FSLN might have remained divided and
missed the opportunity to attack Somoza when he was isolated and
weakened.

In reality the crucial financial support for the FSLN came from the
nations of Costa Rica, Panama, and Venezuela.[17] Most of the FSLN'S
armaments were purchased on the international arms market. Cuba's
backseat role in the final months prior to the triumph did not represent any hesitancy about the FSLN, but rather a conscious decision
based on logistical and political reasoning. First, all the nearby nations,
particularly Costa Rica, were in a better position to provide the
necessary logistical support. Second, and most important, Cuba feared
that the United States was seeking a pretext to intervene militarily and
deny victory to the Sandinistas. Castro reasoned that only a direct
Cuban intervention would provide that pretext, so Cuba deliberately
stayed on the sidelines until the Sandinista victory was secured. That
Castro's fears were well founded can be seen in the anti-Cuban rhetoric
used by the United States in the OAS in the weeks preceding Sandinista
victory.

Once the Sandinistas had assumed power, Cuba's restraint was no
longer necessary, but Cuba's aid to Nicaragua must be viewed in the
context of the assistance from other nations of the world. What concrete aid has Cuba given Nicaragua? In every year since the revolution
in 1979, Cuba has provided 2000 volunteer teachers. In addition, some
2000 Nicaraguan students are permanently enrolled in primary and
secondary schools on Cuba's Isle of Youth. The cost of these students'
education and living expenses is covered entirely by Cuba. Hundreds
of these students have already graduated as middle-level technicians
and skilled workers. In health care, more than 1500 Cuban doctors have
worked in Nicaragua, performing 65,000 operations, assisting at 30,000
births, and providing more than 5 million consultations with individual

patients.[18] Other Cuban medical personnel have served as teachers in the areas of hospital administration and maintenance and repair of medical equipment. Cuban medical personnel have been stationed in all parts of Nicaragua, including remote areas that have been attacked by the Contras. Several Cuban medical personnel have been killed in these attacks.

Some 150 Nicaraguan workers in various trades receive educations in Cuba each year. This is in addition to the 500 sugar mill workers who have been trained in Cuban to run Nicaragua's new Tipitapa-Malacatoya refinery, which was inaugurated in January 1985. Planning, financing, and construction of the mill was carried out largely with Cuban aid, and during his speech inaugurating the mill, Castro canceled all debts the Nicaraguan government had incurred in the construction of the facility.[19] Ten fishing boats have been donated by Cuba, and their crews trained in Cuban fishery schools. Other areas where the Cubans have provided technical assistance include grain storage and textiles, rubber, and chemical production. Brigades of Cuban construction workers have been instrumental in building the first overland route linking Nicaragua's Pacific and Atlantic coasts.

Cuba has also provided Nicaragua with important technical military assistance, although by no means at the levels that have often been claimed by the Reagan administration. When the Sandinistas triumphed as a guerrilla army in 1979, they faced a significant task in constructing a modern army. After repeated rebuffs for military assistance by the United States and Western Europe, Nicaragua sought and received military assistance from the socialist world.[20] In this basic framework, the Soviet Union and other East European countries have supplied the military equipment, while Cuba has supplied the military advisers. The scope and importance of this assistance have grown with the continuing expansion of the U.S.-sponsored "contra" war. Approximately 800 Cuban military advisers are primarily engaged in training operations in Nicaragua.[21] (It should be noted that both Cuba and Nicaragua have stated that these advisors would be withdrawn within the framework of a regional peace treaty for Central America.)[22]

The most interesting aspect of Cuban-Nicaraguan relations has been in the political arena. Contrary to many opinions, Cuba has often served as a moderating influence on the Nicaraguan leadership. From the beginning Fidel Castro and the Cuban Communist party counseled the Sandinistas to adopt a mixed economy and to maintain, if at all possible, good relations with Western Europe and particularly with the United States. As a Cuban foreign policy analyst has stated, "we suffered extreme hardship in the early years of our revolution because of isolation, and we did not wish for Nicaragua to suffer through the same problem."[23] The Cubans judged that the world of the 1980s was

not the Cold War world of the 1960s and that the Nicaraguans had a
real chance of gaining wide international support. In another sense
it is a case of Cuba, a mature, revolutionary power, imparting its wisdom
of twenty-five years of experience to a young revolutionary nation. The
Cubans also recognized that Nicaragua's revolution was even more
broad-based than their own and that the FSLN had a significant base
with which to work. Castro, while appreciative of Cuba's relations with
the Soviet Union, did not wish to see Nicaragua tied to the Soviet Union
in the same manner. Since it is unlikely the Soviet Union is prepared
to integrate Nicaragua into the Council of Mutual Economic Assistance
(CMEA) in the way that Cuba is, to survive Nicaragua must remain
economically involved with the Western nations. The CMEA is the
socialist common market that provides Cuba with three-quarters of its
trade activity. While Soviet assistance to Nicaragua has been significant, Nicaraguan delegations to Moscow have not always returned with
the level of aid that they desired. Even the current level of Soviet
assistance is probably a direct result of Cuba's continued promotion
of the Nicaraguan cause with her Soviet ally. There is considerable
evidence that the Soviet leadership has remained wary about the
political commitments of the politically diverse Sandinista leadership
and the danger of a major confrontation with the United States over
Central America.[24] Cuban-Nicaraguan relations represent an excellent
example of how Soviet and Cuban interests converge, with some distinctly different perspectives held by the Cuban leadership.

Political scientist Max Azicri made an important point about Cuban-
Nicaraguan relations when he stated: "The Cuban-Nicaraguan experience represents a reservoir of experience accumulated after years
of engineering radical approaches and techniques for socio-economic
and political development."[25] While the Nicaraguan revolution is by
no means a carbon copy of the Cuban revolution, the Nicaraguan
leadership has directly opted for several specific programs and
frameworks that have been judged to be successful in Cuba. The two
most important areas of emulation have been the literacy campaign
and the role of the mass organizations.

Within days of assuming power the Sandinista leadership announced
a far-reaching National Literacy Crusade for the following year modeled
after the successful Cuban program of 1960–61. The drive succeeded
in reducing Nicaragua's illiteracy rate from 50% to 12%. Carried out
in close collaboration with Cuban advisers, the campaign also served
to bridge the age-old gap between the cities and the countryside, as
it involved thousands of city youths living for extended periods with
campesino families.[26]

Again emulating Cuba, the Nicaraguan leadership saw the need to
create a wide variety of mass organizations to bring the general popu-

lace into the process of decision-making to counter the lack of democratic institutions and increase civic participation. Paralleling the Cuban Committees for the Defense of the Revolution, the Sandinistas established the Sandinista Defense Committees, neighborhood organizations charged with a variety of tasks ranging from promotion of health and education to civil defense. Other parallel mass organizations include the Sandinista July 19 Youth, the Sandinista Trade Union (CST), and the Rural Workers Association (ATC). All these organizations and many others have been crucial in mobilizing support for the FSLN and its revolutionary projects.[27]

Cuba's Setbacks

While on balance the opportunities created for Cuba by the Nicaraguan revolution have been beneficial to Cuba's standing in the hemisphere, Cuba has encountered setbacks in Central America and the Caribbean in the last five years. In 1980 Castro's friend and ally in Jamaica, Michael Manley, was defeated in an election heavily manipulated by the United States.[28] The Salvadoran revolutionary movement failed to seize power in early 1981, and the subsequent substantial U.S. backing of the Duarte government makes a future rebel victory unlikely. There is no doubt that in the wake of the Sandinistas, Cuba thought a victory by the Salvadoran revolutionaries was imminent; they collaborated to provide technical and logistical support to the Farabundo-Marti National Liberation Front (FMLN).[29] The failure of the FMLN to gain power and the subsequent attacks by the United States on both Nicaragua and Cuba for their assistance to the FMLN represented an important setback for Cuban foreign policy in the region. By all accounts, Nicaraguan and Cuban direct assistance to the FMLN ended after 1981.[30] In 1982 in Guatemala the revolutionary forces suffered a devastating setback at the hands of dictator Rios Montt. In October 1983 the revolutionary government of Grenada, which was receiving significant Cuban assistance, suffered through the assassination of its leader, Maurice Bishop, and a subsequent U.S. invasion to install a pro-American government. Fifteen Cuban construction workers were killed resisting the U.S. invasion.

These setbacks have not gone unnoticed in Havana and have clearly been sobering for the Cuban leadership. To understand Cuba's current outlook on the world and its hopes for revolutionary change, it is instructive to analyze closely the current debt crisis that has been made by Fidel Castro. On numerous occasions Fidel has stuck to his somewhat surprising theme that a settlement of the debt question is essential if revolutionary upheaval throughout Latin America is to be avoided. Such sentiments are sharply at odds with the revolutionary

Castro of the 1960s calling for continent-wide guerrilla warfare, but many events have intervened to temper Castro's views. Castro has not renounced revolutionary change, as evidenced by his current support for Nicaragua and earlier assistance to Grenada. But the more mature Castro of the 1980s recognizes that revolutionary change will occur in Latin America only under very special circumstances. Today Fidel is also more wary than ever of American power. The Grenada events proved graphically that the United States was willing to use force in the Caribbean basin region, and that there was little that Cuba or the Soviet Union could do to block American military action. It is clear to Cuba that the Soviet Union is not prepared to intervene in the hemisphere against obviously superior U.S. firepower. While the Grenada events did not reduce Cuba's support for Nicaragua, the Nicaraguan leaders are well aware that direct Cuban or Soviet assistance in the event of an American invasion is unlikely. Castro genuinely fears the development of conflict situations where the US and the USSR would be brought to the brink of nuclear war. One result of his long contact with the Soviet Union is an acceptance of the basic Soviet political line of "peaceful coexistence" with the capitalist world as a necessary outgrowth of the nuclear stalemate.

These setbacks for Cuba should not obscure the reality that Cuba's isolation in Latin America is rapidly ending. She will likely continue to play a role in the growing Latin American reality. U.S. and Cuban interests in Latin America are obviously at odds, but the issues are not irreconcilable. Latin America is changing; Cuba, the mature revolutionary power, has changed; and a change in American understanding of Cuba is essential.

Notes

1. Jorge Dominguez, "Cuba's Relations with Caribbean and Central American Countries," 167.

2. Fidel Castro, *Second Declaration of Havana* (New York: Pathfinder Press, 1978).

3. For an excellent treatment of this era in Cuban history and foreign policy, see K.S. Karol, *Guerrillas in Power: The Course of the Cuban Revolution*; and Herbert Matthews, *Revolution in Cuba: An Essay in Understanding*.

4. John Stockwell, *In Search of Enemies: A CIA Story* (New York: W.W. Norton, 1978).

5. Pamela Falk, *Cuban Foreign Policy*, 165.

6. Ibid., 90.

7. Declaration of the government of Cuba, May 2, 1982.

8. Richard Holloran, "U.S. Officials Fear a Prolonged War," *New York Times*, June 5, 1982.

9. Joseph Treaster, "Castro Once Isolated, Forms New Bonds in South America," *New York Times*, May 19, 1985.

10. Tad Szulc, "As Castro Rises to Lead the Way in Latin America," *Minneapolis Star and Tribune*, May 7, 1985.

11. Fidel Castro, *On Latin America's Unpayable Debt and Its Unforeseen Consequences* (Havana: Editora Politics, 1985).

12. For detailed treatment of the founding of the FSLN and its early years, see George Black, *Triumph of the People* (London: Zed Press, 1982). Also see Harry Vanden, "The Ideology of the Insurrection," in Thomas Walker, ed., *Nicaragua in Revolution* (New York: Praeger, 1982).

13. The best treatment of Sandino is Gregorio Selser, *Sandino* (New York: Monthly Review Press, 1982). Also see Richard Millet, *Guardians of the Dynasty* (Maryknoll, N.Y.: Orbis, 1977).

14. Carlos Fonseca, *Long Live Sandino* (Managua: FSLN Department of Propaganda, 1984).

15. William Leogrande, "Cuba and Nicaragua" in Barry Levine, *The New Cuban Presence in the Caribbean*, 45.

16. Cole Blasier, *The Giants Rival: The USSR and Latin America*.

17. Mitchell Seligson and William Carroll, "The Costa Rican Role in the Sandinista Victory" in Walker, *Nicaragua in Revolution*.

18. *Granma Weekly Review*, January 20, 1985.

19. *Barricada International*, January 21,1985.

20. For a detailed treatment of Sandinista attempts to secure military assistance in the West, see Robert Matthews, "The Limits of Friendship: Nicaragua and the West," *NACLA Report on the Americas*, May–June 1985, 25–30.

21. Marc Edelman, "Lifelines—Nicaragua and the Socialist Countries," *NACLA Report on the Americas*, May–June 1985, 51. Edelman quotes figure of 786 given by Daniel Ortega on March 19, 1985. Reported in *New York Times*, March 20, 1985.

22. Resolution on International Policy, Third Congress of the Cuban Communist Party, *Granma Weekly Review*, February 23, 1986. For Nicaraguan position, see *Barricada International*, July 3, 1986.

23. Based on interview with Cuban Foreign Ministry official, Havana, July 17, 1984.

24. Personal interview with Soviet international relations specialist, Moscow, January 23, 1986.

25. Max Azicri, "A Cuban Perspective on the Nicaraguan Revolution," in Walker, *Nicaragua in Revolution*, 348.

26. For an excellent in-depth treatment of the literacy campaign, see Valerie Miller, *Between Struggle and Hope: The Nicaraguan Literacy Campaign* (Boulder, Colo.: Westview Press, 1985).

27. For an in-depth treatment of Nicaragua's mass organizations, see Luis Hector Serra. "The Grass-Roots Organizations," in Thomas Walker, ed. *Nicaragua—The First Five Years* (New York: Praeger Press, 1985).

28. See Fred Landis, "CIA Psychological Warfare Operations: Case Studies on Chile, Jamaica, and Nicaragua," *Science for the People* (January–February 1982): 6–37.

29. Dominguez, "Cuba's Relations," 173–74.

30. Ibid., 175.

Bibliography

Achtenberg, Emily, and Peter Maracruse. "Toward the Decommodification of Housing." In Rachel Bratt, Chester Hartman, and Ann Meyerson, eds., *Critical Perspectives on Housing*. Philadelphia: Temple University Press, 1986.

Appelbaum, Richard. "Swedish Housing in the Postwar Period: Some Lessons for American Housing Policy." In Rachel Bratt, Chester Hartman, and Ann Meyerson, eds., *Critical Perspectives on Housing*. Philadelphia: Temple University Press, 1986.

Baloyra, Enrique. "Internationalism and the Limits of Autonomy: Cuba's Foreign Relations." In Heraldo Munoz and Joseph Tulchin, eds., *Latin American Nations in World Politics*. Boulder, Colo.: Westview Press, 1984.

Beauvais, Jean Paul. "Achievements and Contradictions of the Cuban Worker's State." In Fitzroy Ambursly and Robin Cohen, eds., *Crisis in the Caribbean*. New York: Monthly Review Press, 1983.

Benjamin, Medea, Joseph Collins, and Michael Scott. *No Free Lunch: Food and Revolution in Cuba Today*. San Francisco: Institute for Food and Development Policy, 1984.

Betto, Frei. *Fidel Castro y Religion*. Mexico: Siglo Veinti Uno, 1986.

Blasier, Cole. *The Giants Rival: The USSR and Latin America*. Pittsburgh: University of Pittsburgh Press, 1983.

Bonachea, Ramon L., and Marta San Martin. *The Cuban Insurrection 1952–1959*. New Brunswick, N.J.: Transaction Books, 1974.

Bonachea, Rolando, and Nelson Valdes. "Labor and Revolution: Introduction." In Bonachea and Valdes, eds., *Cuba in Revolution*. New York: Anchor Books, 1972.

Bray, Donald W., and Timothy F. Harding. "Cuba." In Ronald H. Chilcote and Joel C. Edelstein, eds., *Latin America: The Struggle with Dependency and Beyond*. New York: John Wiley & Sons, 1974.

Brundenius, Claes. *Revolutionary Cuba: The Challenge of Economic Growth with Equity*. Boulder and London: Westview Press, 1984.

_____. "Cuba: Redistribution and Growth with Equity." In Halebsky and Kirk, eds., *Cuba: Twenty-five Years of Revolution*.

Carciofi, Ricardo. "Cuba: Redistribution and Growth with Equity." In Halebsky and Kirk, eds., *Cuba: Twenty-Five Years of Revolution*.

Cardenal, Ernesto. *In Cuba*, trans. Donald Walsh. New York: New Directions.

Central Committee of the Communist Party of Cuba. *Constitution de la Republica de Cuba*. Havana: N.P., 1976.

Communist Party of Cuba. *Statutes of the Communist Party of Cuba*. Havana: Political Publishing House, 1981.

_____. *Second Congress of the Communist Party of Cuba: Documents and Speeches*. Havana: Political Publishers, 1981.

Cuban Economic Research Project (CERP). *Labor Conditions in Communist Cuba*. Miami: University of Miami Press, 1963.

Danielson, Ross. *Cuban Medicine*. New Brunswick, N.J.: Transaction Books, 1979.

Del Aquila, Juan. *Cuba: Dilemmas of a Revolution*. New York: Westview Press, 1984.

Diaz-Briquets, Sergio. *The Health Revolution in Cuba*. Austin: University of Texas Press, 1983.

Diperna, Paula, *The Complete Travel Guide to Cuba*. New York: St. Martin's Press, 1979.

Direccion Politica de las Fueryas Armadas Revolucionarias de la Republic de Cuba. *Defensores de la Patria y el Socialismo*. Havana: Editorial Orbe, 1981.

Dominguez, Adolfo Valdiva. "Stimulating Community Involvement Through Mass Organizations in Cuba: The Women's Role." *International Journal of Health Education*, 20, no. 1 (1977).

Dominguez, Jorge. *Cuba: Order and Revolution*. Cambridge and London: Harvard University Press, 1978.

_____. "Revolutionary Politics: The New Demands of Orderliness." In Dominquez, ed., *Cuba: Inernal and International Affairs*. Beverly Hills, Calif.:, 1982.

_____. "Cuba's Relations with the Caribbean and Central America." In Alan Adelman and Reid Reading, eds., *Confrontation in the Caribbean Basin*. Pittsburgh: Center for Latin American Studies, 1984.

Eckstein, Susan. "Cuban Internationalism." In Halebsky and Kirk, eds., *Cuba: Twenty-Five Years of Revolution*.

Edelstein, Joel C. "Economic Policy and Developmental Models." In Halebsky and Kirk, eds., *Cuba: Twenty-Five Years of Revolution*.

Erisman, Michael. *Cuba's International Relations*. Boulder, Colo: Westview Press, 1985.

Falk, Pamela. *Cuban Foreign Policy*. Lexington, Mass., and Toronto: Lexington Books, 1986.

Franqui, Carlos. *Family Portrait with Fidel*. New York: Random House, 1984.

Fuller, Linda. "The Politics of Workers' Control in Cuba, 1959–1983: The Work Center and the National Arena." Ph.D. dissertation, University of California, Berkeley, 1985.

Fuller, Linda, "Changes in the Relationship Among the Unions, Administration and the Party at the Cuban Workplace, 1959–1982." *Latin American Perspectives* 13, no. 2 (Spring 1986).

Gilly, Adolfo. *Cuba: Coexistencia a revolucion*. Buenos Aires: Ediciones Monthly Review, 1965.

Gray, Richard B. *Jose Marti, Cuban Patriot*. Gainesville: University of Florida Press, 1962.

Green, Gil. *Revolution Cuban Style*, 2nd ed. New York: International Publishers, 1970.

Groundwork Institute. *Las Arboledas Sketchbook: Design for a New Community in Cuba.* Berkeley, Calif.: Groundwork Institute (in conjunction with the Centro Tecnico de la Vivienda y el Urbanismo, Havana, Cuba), 1984.

Grundy, Paul H., and Peter P. Budetti. "The Distribution and Supply of Cuban Medical Personnel in Third World Countries." *American Journal of Public Health* 70, no. 7 (July 1980).

Grupo Cuban de Invest. *UN estudio sobre Cuba.* Miami: University of Miami Press, 1963.

Halebsky, Sandor, and John M. Kirk, eds. *Cuba: Twenty-Five Years of Revolution.* New York: Praeger, 1985.

Halperin, Maurice. *The Taming of Fidel Castro.* Berkeley and Los Angeles: University of California, 1981.

Hamberg, Jill. "The Dynamics of Cuban Housing Policy." In Rachel Bratt, Chester Hartman, and Ann Meyerson, eds., *Critical Perspectives on Housing.* Philadelphia: Temple University Press, 1986.

Hansen, Joseph. *Dynamics of the Cuban Revolution.* New York: Pathfinder Press, 1978.

Harnecker, Marta. *Cuba: Dictatorship or Democracy?* Westport, Conn.: Lawrence Hill & Company, 1980.

Harrison, Paul. "Cuba's Health Care Revolution." *World Health* (December 1980).

Harsch, Ernest, and Tony Thomas. *Angola: The Hidden History of Washington's War.* New York: Pathfinder Press, 1976.

Hernandez, Roberto, and Carmelo Mesa-Lago. "Labor Organization and Wages." In Carmelo Meso-Lago, ed., *Revolutionary Change in Cuba.* Pittsburgh: University of Pittsburgh Press, 1971.

Jacob, Paul. "Experimental Housing, Havana, Cuba, Participation and Experimentation in Housing." In C. Richard Hatch, ed., *The Scope of Social Architecture.* New York: Van Nostrand Reinhold, 1984.

Karl, Terry. "Work Incentives in Cuba." *Latin American Perspectives* 2 (Supplement). (1975).

Karol, K.S. *Guerrillas in Power: The Course of the Cuban Revolution.* New York: Hill & Wang, 1970.

Langley, Lester. *The Cuban Policy of the United States: A Brief History.* New York: John Wiley & Sons, 1968.

Leogrande, William. "Mass Political Participation in Socialist Cuba." In John A. Booth and Mitchell A. Selgeson, eds., *Political Participation in Latin America, Vol. 1: Citizen and State.* New York: Holmes & Meier, 1978.

Levine, Barry. *The New Cuban Presence in the Caribbean.* Boulder, Colo.: Westview Press, 1983.

Lewis, Oscar, and Ruth Lewis. *Living the Revolution: Four Women.* Urbana: University of Illinois Press, 1977.

MacEwan, Arthur. *Revolution and Economic Development in Cuba.* New York: St. Martin's Press, 1981.

Margulis, Lynn, and Thomas H. Kunz. "Glimpses of Biological Research and Education in Cuba." *BioScience* 34, no. 10 (November 1984).

Matthews, Herbert L. *Revolution in Cuba: An Essay in Understanding.* New York: Charles Scribner's Sons, 1975.

Mesa-Lago, Carmelo. *Cuba in the 1970's.* Albuquerque: University of New Mexico Press, 1978.

———. *The Economic Development of Revolutionary Cuba.* New York: Praeger, 1981.

———. *The Economy of Socialist Cuba.* Albuquerque: University of New Mexico Press, 1981.

Montaner, Carlos Alberto. *Secret Report on the Cuban Revolution*. New Brunswick, N.J.: Transaction Books, 1981.

Morray, J.P. *The Second Revolution in Cuba*. New York: Monthly Review Press, 1962.

Munck, Ronaldo. *Politics and Dependency in the Third World*. London: Zed Books, 1984.

O'Connor, James. *The Origins of Socialism in Cuba*. Ithaca: Cornell University Press, 1971.

Perez-Stable, Marifeli. "Institutionalism and Workers' Response." *Urban Studies* 6 (January–July 1976).

_____. "Whither the Cuban Working Class?" *Latin American Perspectives* 2 (Supplement) (1977).

_____. "Class, Organization, and *Conciencia*: The Cuban Working Class after 1970." In Halebsky and Kirk, eds., *Cuba: Twenty-Five Years of Revolution*.

Rabkin, Rhonda Pearl. "Cuban Political Structure: Vanguard Party and the Masses." In Halebsky and Kirk, eds., *Cuba: Twenty-Five Years of Revolution*.

Randall, Margaret. *Cuban Women Now: Women in Cuba Twenty Years Later*. Toronto: The Women's Press, 1974.

Reckord, Barry. *Does Fidel Eat More Than Your Father?* London: Andre Deutsch, 1971.

Rizo, Enrique Capablanca. *La Plaza Vieja: Propuesta de Restauracion*. Havana: Centro Nacional de Conservacion, Restauracion, Museologia, 1982.

Robaina, Tomas Fernandez. *Recuerdos secretos de dos mujeres publicas editorial letras Cubanas*. Havana, 1984.

Ruiz, Ramon Eduardo. *Cuba: The Making of a Revolution*. New York: W.W. Norton, 1970.

Salas, Luis. *Social Control in Cuba*. New York: Praeger, 1979.

Segre, Roberto. *La vivienda en Cuba en el siglo XX: Republica y Revolucion*. Mexico: Editorial concepto, 1980.

_____. "Microbrigades and Participation: Cuba, Architecture in the Revolution." In C. Richard Hatch, ed., *The Scope of Social Architecture*. New York: Van Nostrand Reinhold, 1984.

Silverman, Bertram, ed. *Man and Socialism in Cuba: The Great Debate*. New York; Atheneum, 1973.

_____. "Organizacion economica y conciencia social: algunos dilemas." In David Barkin and Nita Maritzas, eds., *Cuba: Camino Abierto*. Mexico City: Sigeo XXI, 1973.

Sirianni, Carmen. *Workers' Control and Socialist Democracy: The Soviet Experience*. London: Verso Editions and NLB, 1982.

Smith, Wayne, "US–Cuba Relations: Twenty-Five Years of Hostility." In Halebsky and Kirk, eds., *Cuba: Twenty-Five Years of Revolution*.

_____. *The Closest of Enemies*. New York: W.W. Norton, 1987.

Spalding, Hobart, Jr. *Labor in Latin America*. New York: New York University Press, 1977.

Stubbs, Jean. *Tobacco on the Periphery*. Cambridge: Cambridge University Press, 1985.

Suchlicki, Jaime. *University Students and Revolution in Cuba, 1920–1968*. Coral Gables: University of Miami Press, 1969.

_____. *Cuba: From Columbus to Castro*. New York: Charles Scribner, 1974.

_____. *Cuba: Continuity and Change*. Coral Gables: University of Miami, 1984.

Szulc, Tad. *Fidel: A Critical Portrait*. New York: William Morrow, 1986.

Thomas, Hugh. *Cuba: The Pursuit of Freedom*. New York: Harper & Row, 1971.
— — —. *The Cuban Revolution*. New York: Harper Torchbooks, 1977.
Ubell, R.N. "High-Tech Medicine in the Caribbean: 25 Years of Cuban Health Care." *New England Journal of Medicine* (1983).
Zeitlin, Maurice. *Revolutionary Politics and the Cuban Working Class*. New York: Grove Press, 1967.
Zimbalist, Andrew. "Cuban Economic Planning: Organization and Performance." In Halebsky and Kirk, eds., *Cuba: Twenty-Five Years of Revolution*.

Contributors

WILBER A. CHAFFEE, JR., is associate professor of government at Saint Mary's College of California. His research combines studies of Latin American politics with an interest in political-economic analysis. He has published articles in the *Latin American Research Review, Revista/Review Interamericana*, and *The American Journal of Economics and Sociology*.

GARY PREVOST is chair and associate professor of government at Saint John's University, Collegeville, Minnesota. He is coeditor of *Politics and Change in Spain*, author of several articles on Spanish and Nicaraguan politics, and recipient of two NEH grants. He is currently working on a book on the political philosophy of the FSLN.

DAVID LEE CRAVEN is professor of art history at the State University of New York–Cortland. He coauthored *Art of the New Nicaragua* and is the author of more than twenty-five published articles. He has been awarded grants by the NEA, NEH, and the New York Council for the Humanities.

LINDA FULLER is assistant professor of sociology at the University of Southern California. Her research on Cuban labor in 1982 and 1983 was published in *Latin American Perspectives*.

HOWARD GLAZER, AIA, has been the principal of "The Architects Forum" of Portland, Oregon, since 1959. He has designed and consulted on numerous housing developments in the United States and in Latin America.

NORA HAMILTON is associate professor of political science at the University of Southern California. She is the author of *The Limits of State Autonomy: Post-Revolutionary Mexico*, the coeditor of *Modern Mexico: State, Economy and Social Conflict*, and is currently coediting a book based on the 1986 conference "The United States and Central America: A Five-Year Assessment." She is a member of the editorial board of *Latin American Perspectives* and of the board of Policy Alternatives for the Caribbean and Central America.

DAWN KEREMITSIS is professor and former chair of the history department at West Valley College, Saratoga, California. Twice a holder of Fulbright grants, she is the author of *La industria textile mexicana en el siglo xix* and numerous articles on women workers in Latin America.

J. C. ROSENBERG is chief of surgery at Hutzel Hospital, Wayne State University. He has lectured on advances in organ transplantation and has been a consultant for Cuba's senior medical professionals.

Index

Please remember that this is a library book,
and that it belongs only temporarily to each
person who uses it. Be considerate. Do
not write in this, or any, library book.